Pakistan

WORLD BIBLIOGRAPHICAL SERIES

General Editors:
Robert G. Neville (Executive Editor)
John J. Horton   Ian Wallace
Hans H. Wellisch   Ralph Lee Woodward, Jr.

John J. Horton is Deputy Librarian of the University of Bradford and currently Chairman of its Academic Board of Studies in Social Sciences. He has maintained a longstanding interest in the discipline of area studies and its associated bibliographical problems, with special reference to European Studies. In particular he has published in the field of Icelandic and of Yugoslav studies, including the two relevant volumes in the World Bibliographical Series.

Ian Wallace is Professor of Modern Languages at Loughborough University of Technology. A graduate of Oxford in French and German, he also studied in Tübingen, Heidelberg and Lausanne before taking teaching posts at universities in the USA, Scotland and England. He specializes in East German affairs, especially literature and culture, on which he has published numerous articles and books. In 1979 he founded the journal *GDR Monitor*, which he continues to edit.

Hans H. Wellisch is Professor emeritus at the College of Library and Information Services, University of Maryland. He was President of the American Society of Indexers and was a member of the International Federation for Documentation. He is the author of numerous articles and several books on indexing and abstracting, and has published *The Conversion of Scripts* and *Indexing and Abstracting: an International Bibliography*. He also contributes frequently to *Journal of the American Society for Information Science, The Indexer* and other professional journals.

Ralph Lee Woodward, Jr. is Chairman of the Department of History at Tulane University, New Orleans, where he has been Professor of History since 1970. He is the author of *Central America, a Nation Divided*, 2nd ed. (1985), as well as several monographs and more than sixty scholarly articles on modern Latin America. He has also compiled volumes in the World Bibliographical Series on *Belize* (1980), *Nicaragua* (1983), and *El Salvador* (1988). Dr. Woodward edited the Central American section of the *Research Guide to Central America and the Caribbean* (1985) and is currently editor of the Central American history section of the *Handbook of Latin American Studies*.

VOLUME 10

Pakistan

David Taylor

Compiler

CLIO PRESS

OXFORD, ENGLAND · SANTA BARBARA, CALIFORNIA
DENVER, COLORADO

British Library Cataloguing in Publication Data

Taylor, David, *1945 Mar. 25*–
Pakistan. — (World bibliographical series, 10).
1. Pakistan – Bibliographies
I. Title   II. Series
016.9549′1

ISBN 1–85109–081–9

Clio Press Ltd.,
55 St. Thomas' Street,
Oxford OX1 1JG, England.

ABC-CLIO,
130 Cremona Drive,
Santa Barbara,
CA 93117, USA.

Designed by Bernard Crossland.
Typeset by Columns Design and Production Services, Reading, England.
Printed and bound in Great Britain by
Billing and Sons Ltd., Worcester.

THE WORLD BIBLIOGRAPHICAL SERIES

This series, which is principally designed for the English speaker, will eventually cover every country in the world, each in a separate volume comprising annotated entries on works dealing with its history, geography, economy and politics; and with its people, their culture, customs, religion and social organization. Attention will also be paid to current living conditions – housing, education, newspapers, clothing, etc.– that are all too often ignored in standard bibliographies; and to those particular aspects relevant to individual countries. Each volume seeks to achieve, by use of careful selectivity and critical assessment of the literature, an expression of the country and an appreciation of its nature and national aspirations, to guide the reader towards an understanding of its importance. The keynote of the series is to provide, in a uniform format, an interpretation of each country that will express its culture, its place in the world, and the qualities and background that make it unique. The views expressed in individual volumes, however, are not necessarily those of the publisher.

VOLUMES IN THE SERIES

To my parents

Contents

Contents

Contents

Introduction

The Islamic Republic of Pakistan has existed within its present borders, in the north-western part of the Indian subcontinent, only since 1971. For the first twenty-four years after independence in 1947 the majority of the country's population lived in the eastern wing in East Bengal, but after a bloody civil war this broke away from the dominant western wing and became the independent state of Bangladesh. The year 1947 itself had also seen horrendous violence and transfers of population within the newly partitioned British Indian empire. Fifteen to twenty per cent of the population of Pakistan immediately after independence were refugees from India, taking the place of Hindus and Sikhs who had fled in the opposite direction. Even before 1947 the territories which today make up Pakistan – Punjab, Sindh, the North-West Frontier and Balochistan – had had a complicated past. Subject to the political and cultural pulls of Iran and Central Asia as well as of the Indian subcontinent, they had often been frontier areas, and the British especially had treated them as such. Until the advent of large-scale irrigation schemes in the 19th and 20th centuries population densities were much less than elsewhere in the subcontinent.

It was only after the First World War and the eventual formulation of the demand for a homeland for South Asia's Muslims by the Muslim League and its principal leader Mohammed Ali Jinnah, the founder of Pakistan, that attention became focused on a specific territory as well as on the political demands of the whole community. When suddenly Pakistan achieved independence as a modern territorial state in 1947 a whole range of political questions demanded answers that the leadership was not in a position to provide. Since independence, efforts have been made to solve them by placing greater emphasis on the idea of an Islamic state, but this too has been problematic, with several sharply contrasted models on offer. Meanwhile, questions of class and region have become ever more acute, while the international environment in the aftermath of the Afghan crisis of 1979 has been a demanding one.

Introduction

An understanding of Pakistan today requires therefore a more than usually wide frame of reference. Its history is simultaneously that of its geographical territory and of the Muslims of South Asia. Intellectual or political developments elsewhere in the Islamic world often have a direct impact. While in some respects, therefore, it is deeply rooted both in its territory and in its culture, the traumatic circumstances of its creation, the civil war of 1971, and continuing political instability have meant that the relevance of the past has not always been clear. Pakistan is at the same time a part of the Third World, facing crises of poverty and underdevelopment which elude simple solutions.

The country and its people

Pakistan is made up of four major provinces each of which corresponds to some extent to a linguistic and cultural unit, although there are many inconsistencies and overlaps. In population terms the largest province is the Punjab, with its political and cultural centre in Lahore. Some fifty-six per cent of Pakistan's citizens live in the province, most of whom speak Punjabi. Irrigation from the Indus and its tributaries has meant that parts of the province have become the principal agricultural regions of the country, growing wheat and cotton, while industry in recent years has made rapid progress in Lahore, Faisalabad, and some other areas in the north-east. Martial traditions reflect the region's turbulent past, and these were reinforced by a British policy of recruiting its soldiers from the area. Today, the bulk of Pakistan's army is Punjabi. The institution of *biraderi* or brotherhood remains of great importance, both socially and politically.

The North-West Frontier Province, usually abbreviated to NWFP, lies between Punjab and the Afghan frontier and was administered with the former until 1901. Its population forms thirteen per cent of the country's total. The dominant element are the Pukhtuns (also called Pushtuns or Pathans), who speak a distinct language and whose social organization is based on tribal units. Also important is a strict code of behaviour called *pukhtunwali* which emphasizes the imperatives of hospitality, revenge and honour. There are other ethnic groups in NWFP, especially in Hazara district, who speak dialects of Punjabi. There has been some agricultural development in the region, and a limited amount of industrial development, but much of the economy depends on remittances from men working elsewhere in Pakistan or abroad. The province has been very much affected by the movement of refugees from Afghanistan after 1979.

This has had political and economic consequences, and has also been connected with the rise of drug smuggling in the area. Further to the south along the Indus river lies the province of Sindh (earlier Sind). Much of its surface is desert but some has become highly fertile as a result of irrigation projects. Twenty-three per cent of the population lives in Sindh, but by no means all are Sindhi-speakers. In the cities, especially the country's principal commercial and industrial centre Karachi, whose population is now at least seven million, Sindhis are a minority. The dominant element are the mainly Urdu-speaking *muhajirs* or refugees who came from India at the time of independence. There are also substantial numbers of Punjabis and Pukhtuns who have come in recent years.

The smallest province in terms of population but largest in geographical area is Balochistan (earlier Baluchistan). It has substantial mineral resources but these have yet to be fully developed. Agriculturally it has made little progress. In historical and cultural terms, Balochistan, still basically a tribal society, has links as much with the Middle East as with South Asia, and there are indeed many Baluch in Iran and Afghanistan as well as in Pakistan. A significant number of non-Baluch are to be found in the towns and elsewhere.

The other political units of Pakistan include the centrally administered areas. These are made up first of the tribal areas or agencies along the Afghan border. Inhabited by Pukhtun tribes, these are part of Pakistan but not all of the country's laws are applied there. Secondly, in the high mountains of the North, the Gilgit Agency is also centrally administered. This region, together with Baltistan in the northern part of Kashmir, is often referred to as the Northern Areas. Although very sparsely populated, its tribal groups have often attracted attention for their distinct cultural patterns. It has been made much more accessible in recent years by the opening of the Karakoram Highway from Pakistan to China. Also administered centrally is the Federal Capital Territory of Islamabad.

Mention must also be made of Azad Jammu and Kashmir (generally called Azad Kashmir). Following the partition of India in 1947 and the war with India in 1947-48, the former princely state was divided on a de facto basis between India and Pakistan. But while India has incorporated its section into its national territory (and claims sovereignty over the remainder, including the Northern Areas which Pakistan does not consider to be disputed) Pakistan insists that until the plebiscite provided for by the United Nations in its resolution in 1949 is held, the status of the whole state remains undecided. It therefore treats the area under its control as a quasi-independent jurisdiction. One consequence of this is that Azad

Introduction

Jammu and Kashmir is usually excluded from official surveys and statistics. The population is estimated at less than two million.

The history of Pakistan

The earliest archaeological evidence for human habitation in South Asia in fact comes from Pakistan, and the first urban civilization in the subcontinent had its centre in the Indus valley. The two cities of Harappa (in the Punjab) and Mohenjo-daro (in Sindh) together with Kalibangan and Lothal in India are the most important known centres of a distinctive culture which flourished from around 2500 BC and declined during the course of the second millennium BC. It was a literate culture but the script remains largely undeciphered and the archaeologist has to rely on the extensive and impressive remains to reconstruct the characteristics of the civilization.

From the middle of the second millennium successive waves of migrants from the Iranian plateau and later on from Central Asia passed into India from the north-west. Alexander the Great reached the Punjab in 327 BC but Greek control in the north-west lasted only a brief while before the Mauryan empire extended its control over the area. After its decline, however, there was a period in the 2nd century BC when Indo-Greek (Bactrian) dynasties ruled in the Punjab. They in turn were succeeded by a number of other dynasties, for example the Shakas, Pahlavas and Kushans, the last of whom ruled in the region up to the 3rd century AD. The Kushans were displaced by the Gupta empire, although its influence hardly penetrated to the north-west which from the 5th century on saw the movement into India of fresh waves of tribes from Central Asia. For much of the classical period, indeed, the history of what were essentially sparsely inhabited borderlands is obscure. There are, however, extensive archaeological remains at Taxila (near present-day Islamabad) which testify to the vigour of Buddhism in the region during the Mauryan and Kushan periods, as well as to the earlier cultures of what was then called Gandhara.

The first contact South Asia had with Islam was when Muhammad bin Qasim, the Arab governor of Basra, invaded Sindh in the 8th century and established a brief sway over the lower Indus valley. In the 11th century the Ghaznavid rulers, Turks who had established themselves in Afghanistan, succeeded in dominating much of what is now Pakistan. In 1206 a centre of Muslim power was established within South Asia. This was the Delhi sultanate, which dominated northern India for the next three centuries. It was not, however, a stable régime and had to contend with domestic rebellion, intra-dynastic feuding and constant pressure from outside Muslim groups, notably the Mongols of Central Asia. It was a Mongol dynasty, the Mughals, who from the 16th to the 18th centuries pushed Muslim dynastic control to its widest limits in South Asia. They also established an administrative and fiscal system that allowed the development of the most distinguished intellectual and artistic achievements of South Asian Islam in the pre-modern period. Akbar perhaps achieved the most during his long reign in the second half of the 16th century, but the names of Babur, Humayun, and Aurangzeb, the last of the powerful Mughals, are nearly as important.

During the whole period from the founding of the Delhi sultanate to the decline of the Mughal empire many individual Muslims entered India from outside, mostly to serve as soldiers, officials and artists. The rulers did not staff their administrations exclusively with Muslims, however, nor did they make any concerted efforts to convert their indigenous subjects by force. Yet by the 19th century Muslims formed no more than about a fifth of the population of India, concentrated disproportionately in East Bengal, the north-west and the towns and cities of North India. Most of the Muslims were converted members of the indigenous population. The process had been a gradual one and had taken place largely under the influence of Muslim holy men belonging to the mystical sufi orders. Settling in various parts of India, they had gradually drawn some sections of the population to a religious identity as Muslims that did not demand too drastic a break with traditional beliefs and practices.

By the 18th century the Mughal empire was in decline and was gradually replaced first by regional rulers and then by the colonial power of the British East India Company. In 1803 Delhi was captured and the Mughal emperor reduced to the status of a Company pensioner. Sindh was taken from the local Talpur dynasty in 1843 and the Punjab from the Sikhs in 1849. In 1858, following the revolt of the previous year (once known as the Indian Mutiny), the British government assumed direct control of India and abolished both the East India Company and the last shadow of the Mughal empire. The mid-19th century also marked the beginning of the construction of the infrastructure of a modern state and economy. Railways were built, examinations introduced for the senior ranks of the civil service, and new irrigation schemes begun to improve the output of commercial crops like wheat and cotton. Although the primary purpose of such changes was of course to integrate India into the British imperial system, they also provided a focus for new patterns of thought and action among the various communities and regions in the country.

Introduction

For some of the Muslims of South Asia the impact of the British meant in a direct way the loss of political and cultural dominance, and it was among these groups in North India that new movements sprang up in the later part of the 19th century. Two small towns near Delhi became associated with divergent positions on how to respond to the political and cultural challenge of the British. The first was Deoband, where a group of *ulama* (learned men) settled after the 1857 defeat. Drawing on the work of earlier reformers, notably that of Shah Wali Allah in the 18th century, they set out to purify Islam of medieval accretions and to keep closely to the teachings of the Quran and the traditions of the Prophet. Through its direct training of young students who went on to staff the mosques and to teach, and through its network of schools, Deoband has had an enormous influence on the modern development of Islam in South Asia (although it must be emphasized that alternative focuses exist, especially the Barelvi group which takes a more indulgent view of traditional practices). In political terms, Deoband's attitudes to the colonial presence ranged from indifference to outright hostility. The second, 'modernist' response came from Aligarh, where a descendant of the Mughal aristocracy Sayyid Ahmad Khan established the Muhammadan Anglo-Oriental College in 1875 (originally as a school) after his retirement from British service. Addressing himself directly to the Muslim élite of North India, Sayyid Ahmad Khan preached the compatibility of European science and Islamic teaching on the one hand and of British power and Muslim self respect on the other.

The Muslim League, founded in 1906 as a pressure group for the protection of Muslim interests, grew directly out of Sayyid Ahmad Khan's work, and initially its office was located at Aligarh. The British responded favourably by creating what were known as separate electorates for Muslim voters in the new legislative councils that were being established. It soon became clear, however, that other possibilities existed for the expression of Muslim élite interests besides cooperation with the British, and under the leadership of men like the Ali brothers Mohamed and Shaukat some rejected co-operation with the British and began to cooperate with the Indian National Congress. Ideas of pan-Islamic solidarity became important. Two episodes in this period are of especial importance. The first was an agreement reached with the Congress in 1916, the Lucknow Pact, which confirmed the Muslim demands for recognition as a separate political unit with legitimate demands such as reservation of seats in legislative institutions. The second was the Khilafat movement which began in 1919 and was at its peak from 1920 to 1922. The object of the movement was to secure better treatment for Turkey, which had been defeated in the First World War, and whose ruler held the position of Caliph of the Islamic world. The campaign, which was linked to Gandhi's first major confrontation with the British, was led jointly by the Ali brothers and members of the *ulama*, who for the first time used the techniques of mass agitation to make their point. Although it failed to achieve its ostensible object, the Khilafat movement created an awareness of new possibilities and new horizons.

By the early 1930s the rapid pace of political development, in particular the ability of the Congress to challenge British power, meant a refining and limiting of the political options open to the Muslim population and to its élite leadership. The Congress had made it clear in 1928 that cooperation had to be on the basis of universal franchise with only limited and short-term special protection for Muslims. The sense of foreboding felt by many Muslims was articulated in 1930 by Muhammad Iqbal, an enormously influential poet and philosopher with a vision of Islam as a dynamic and creative force. Iqbal argued that the Muslim genius could flourish only if there were to be a separate Muslim state in the north-west of India. By the time he died in 1938 the leadership of the Muslim League had been assumed by Jinnah and on 23 March 1940 the party passed what has become known as the Pakistan Resolution, demanding independent states for the Muslim-majority areas of South Asia (it was only in 1946 that the resolution was amended to demand a single state).

From 1940 to 1947 events moved rapidly under the impetus first of the Second World War and then of the desire of the postwar government in Britain to grant independence. Jinnah seems to have played a careful hand in the tortuous negotiations that took place, although it has been argued that in many ways the outcome – a fully independent Pakistan but located within a divided Punjab and a divided Bengal – was not what Jinnah had wanted at all. The last stages of the negotiations were in any case overshadowed by mounting violence between Hindu, Sikh and Muslim in which hundreds of thousands were killed and many millions forced to become refugees. Any possibility of normal relations with India after independence was dashed by the armed conflict that broke out over the fate of the princely state of Kashmir. Occupying a strategic position between India and Pakistan to the south and China to the north, Kashmir had a majority-Muslim population but a Hindu ruler.

Pakistan after independence

At independence on 14 August 1947 the initiative remained in the hands of Jinnah, whose authority was unquestioned. He was already a sick man, however, and he died on 11 September 1948. His place was taken by Liaquat Ali Khan, his close ally but politically a lesser figure. Beyond Liaquat there were simply provincial leaders squabbling over the spoils of office: yet the tasks were enormous, greater, for example, than in India. New political institutions had to be created almost from nothing. What had previously been peripheral areas had to be welded into a new country, and a just formula had to be found to balance the interests of the two wings and of the provinces within the western wing. The meaning of an Islamic state had also to be defined, although at this stage the modernist view was the dominant one.

Pakistan's political history to the present time can be divided into five periods, separated from each other by military coups or other violent interruptions. The first phase lasted from 1947 until the coup that brought Ayub Khan to power in 1958. Liaquat Ali Khan was assassinated in obscure circumstances in 1951 and from then on a succession of weak civilian governments wrestled with the problems of framing a constitution and of creating a party that could integrate the various social groups and regions. Although a constitution was finally put together in 1956, the political situation had degenerated to a point where there was little chance of it being worked successfully. Already, the senior ranks of the army and the bureaucracy had emerged as the real decision-makers. Pakistan had also moved firmly into the Western sphere of influence, both militarily through its membership of the US-sponsored SEATO (South-East Asia Treaty Organization) and CENTO (Central Treaty Organization) pacts and economically through the policies it adopted.

It was therefore no great surprise when in October 1958 the president – a senior civil servant – and the army commander, General Ayub Khan, seized power. Ayub Khan shortly afterwards eased out his colleague and assumed the presidency as well. He made no secret of his view that a country like Pakistan was not suited to Western parliamentary institutions with direct elections and he therefore created a constitution based on indirect elections. This was deliberately designed to root Pakistan's political institutions in the countryside among the 'natural leaders' of rural society. It was from an electoral college thus constituted that Ayub Khan was re-elected president at the beginning of 1965.

This election was the high point of his period of power, however. Pakistan fought an ill-advised war with India in September 1965 to try to wrest Kashmir by force. The stalemate that resulted damaged Ayub's domestic standing and opened the way for his ambitious foreign minister, Zulfikar Ali Bhutto, to make a bid for power. Bhutto did this by establishing his own party, the Pakistan People's

Party (PPP), in 1967 with a radical programme of social and economic change. He was helped by the consequences of Ayub's economic policy which, under American guidance, had stimulated rapid economic growth but had also widened the already great disparities between rich and poor. In late 1968 disturbances spread throughout the country and forced Ayub to stand down in March 1969, to be replaced by General Yahya Khan, the then army chief.

The most important challenge to Yahya Khan came in fact not from the PPP but from East Pakistan, where the Awami League under Sheikh Mujibur Rahman was demanding a degree of autonomy that seemed to the West to be tantamount to independence. Yahya and his advisers decided to risk holding elections on the basis of universal suffrage, calculating perhaps that divisions between the political leaders of the two wings would allow the military a decisive voice. These elections, the first in fact to be held in Pakistan, took place in December 1970 and resulted in a stunning victory for the Awami League which won all but two seats in East Pakistan and thus an absolute majority in the country as a whole. Meanwhile the PPP had secured a convincing but not overwhelming position in the West. In this situation much depended on the goodwill of the three main players, Mujib, Bhutto and Yahya Khan, but each had his own aims and was unwilling to subordinate them to some wider objective. After several months of negotiation, not all of it in good faith, the government clamped down on East Pakistan in March 1971 and thus initiated what soon became a civil war in which hundreds of thousands died. While the Pakistan army ruthlessly repressed all expressions of Bengali nationalism, it was unable to establish complete control over the countryside where a resistance movement, the Mukti Bahini, had emerged. Eventually India, which was host to millions of refugees from East Bengal, intervened militarily and soon defeated the Pakistan army. Bangladesh became a reality in December 1971 and has pursued its own fraught course since then.

There was no role left for Yahya Khan in the truncated Pakistan, and elements in the army ensured that Bhutto, as the only popular political figure in the country, became the new president. Bhutto moved swiftly to establish his political control and to implement his manifesto, for example by taking over control of most of the country's large-scale industry. A new constitution was framed in 1973 which reintroduced parliamentary democracy. Despite these achievements, Bhutto was unable to establish a stable government, perhaps because of his own imperious personality, and he faced increasing hostility from a wide range of sources. Most of his early political associates in the PPP left or were driven out, to be replaced by local political bosses. Opposition parties were harassed and in some cases their leaders put on trial. Matters came to a head in 1977 when elections were held under the new constitution. The PPP won, but there were widespread and plausible allegations of rigging by party members. The immediate result was a storm of protest organized by the opposition Pakistan National Alliance. Taken aback by its strength, Bhutto tried to negotiate a compromise but before one could be reached the army again intervened under the leadership of General Zia-ul-Haq, the chief of staff. While promising fresh elections as soon as possible, Zia also claimed that it was his duty to bring politicians to account. Bhutto was put on trial for alleged involvement in the murder of the father of a political opponent, and was executed in April 1979.

General Zia ruled Pakistan for eleven years, and attempted a transformation of the country as radical in its way as anything tried by his predecessors. His vision of Pakistan was based on the notion of social and political discipline deriving from a commitment to thoroughgoing Islamization of the country's institutions. This took him into the fields of criminal justice, economic policy and finally constitutional change. In 1985 he held non-party elections and lifted Martial Law but only after rewriting the 1973 constitution in such a way as greatly to enhance the powers of the presidency. The new prime minister Mohammad Khan Junejo was initially Zia's creation. When he tried subsequently to establish some independent room for himself, he was dismissed in May 1988.

Zia promised to hold fresh elections at the end of 1988 but in August he died in an air crash which was almost certainly the result of sabotage, although the perpetrators have never been named. Despite ruling for longer than any other leader of Pakistan, Zia never succeeded in generating widespread support for his régime. Apart from limited support from fundamentalist Islamic groups, he achieved passive acceptance but not popular acclaim. He was actively opposed by regional movements in Sindh and Balochistan, and was unpopular with women. One factor which strengthened his position was the Afghan crisis which erupted at the end of 1979. This guaranteed American aid and allowed Zia to cultivate new interests in the country. After some years, however, the lack of progress towards a solution and the continuing presence in Pakistan of millions of refugees began to have its effect and the Afghan issue became something of a wasting asset for Zia.

After Zia's death the presidency was assumed by Ghulam Ishaq Khan, a career civil servant who had been chairman of the Senate. Despite anxieties about renewed military intervention, elections were held in November which made the PPP the largest party but without an absolute majority. The late Mr Bhutto's daughter Benazir became prime minister and took up the burden, unsolved by any of her predecessors, of defining Pakistan's place in the world.

Economic and social development

Pakistan in its forty-two years of independence has made progress in some areas but has yet to make a breakthrough to steady, self-reliant growth. Once the immediate shock of partition was handled, some economic progress was made as the gaps left were filled up. From 1955 Pakistan adopted the practice of formulating five-year development plans. It was with the 1960s, however, that a clearly defined economic strategy was set out with the aid of American advisers. This was based on encouraging private entrepreneurs to move into fast-yielding industries such as textiles. The results were striking when measured in terms of overall growth, but were achieved at the expense of significantly increased disparities between rich and poor. Of particular significance was the strong feeling in East Pakistan that the boom had been financed by foreign exchange earnings from jute transferred to West Pakistan-based entrepreneurs through manipulations of the exchange rate.

After the secession of Bangladesh industry languished, partly because of the policies pursued by the Bhutto government. Agricultural production, however, which had benefited in the late 1960s from the impact of the 'green revolution' in technology, continued to increase. The economy also benefited from the rapid rise in remittances of foreign exchange from Pakistanis working abroad, especially in the Middle East. Generally, however, the 1970s were a bad period for the economy. During the Zia period the economy recovered in some respects, although little progress was made in tackling questions of structural change and development. Increasing foreign debt and large budget deficits became serious concerns, and in 1988 Pakistan had to go to the International Monetary Fund for loans to tide over a major foreign exchange crisis. These came with the usual conditionalities.

Although Pakistan's economy has grown somewhat over the years, and per capita income in 1987 was $350, substantially above many other low-income countries, its social infrastructure is still very undeveloped. Health and other facilities leave much to be desired in the rural areas, and slums are a major problem in Karachi. Education particularly is an area where little progress has been made; the literacy rate is below thirty per cent, and among rural women much less. Income inequalities remain very marked both between urban and rural areas and within each sector. The extremes of poverty which exist elsewhere in South Asia are rarely to be found in

Introduction

Pakistan, but there are many families living in very depressed circumstances. By contrast there is a small but very wealthy élite in the big cities, some of whom are also rural landlords.

International relations

Pakistan's international relations were for many years dominated by the Kashmir issue. The initial conflict over Kashmir in 1947-48 was brought to an end with a UN-sponsored ceasefire which included provision for a plebiscite in the state. India's refusal to implement this led Pakistan to join the US-sponsored CENTO and SEATO alliances and to receive military aid from the USA. These steps did not, however, produce the results it had hoped for. In 1965 the Ayub Khan government tried by force to seize Kashmir, but the war ended in stalemate and a Soviet-sponsored ceasefire. The only other military conflict between the two countries was in 1971 when India intervened in the civil war. Pakistan's decisive defeat meant an end to any realistic hopes of being able to match India's growing military strength, and the Simla agreement of July 1972 between Mr Bhutto and Mrs Indira Gandhi, the Indian prime minister, set the seal on this with a tacit understanding that the status quo in Kashmir would continue.

Since 1972 successive Pakistan governments have continued to worry about what they see as India's hegemonic ambitions in South Asia and have taken both military and diplomatic steps to counteract them. A nuclear programme has been under way since the 1970s and although strict secrecy is preserved it seems almost certain that there is a military dimension. The Afghan crisis set off by the Soviet intervention of 1979 has enabled Pakistan to get access to advanced weapon systems from the USA. On the diplomatic front, the friendly relationship with China which developed in the early 1960s has been maintained and is regarded as a cornerstone of foreign policy. Perhaps the most significant development in recent years, however, has been greater integration of Pakistan into the Islamic world. This process began in the early 1970s during the Bhutto years and continued under Zia. Economic, cultural and military relationships have all been important. The Afghan crisis has also been important in reinforcing links with other Muslim countries. Pakistan has been able to maintain close and friendly ties with a wide range of countries in the Middle East. Within South Asia itself Pakistan maintains close links with the other countries, including Bangladesh, and has been a supporter of the South Asian Association for Regional Cooperation (SAARC).

Pakistani culture and literature

It will have become clear from the historical sketch above that Pakistan's culture today is firmly grounded in the Islamic faith of its people. The Islam that is practised is increasingly based on a Sunni orthodoxy that is the preserve of the learned scholars. Even so, one should not suppose that there is no room for differences of interpretation and expression, between, for example, the fundamentalists grouped together in the Jamaat-i-Islami and the more traditional approach of the Deoband or Barelvi scholars. Nor should one suppose that the importance of sufism has diminished. For many Pakistanis their initiation as a pir's disciple is of enormous emotional and spiritual importance. There is also a substantial Shia minority in the country. The numbers are uncertain but are commonly put at between ten and twenty per cent. Among the educated élite modernist interpretations of Islam are important, expressed today more in terms of Iqbal's ideas than in those of Sayyid Ahmad Khan. Secularist thought also exists, although often on the defensive. In specific areas, for example women's rights, there have been lively debates.

The artistic tradition of Pakistan can hardly be disentangled from the traditions of the whole subcontinent, especially but not exclusively the Islamic ones. The music of Pakistan, for example, is the music of North India. Elite culture remains closely linked to the Urdu language and its literary forms, even among many for whom it is not their first language. In recent years, however, there has been a considerable upsurge in regional literary activity, often linked to political demands for greater regional autonomy.

Pakistan and the future

Benazir Bhutto's accession to power in 1988 was in some ways a remarkable event. She became one of the world's youngest leaders and the first woman to achieve such a position in a Muslim country. In other respects, though, her position was less surprising. In the first place she came from a leading political family, and would clearly not have become prime minister otherwise. Secondly, she was constrained in the way that so many of her predecessors had been by the entrenched structures of Pakistani society. She knew that if she diverged too sharply from the status quo the armed forces would be likely to intervene, and in any case her political position was weak. Thirdly, there is a huge and difficult agenda to be tackled, much of it inherited from the past. Items on the list include the economy, which despite growth in the 1980s remains fragile, and the social infrastructure in such fields as health and education. In the 1980s, partly as a consequence of the Afghan crisis, smuggling, especially in arms and drugs, has become a major factor in Pakistan society and has been one of several factors that have led to a sharp upsurge in violence on the streets, especially in Karachi. Although Soviet troops were withdrawn from Afghanistan in 1989, there seems little prospect of an internal settlement that would allow the millions of refugees in Pakistan to return, and at least some portion of them may become semi-permanent residents. The shape of the country itself is still under challenge, with strong regional movements in several parts of the country. Although the prospect of a further partition is unlikely, politics will continue to reflect a very strong regional emphasis.

Pakistan has not so far achieved its founders' vision of a state which would allow all its citizens, through their Islamic faith, to lead a productive and satisfying life. Nor has it been able to transform itself into an Islamic state in a literal sense of the term. There is concern in many quarters over the country's inability to sustain democratic institutions and over its position internationally, but little prospect of a radical alternative that would achieve a political breakthrough. Although in the 1990s these frustrations may place great strain on the social fabric, they are hardly unique to Pakistan. The measure of the achievement since 1947 is that the majority of Pakistanis see the solution to their problems as having to come from within the country.

The bibliography

The aim of this bibliography is to present an accurate map or template of its subject, the history and culture of Pakistan, but it must be said that there are certain insuperable difficulties which mean that it can at best be only a partial representation. These difficulties revolve round the interrelated questions of language and of the authors' own concerns. A bibliography which confines itself to works in English and other European languages, or to works translated into those languages, is of course limited in the range of authors included. However brilliant an author may be, if he or she has not been translated from Urdu, Punjabi or whatever, he or she is excluded. This is regrettable in itself but also conceals the more important problem that those who write in, or who translate into, English, have their own assumptions about what is important. This is so whether the authors concerned are Pakistani or foreign. In both cases, even if with somewhat different emphases, the focus is likely to be, for example, on the modernist elements in recent Islamic thought. Although it is true that the fundamentalist views of someone like Maulana Maududi are easily available in English, the same is not true of the perspectives of, for example, the Barelvi sect to which belong very many ordinary Pakistanis in town and country, or of the Shia minority. In the field of literature the number of translations from Urdu into English compared to the number from Punjabi or other languages, although it reflects what is available, gives a false impression of the relative standing of the languages within Pakistan today, not least because of the large number of Urdu works written before 1947 outside what is now Pakistan. Yet it would be impossible to describe the literature of Pakistan without including the major classical Urdu poets. Inevitably, therefore, the bibliography gives greater space to some aspects of Pakistan than others.

Two problems confront all who write in English on Pakistan or South Asia: transliteration and alphabetization. Rules for both are available, but they frequently fail to reflect the reality of Pakistani usage and are not widely used except in specialist journals and libraries. To have used them would have hindered rather than helped the reader. As far as transliteration is concerned I have used the most widely accepted forms current in South Asia today. Diacritical marks have not been used (although they are of course reproduced where they occur in titles of books and articles). Using similar criteria, I have arranged both entries and indexes according to the last element of an author's name, although it must be stressed that Muslim personal names are not based on the same principles as Western ones. Some catalogues and indexes, however, use alternative systems, and it is always worth looking for an author or individual subject under all elements of his or her name. I have made an exception to the 'last name' rule for pre-modern writers such as Abul Fazl or Wali Allah, who are universally known by their full names, although even here titles, such as Shah, can be misleading.

Items for the bibliography have been located in many different collections and libraries, and I am grateful to those many librarians who have never raised an eyebrow at the apparently eclectic collection of books that I have asked for. I must mention especially the libraries of my own institution, the School of Oriental and African Studies of the University of London, the Institute of Commonwealth Studies, the London School of Economics, the India Office Library and Records, the British Library, and the Indian Institute in the Bodleian Library, Oxford, but this list is far from exhaustive. I am also grateful to booksellers in Pakistan and Britain who never objected to my prolonged browsing along their shelves. I have tried not to impose too much on the goodwill of my colleagues, although many have been aware of the progress of the work and have always been ready with advice and suggestions. Two friends who have been especially helpful are Dr Mohammad Waseem and Professor Christopher Shackle. My wife Pamela has as always been my most careful editor and critic. My children's contributions, not always so constructive, have been just as welcome.

David Taylor
December 1989

Chronology

ca. 2500-1750 BC	Indus valley civilization
327 BC	Invasion by Alexander the Great
ca. 272-232 BC	Reign of Ashoka
712 AD	Arab conquest of Sindh
1206	Establishment of Delhi sultanate
1526	Establishment of Mughal dynasty in India
1556-1605	Reign of Akbar
1707	Death of Aurangzeb
1803	British conquest of Delhi
1843	British conquest of Sindh
1849	British conquest of the Punjab
1857	The Great Rebellion or Indian Mutiny
1867	Establishment of the Deoband seminary
1875	Establishment of the Aligarh College
1906	Establishment of the Muslim League
1916	The Lucknow Pact between the Muslim League and the Indian National Congress
1919-c.1922	Khilafat movement
1930	Muhammad Iqbal's speech to the Muslim League calling for a Muslim state
1940	The Pakistan Resolution passed at Lahore
1947	Independence and partition
1947-8	Kashmir issue emerges; war with India

Chronology

1948	Death of M. A. Jinnah
1956	Promulgation of first constitution
1958	Military coup by General Ayub Khan
1965	Ayub Khan re-elected president; war with India
1968-9	Fall of Ayub Khan; martial law declared by General Yahya Khan
1971	Bangladesh civil war; war with India; partition of Pakistan
1973	New constitution promulgated
1977	Parliamentary elections; allegations of rigging; anti-government agitation; military coup by General Zia-ul-Haq
1978-9	Trial and execution of Z. A. Bhutto
1979	Soviet intervention in Afghanistan
1984	Referendum on Islamization programme of President Zia
1985	Non-party elections; martial law lifted
1988	Death of President Zia in air crash; elections; accession to power of Benazir Bhutto
1989	Soviet withdrawal from Afghanistan completed

Heads of State and Prime Ministers

(Governors-general)

1947-8	M. A. Jinnah
1948-51	Khwaja Nazimuddin
1951-5	Ghulam Mohammad
1955-6	Iskander Mirza

(Presidents)

1956-8	Iskander Mirza
1958-69	Ayub Khan
1969-71	Yahya Khan
1971-73	Zulfikar Ali Bhutto
1973-8	Fazl Elahi Chaudhuri
1978-88	Zia-ul-Haq
1988-	Ghulam Ishaq Khan

Prime ministers

1947-51	Liaquat Ali Khan
1951-3	Khwaja Nazimuddin
1953-5	Muhammad Ali Bogra
1955-6	Chaudhri Muhammad Ali
1956-7	H. S. Suhrawardy
1957	I. I. Chundrigar
1957-8	Firoz Khan Noon
1973-7	Zulfikar Ali Bhutto
1985-8	Mohammad Khan Junejo
1988-	Benazir Bhutto

The Country and Its People

1 **We live in Pakistan.**
Mohamed Amin. Hove, England: Wayland, 1984; New York:
Bookwright Press, 1985. 60p. map.
Lavishly illustrated with excellent colour photographs, this book is intended primarily
for educational use by younger children. It consists of 26 statements by individual
Pakistanis about their lives, work and beliefs. Those included range from a farmer to a
woman television news reader, but there is a strong emphasis on modern urban life.

2 **Journey through Pakistan.**
Mohamed Amin, Duncan Willetts, Graham Hancock. London; Sydney;
Toronto: Bodley Head, 1982. 255p. map.
A book of glossy photographs of all parts of the country from the spectacular northern
mountains to the port and beaches of Karachi. The emphasis is on the scenic and
picturesque. There is a text which serves as a useful and informative commentary on
the photographs. The same authors produced the similar *Beauty of Pakistan* (Karachi:
SAY Publishing, 1983).

3 **Pakistan: a nation in making.**
Shahid Javed Burki. Boulder, Colorado; London: Westview Press;
Karachi: Oxford University Press, 1986. 226p. bibliog.
An account for the general reader of Pakistan's political history, its economic and
social development and its foreign relations. The author is a Pakistani economist who
has worked for many years as a senior official of the World Bank. His major thesis is
that the circumstances of Pakistan at the time of its creation forty years ago are no
longer an adequate basis either for understanding the country today or for the
construction of a national identity.

1

The Country and Its People

4 **Let's visit Pakistan.**
John C. Caldwell. London; Toronto; Bridgeport, Connecticut: Burke, 1983. 3rd ed. 96p. map.
Designed for junior classes in schools, this book offers a broad, historically based introduction to Pakistan. First published in 1966, some of the text has been only rather sketchily revised since then and some of the illustrations also now appear a little dated.

5 **The Pathans 550 BC – AD 1957.**
Olaf Caroe. London: Macmillan; New York: St Martin's Press, 1958. 521p. 6 maps.
Still unsurpassed as a general history and survey of the tribes of the North-West Frontier Province, although in the later sections the account is very much from the perspective of the British Raj. The author was a distinguished member of the Indian Civil Service and a governor of the province just before independence.

6 **An introduction to South Asia.**
B. H. Farmer. London; New York: Methuen, 1983. 253p.
A brief and businesslike general introduction to the subcontinent. Farmer discusses the physical environment, history, political and economic development, and international relations of the region. Where appropriate, there are separate sections for Pakistan.

7 **An anthropological reconnaissance in West Pakistan, 1955. With appendixes on the archaeology and natural history of Baluchistan and Bahawalpur.**
Henry Field. Cambridge, Massachusetts: Peabody Museum, 1959. 332p. maps. bibliog. (Papers of the Peabody Museum of Archaeology and Ethnology, Harvard University, vol. 52).
The volume contains the detailed scientific findings of an expedition to Baluchistan and Bahawalpur in 1955, the purpose of which was to fill in some of the known lacunae in prehistory, early history and physical anthropology in these two areas lying on each side of the Indus valley. Although described as an anthropological expedition, much of the work done was of a somewhat miscellaneous character. Field himself was particularly concerned with the use of anthropometrical techniques. Seventeen appendices, by a number of hands, cover such fields as archaeology, botany, entomology, etc.

8 **Pakistan past and present: a comprehensive study published in commemoration of the centenary of the birth of the founder of Pakistan.**
Edited by Hamid Jalal (et al.). London: Stacey International, 1977. 288p. maps. bibliog.
Published in connection with the Jinnah centenary, this extensively illustrated book is by many authors but has been moulded by the editors into a more or less continuous account of Pakistan. Sections cover Jinnah's life, Pakistan's history from the Harappan civilization, the land and the people, economic and social topics, cultural traditions, and Pakistan's place in the world.

9 **All round view.**
Imran Khan. London: Chatto & Windus, 1988. 210p.

This mainly autobiographical book is primarily about the author's own cricketing career in England and Pakistan, but it has a little family background (he comes from a family of cricketers) and some sharp criticism of the cricketing authorities in Pakistan. Imran Khan published an earlier autobiography (*Imran: the autobiography of Imran Khan*, with Patrick Murphy. London: Pelham Books, 1983) which covers the same ground but deals almost exclusively with the cricketing side. The name Khan is also synonymous with Pakistan's prominent position in squash. The exploits of Jahangir Khan and other members of his family are covered by Keith Miles in *Jahangir and the Khan Dynasty* (with Rahmat Khan, London: Pelham Books, 1988).

10 **Sind: a general introduction.**
H. T. Lambrick. Hyderabad, Pakistan: Sindhi Adabi Board (distributed by Oxford University Press, Pakistan), 1964. 274p. 15 maps. (History of Sind Series, vol. 1).

This first volume in what will, if completed, be the standard history offers an overview of Sindh through the ages, with special emphasis on the influence of geographical and climatic factors. Of central importance is the river Indus, which gave the province its name and whose annual flooding and occasional changes of course have quite literally been responsible for the present shape of the land. The book does not cover the colonial or post-1947 periods, when the river was tamed into providing massive irrigation facilities. It does, however, include a chapter on the Sindhi language.

11 **Pakistan: das Land und seine Menschen, Geschichte, Kultur, Staat und Wirtschaft.** (Pakistan: the land and its people, history, culture, state and economy.)
Edited by M. Usman Malik, Annemarie Schimmel. Tübingen, West Germany; Basel, Switzerland: Horst Erdmann, 1976. 563p. 12 maps. bibliog.

A comprehensive survey of all aspects of Pakistan's history and culture, together with information on geology and flora and fauna. Well illustrated with photographs, maps, statistical tables and charts showing, for example, the educational pattern, it has a useful bibliography of works in both German and English.

12 **Peoples of South Asia.**
Clarence Maloney. New York: Holt, Rinehart & Winston, 1974. 584p. 8 maps. bibliog.

A basic American college textbook on South Asian society which gives plenty of attention to Pakistan. It provides coverage of a large number of topics which range from social structure to socio-linguistics.

13 **Pakistan: society and culture.**
Edited by Stanley Maron. New Haven, Connecticut: Human Relations Area Files, 1957. 192p. 5 maps. bibliog.

A collection of primarily anthropological articles on aspects of society in Pakistan intended for a general reader. The style is descriptive. Punjab and the North-West

Frontier Province are covered but not Sindh or Baluchistan. There is also a piece on women in Pakistan.

14 The tigers of Baluchistan.
Sylvia Matheson. London: Arthur Barker, 1967. 213p. maps. bibliog.

A rather breathless account by a writer and journalist of five years in the late 1950s spent among the Bugti tribesmen (the 'tigers' of the title) of Baluchistan. The author's main concern is the value system of the tribesmen, particularly the emphasis on honour and revenge. Her husband was an engineer working on the development of natural gas reserves in the area, and the book is also interesting for the light it sheds on the impact of these operations on local life.

15 Saints of Sind.
Peter Mayne. London: John Murray, 1956. 200p. map.

This is essentially a travelogue but focused entirely on the principal sufi shrines of Sindh, which have always provided social as well as religious leadership to the region. The tone of the writing may strike some as relentlessly personal and anecdotal, but the author writes with knowledge and experience. Two chapters are devoted to the Pir of Pagaro.

16 Area handbook for Pakistan.
Richard Nyrop (et al.). Washington, DC: American University, Foreign Area Studies Division, 1984. 5th ed. 372p. maps. bibliog.

Originally published in 1958, this is a descriptive work intended in the first instance for US personnel working in or visiting Pakistan. The basic facts about Pakistan are conveyed succinctly in sections on history and society, politics, the economy and military forces.

17 The Pakistani way of life.
Ishtiaq Husain Qureshi. London: Heinemann, 1956. 81p. bibliog.

Although brief and published not many years after the creation of Pakistan, this can still be seen as a significant statement of the aspirations of many of the country's élite. The author was Education Minister in the 1950s and an eminent academic.

18 The Cambridge encyclopedia of India, Pakistan, Sri Lanka, Nepal, Bhutan and the Maldives.
Edited by Francis Robinson. Cambridge, England: Cambridge University Press, 1989. 520p. maps. bibliog.

An up-to-date survey of the whole subcontinent produced by numerous scholars from the region and from outside. Although termed an encyclopedia, it is arranged by subject rather than alphabetically, with short articles covering aspects of history, economics, society and culture. It is attractively designed and illustrated.

19 Indian cookery.
Sameen Rushdie. London: Century, 1988. 256p.

The author spent much of her early life in Pakistan and includes some regional dishes in this collection of recipes designed to introduce South Asian or Indian cookery to a wider audience abroad. Another well-known writer on Indian cuisine is Madhur Jaffrey. Among her books is *An invitation to Indian cooking* (New York: Knopf, 1973; London: Jonathan Cape, 1976).

20 **Pakistani village.**
Ailsa Scarsbrook, Alan Scarsbrook. London: A. & C. Black, 1979. 25p. map.
Provides photographs and a short text on life in a village in northern Punjab near Rawalpindi, seen through the eyes of a young boy. This book is designed for use by lower age groups in schools.

21 **Lords of the Khyber: the story of the North-West Frontier.**
André Singer. London: Faber & Faber, 1984. 234p. map. bibliog.
A modern study intended for a general readership. The author is a trained anthropologist as well as film-maker, and brings a number of perspectives to bear on his description of Pukhtun history and society. Although many of the dramatis personae are European, the centre of attention remains the Pukhtun. Singer believes that the Soviets have made many of the same mistakes as earlier invaders by failing to understand the true nature of Pukhtun society. The book could be read alongside Caroe, *The Pathans 550 BC – AD 1957* (q.v.) as a basic introduction to the North-West Frontier.

22 **The way of the Pathans.**
James W. Spain. London: Robert Hale, 1962. 190p. map.
This is an anecdotal account of the Pukhtun areas of the North-West Frontier Province by an American diplomat who was stationed in Pakistan in the 1950s and subsequently went on to carry out more systematic research on the peoples of the area. The fruits of the latter were published as *The Pathan borderland* (The Hague: Mouton, 1963).

23 **Muslim peoples: a world ethnographic survey.**
Edited by Richard V. Weekes. Westport, Connecticut; London: Greenwood Press, 1978. 546p. bibliog.
An anthropologically oriented cooperative work, mainly by American scholars. The aim is to describe the major ethnic groups within the worldwide Muslim population. Pakistan is covered in terms of Punjabis, Sindhis, Pashtuns, Baluch, Brahuis, and Kashmiris, and an ethnically diverse group labelled 'Urdu speakers of North India and Pakistan'. For each group there is a separate section giving a succinct description of language, social structure and stratification, distinctive religious practices and recent history.

Pakistan: a political geography.
See item no. 34.

Gazetteer of the province of Sind.
See item no. 36.

Geography

General

24 **The mineral and nuclear fuels of the Indian subcontinent and Burma: a guide to the study of the coal, oil, natural gas, uranium and thorium resources of the area.**
J. Coggin Brown, A. K. Dey. Delhi: Oxford University Press, 1975. 517p. 25 maps.

This is a detailed geological survey for the specialist of the subcontinent's known reserves of mineral and nuclear fuels. While Pakistan has very little of the latter, it has extensive reserves of coal and natural gas and some onshore oil, mostly explored since 1975. The work also includes a technical history of exploration and exploitation of the resources identified.

25 **The North-West Frontier of West Pakistan: a study in regional geography.**
David Dichter, with the collaboration of Nathan Popkin. Oxford, England: Clarendon Press, 1967. 231p. maps. bibliog.

This is a study based on extended fieldwork which seeks to establish a general framework for more detailed research. The main part of the book describes each geographical division in turn, laying particular stress on physical and economic aspects. The tribal agencies and the northern territories are also included.

26 **Pakistan.**
B. L. C. Johnson. London; Exeter, New Hampshire: Heinemann, 1979. 214p. maps.

A comprehensive study of Pakistan from a geographical perspective. The author studies the interaction of man and his environment in the light of a wide range of material drawn from the other social sciences. The book would be useful both as an undergraduate textbook and as an introduction for the general reader.

27 **A geography of Pakistan.**
K. U. Kureshy. Karachi: Oxford University Press, 1977. 4th ed. 199p.
maps. bibliog.
A comprehensive account in the old style of Pakistan's physical, economic and human geography. It includes a statistical appendix on agricultural and industrial production, population and climate. The three earlier editions of the book (1964, 1969, 1973) were written by Kazi S. Ahmad. The present version is substantially rewritten and updated, although it follows the same pattern as the earlier volumes.

28 **Pakistan Geographical Review.**
Lahore: University of the Punjab, Department of Geography, 1949- .
biannual.
The major geographical journal from Pakistan, this covers the full range of geographical topics. It replaced the *Punjab Geographical Review* which began publication in 1942.

29 **A physical and economic geography of Sind (the lower Indus basin).**
Maneck B. Pithawalla. Karachi: Sindhi Adabi Board, 1959. 389p. 41
maps. bibliog.
The first six chapters of this work deal with aspects of Sindh's physical geography, including the hydrography of the Indus, soils, natural vegetation and climate, while the remaining six cover the economic side. Considerable attention is paid to the importance of the Indus river both as a means of communication and as a source of irrigation water.

30 **Pakistan: its resources and development.**
Akhtar Husian [*sic*, Husain] Siddiqi. Hong Kong: Asian Research
Service, 1979. 276p. 26 maps.
This is essentially an economic geography of Pakistan, which takes full advantage of a wide range of sources, both official and unofficial, to produce a rounded picture of Pakistan's resource endowment and the extent to which it has been developed. A concluding chapter looks at regional patterns of development.

31 **India and Pakistan: a general and regional geography.**
O. H. K. Spate, A. T. A. Learmonth. London: Methuen, 1967. 3rd
ed. 877p. maps. bibliog.
Although a little dated, this remains the most comprehensive and reliable geographical survey of the Indian subcontinent. The authors are generous in their definition of the geographical and discuss many aspects of historical and economic development. Due attention is paid to Pakistan throughout, with separate sections where appropriate. The specifically regional chapters of the work were published as a separate volume in 1972: *India, Pakistan and Ceylon: the regions*, by Spate, Learmonth and B. H. Farmer (London: Methuen). Spate contributed a much briefer review of the subcontinent to *The changing map of Asia: a political geography*, edited by W. Gordon East, Spate and Charles Fisher (London: Methuen, 1971, 5th ed.).

32 **South Asia: a systematic geographic bibliography.**
B. L. Sukhwal. Metuchen, New Jersey: Scarecrow Press, 1974. 827p.
A well-prepared but unannotated bibliography which lists 1,622 entries for Pakistan arranged according to standard geographical categories. Unpublished US dissertations are included, as are numerous journal articles from Pakistan and abroad.

33 **Geology of Kohistan: Karakoram Himalaya, northern Pakistan.**
Edited by R. A. Khan Tahirkheli, M. Qasim Jan. Peshawar: University of Peshawar, Centre of Excellence in Geology, [c.1979]. 187p. maps. bibliog.
The papers included in this collection are intended for the specialist interested in the geology and petrography of the Kohistan region which lies to the north of Peshawar and Islamabad. Kohistan, which is part of the Karakoram range at the northwestern end of the Himalayas, has been explored systematically only since 1968.

34 **Pakistan: a political geography.**
A. Tayyeb. London: Oxford University Press, 1966. 250p. 39 maps. bibliog.
This is perhaps not so much a geography of Pakistan as a book about Pakistan written by a geographer. Tayyeb brings a geographer's awareness of space and the environment to his account of Pakistan's history, its economy and its relations with its neighbours.

35 **Mountain people.**
Edited by Michael Tobias, foreword by Georgina Ashworth, introduction by Jack D. Ives. Norman, Oklahoma; London: University of Oklahoma Press, 1986. 219p. 9 maps. bibliog.
This is a collection of essays devoted to recording the lives of mountain peoples worldwide as they face the environmental pressures of the late 20th century. Two papers are concerned with groups in Pakistan. Kenneth Hewitt describes the Kalash Kafirs of the Hindu Kush and muses on how to see the world through their eyes. Pat Emerson describes the human world of Baltistan.

Fully annotated atlas of South Asia.
See item no. 39.

Gazetteers and maps

36 **Gazetteer of the province of Sind.**
E. H. Aitken. Karachi: Government of Bombay, 1907. 519p. map.
Although in most parts of British India gazetteers were compiled on a district basis, in Sindh it was decided that a single volume should be prepared for what was then a part of the Bombay presidency, albeit under its own chief commissioner. Aitken's work follows the standard colonial pattern, with chapters detailing the physical aspects of the

region, its flora and fauna, its economy, its population divided into ethnic and religious groups, its history and its system of government. It should be noted that there was no direct connection between Aitken's work and that produced as part of the *Imperial gazetteer: provincial series* (q.v.). After independence, a new gazetteer was produced by a retired British official, H. T. Sorley, *The gazetteer of West Pakistan: the former province of Sind (including Khairpur State)* (Karachi: Government of West Pakistan, [c.1968]).

37 **Atlas of Pakistan.**
Rawalpindi: Director of Map Publications, Survey of Pakistan, 1985.
129p.

This is the first officially produced atlas of Pakistan. The country is covered at a scale of 1:1,000,000 and there are 43 thematic maps at 1:5,000,000 dealing with vegetation, climate, crops and industries.

38 **An historical atlas of Islam.**
Edited by William C. Brice. Leiden, The Netherlands: E. J. Brill, 1981. 71p. 57 maps. bibliog.

Intended as a companion to the *Encyclopaedia of Islam* (q.v.), this atlas contains ten maps illustrating Muslim penetration of India and the areas ruled by the subsequent Muslim dynasties. Other maps show the place of India within the Indian Ocean and the wider Islamic world. The brief introduction includes bibliographical notes.

39 **Fully annotated atlas of South Asia.**
Ashok K. Dutt, Margaret Geib. Boulder, Colorado; London: Westview Press, 1987. 231p. maps. bibliog.

This is in fact more a descriptive geography than simply an atlas. The authors devote a chapter to the political and economic geography of Pakistan, as well as covering it as part of the region as a whole. Much of the information is given in the form of charts and tables as well as in numerous clearly drawn, although rather cramped maps.

40 **An atlas of the Mughal empire: political and economic maps with detailed notes, bibliography and index.**
Irfan Habib. Delhi: Oxford University Press, 1982. 105p. maps. bibliog.

This volume is primarily intended for the specialist historian but might be of some use to others, although the black and white maps are not in themselves especially alluring. The Mughal empire is divided into sixteen blocks, for each of which there are two maps at a scale of 1:2,000,000 giving political and economic information respectively. The extensive notes give sources for place-name identification and other information contained on the maps, and contain discussions of the issues raised. As Habib, the leading present-day historian of the Mughals, states in his introduction, the period is remarkably rich in sources for the modern map-maker, and an immense amount of information can be derived from the maps. Susan Gole has demonstrated the range of precolonial map-makers in two books: *Maps of Mughal India, drawn by Colonel Jean-Baptiste-Joseph Gentil, Agent for the French government to the court of Shuja-ud-daula at Faizabad, in 1770* (Delhi: Manohar, 1988), and *Indian maps and plans from earliest times to the advent of European surveys* (Delhi: Manohar, 1989).

41 **The imperial gazetteer of India: the Indian empire.**
Oxford: Clarendon Press, 1907-9. 26 vols.

The first attempt at a comprehensive gazetteer of the Indian empire was produced in 1881, when it was a mere nine volumes. The 1907-9 version, produced at the height of the British Raj, was 26 volumes in length. Four served as general description, one was an index, one an atlas, and the remaining twenty contained alphabetically arranged notes on every place of any significance in the whole country.

42 **The imperial gazetteer of India: provincial series.**
Calcutta: Government of India, Superintendent of Government Printing, 1908-9. maps.

Produced at the same time as the series for the Indian empire (see previous entry), the aim and pattern is similar. Each province is covered in one or two volumes, with sections on the general history of the province and its main subdivisions, followed by a place-by-place gazetteer. Punjab is covered in two volumes, mostly written by H. A. Rose, Baluchistan and North-West Frontier Province each in one by R. Hughes-Buller and H. A. Rose respectively. Sindh is included in the second volume of the Bombay Presidency set.

43 **Indian subcontinent: India, Pakistan, Bangladesh, Sri Lanka.**
Edinburgh: John Bartholomew, [n.d.]. (Bartholomew World Travel Map).

This widely available and frequently reprinted map covers the whole subcontinent at a scale of 1:4,000,000. The physical features, main communications network and urban centres are all clearly shown and there is a 1:200,000 plan of Karachi. The cartography of the map is also used for the *Times Atlas of the World* (London: Times Books, 1980, 6th ed.).

44 **Atlas of the Islamic world since 1500.**
Francis Robinson. Oxford, England: Phaidon, 1982. 238p. 50 maps. bibliog.

The title of this work, intended for a general readership, is somewhat misleading. Although it contains a number of clearly drawn and informative maps, it could equally be described as an illustrated history of the Muslim world or an introduction to Islamic civilization. Photographs of people and places, Persian and Mughal miniatures, and political cartoons are all used to illustrate the author's text. Considerable attention is given to the Muslims of the Indian subcontinent.

45 **A historical atlas of South Asia.**
Edited by Joseph E. Schwartzberg. Chicago, London: University of Chicago Press, 1978. 352p. maps. bibliog. (Association for Asian Studies Reference Series, no. 2).

The product of many years' work by Schwartzberg and his colleagues, this atlas quickly established itself as a uniquely valuable research tool. The numerous large and small maps are divided into fourteen sections covering historical periods from the prehistoric to the contemporary and political, economic and social developments. Each section of maps has a paired chapter of text which provides background information and commentary. The bibliography is also particularly extensive and useful.

Abode of snow: a history of Himalayan exploration and mountaineering.
See item no. 65.

Continents in collision: the International Karakoram Project.
See item no. 69.

Irrigation and drainage in the world: a global review.
See item no. 661.

Lahore: Entwicklung und räumliche Ordnung seines zentralen Geschäfts-bereich. (Lahore: development and spatial organization of its central business area.)
See item no. 685.

Flora and Fauna

46 **Compact handbook of the birds of India and Pakistan.**
Salim Ali, S. Dillon Ripley, plates by John Henry Dick.   Delhi: Oxford
University Press, 1987. 2nd ed. 737p. maps. bibliog.

Ali and his American colleague Ripley are the universally acknowledged founders of modern ornithology in South Asia. Their magnum opus was the *Handbook of the birds of India and Pakistan*, published originally in ten volumes from 1968 to 1975 (Bombay: Oxford University Press). A second edition is gradually being issued. The *Compact handbook*, published originally in 1983, manages, by using small but legible print, to get all the text into a single large volume. The second edition incorporates the revised editions of the first four volumes. It also includes an entirely new set of illustrations, some in colour and some in black and white. Closely connected to the *Handbook* are Salim Ali, *The book of Indian birds* (Delhi: Oxford University Press, 1979, 11th ed.), the best single-volume work for the amateur, and S. Dillon Ripley, *A synopsis of the birds of India and Pakistan* (Bombay: Natural History Society, 1982, 2nd ed.).

47 **The book of Indian reptiles.**
J. C. Daniel.   Bombay: Bombay Natural History Society (distributed
by Oxford University Press, Delhi), 1983. bibliog.

Illustrated with colour and black and white pictures as well as with line drawings, this work describes all the common reptiles to be found in India. Crocodiles, turtles, lizards and snakes are all included. Although the author is concerned primarily with present-day India, there are a number of references to the whole of the subcontinent.

48 **Encyclopedia of Indian natural history: centenary publication of the
Bombay Natural History Society, 1883–1983.**
Edited by R. E. Hawkins, illustrations editors Doris Norden, Bittu
Sahgal.   Delhi: Oxford University Press for the Bombay Natural
History Society, 1986. 620p. map.

Although oriented towards India, many entries in this work are for species to be found in Pakistan also, and distributions there are often noted. The encyclopedia lists some hundreds of species and categories of species of all types of plant and animal life. The entries are written by experts but intended to convey up-to-date, non-technical information to a general readership. There are many well-reproduced drawings and black and white photographs in the text, and 40 plates of colour and black and white illustrations.

49 **The vanishing jungle: the story of the World Wildlife Fund expeditions to Pakistan.**
Guy Mountfort, illustrated by Eric Hosking. Boston: Houghton Mifflin, 1970. 286p. 5 maps. bibliog.

The author led two expeditions to undivided Pakistan on behalf of the World Wildlife Fund in 1966 and 1967. The book itself is as much a travelogue as anything, but it contains a full list of all bird, amphibian, reptile and mammal species observed during the two expeditions. The expeditions themselves were mounted in order to make recommendations to the Government of Pakistan on how to preserve the country's rapidly dwindling wildlife.

50 **Flowers of the Himalaya.**
Oleg Polunin, Adam Stainton. Oxford, England; New York: Oxford University Press, 1984. 580p. maps. bibliog.

Intended as a field guide, this volume identifies all the common species which belong to the Himalayan flora. The fieldwork was carried out in India and Nepal, but many of the species described can be found in Pakistan (alongside others of West or Central Asian provenance). Each of the 1,495 entries is given a full scientific description. There are 689 colour photographs and 316 line drawings. A concise edition, including all the illustrations but with abbreviated descriptions, was published in 1988.

51 **The mammals of Pakistan.**
T. J. Roberts, with a foreword by His Royal Highness Prince Bernhard of The Netherlands. London; Tonbridge, England: Ernest Benn, 1977. 361p. maps. bibliog.

This is a detailed catalogue of Pakistan's mammals, from the smallest mouse to monkeys, leopards, deer and goats and including aquatic mammals such as dolphins. The author maintains that his work is oriented towards the field observer rather than the scientific taxonomist, but the book is rigorously organized and would be useful to specialist zoologists as well as to serious amateurs.

52 **Mountain monarchs: wild sheep and goats of the Himalaya.**
George B. Schaller. Chicago; London: University of Chicago Press, 1977. 425p. map. bibliog.

A scientific study based on over two years' research in Pakistan on the ecology and behavioural patterns of the wild sheep and goat of the Himalayan region. The author is particularly concerned with those species about which little has been written previously, for example the urial, wild goat and bharal. The work is well illustrated both with photographs and with tables of information on distribution, physical characteristics, etc. Schaller also wrote *Stones of silence: journeys in the Himalaya* (London: André Deutsch, 1980), which is based on the same research but takes a broader view of the environment of the regions in which he travelled.

13

Flora and Fauna

An anthropological reconnaissance in West Pakistan, 1955. With appendixes on the archaeology and natural history of Baluchistan and Bahawalpur.
See item no. 7.

The trekker's guide to the Himalaya and Karakoram.
See item no. 82.

Herb drugs and herbalists in Pakistan.
See item no. 699.

Travellers' Accounts

53 **Mountains of the Murgha Zerin: between the Hindu Khush and the Karakoram.**
Elizabeth Balneaves. London: John Gifford, 1972. 239p. bibliog.
This is an account of an extended journey in the northern areas of Pakistan by a writer who had made a number of previous visits to Pakistan. The date is not mentioned but must have been the late 1960s. Another book by the author on Pakistan is *The waterless moon* (London: Lutterworth, 1955).

54 **Travels into Bokhara together with a narrative of a voyage on the Indus.**
Alexander Burnes, introduction by James Lunt. Karachi: Oxford University Press, 1973. 3 vols. map. (Oxford in Asia Historical Reprints).
Burnes, later to be killed in Kabul during the first Afghan war, was one of the first European explorers of Afghanistan and Central Asia. In 1831 he travelled up the Indus to deliver a gift of horses to Ranjit Singh in Lahore (as well, of course, as carrying out surveys of the country for British use). He later travelled through Punjab to Afghanistan and Bokhara. The third volume of his travels, first published in 1834, tells the story of his journey up the Indus. The editor of the reprint is also the author of *Bokhara Burnes* (London: Faber & Faber, 1969).

55 **Scinde; or the unhappy valley.**
Richard F. Burton. London: Richard Bentley, 1851. 2 vols.
Burton was a young officer with Napier during the initial British conquest of Sindh, and he spent several years there in the 1840s. He was one of the first British officials to master the Sindhi language. His experiences there provided the basis for this account of the province and its people. Generally lighthearted in tone (if rather precious in places to modern ears), he nevertheless argues for continuing British rule if Sindh is to progress from what he sees as its unhappy economy and political condition. Burton also wrote *Sindh, and the races that inhabit the valley of the Indus; with notices of the topography and history of the province* (London: W. H. Allen, 1851) which covered

much of the same ground in a more systematic but less lively way. In 1877 he published *Sind revisited: with notices of the Anglo-Indian army; railroads; past, present, and future* (London: Richard Bentley). Despite its separate title that work is in most respects a revised version of *Scinde; or the unhappy valley*, although there are some comments on developments since it was first published.

56 **Breaking the curfew: a political journey through Pakistan.**
Emma Duncan. London: Michael Joseph, 1989. 313p. 2 maps.

The author is an economic journalist who covered Pakistan for the London *Economist* for some time in the mid-1980s. Her book describes various places she visited and people whom she met during visits to the country, and through these vignettes she tackles such issues as the role of the army in politics, corruption, and the position of women. She reports also on meetings with the late President Zia and with Benazir Bhutto.

57 **Up the country: letters written to her sister from the Upper Provinces of India.**
Emily Eden, notes by Edward Thompson, new introduction by Elizabeth Claridge. London: Virago, 1983. 410p.

First published in 1866 and reprinted several times since (in the present version in 1930), this is a classic of early English travel writing on India. Emily Eden was the sister of Lord Auckland, governor-general of India from 1836 to 1842. With him she went, in the pre-railway age, on a progress 'up the country' in 1838-9. In the course of it she visited Lahore and met Ranjit Singh. Her letters to a married sister in England are notable for their wit and observation. Her younger sister Fanny, who travelled with her, also kept a journal in the form of letters to friends which has only recently been published (*Tigers, durbars and kings: Fanny Eden's Indian journals 1837–1838*, transcribed and edited by Janet Dunbar. London: John Murray, 1988). This lacks some of the subtlety and style of Emily's work, but can be read with pleasure either by itself or in parallel. Some of Fanny's original sketches are included as illustrations.

58 **The lion river: the Indus.**
Jean Fairley. London: Allen Lane, 1975. 290p. 6 maps. bibliog.

A popular account of the Indus from its source in Tibet to its mouth near Karachi. Special attention is paid to its European explorers.

See item no. 3
59 **Early travels in India 1583–1619.**
Edited by William Foster. London: Oxford University Press, 1921. 351p. 2 maps. bibliog.

This volume contains the original narratives of seven English travellers, mostly traders and merchants, during the heyday of the Mughals. Several of them passed through what is now Pakistan. Of particular value is William Finch's account of his visit to Lahore in 1611.

60   **Letters from India; describing a journey in the British dominions of India, Tibet, Lahore, and Cashmere during the years 1828, 1829, 1830, 1831 undertaken by orders of the French government.**
Victor Jacquemont, introduction by John Rosselli.   Karachi: Oxford University Press, 1979. 2 vols. map. (Oxford in Asia Historical Reprints).

First published in English in 1834, this work was widely read in the 19th century both in France and in Britain. Its author went to India on a scientific expedition to collect botanical specimens but soon made contacts among British officials and Indian rulers. Although Jacquemont shared most of the European prejudices of his time, his letters to family and friends are marked, in the words of Rosselli's useful introduction to the modern edition, by a 'morning freshness' of perception. During his travels he made extensive visits to both Punjab and Kashmir, although less so to those parts that are now in Pakistan or Azad Kashmir.

61   **Where men and mountains meet: the explorers of the western Himalayas 1820–75.**
John Keay.   London: John Murray, 1977. 277p. 4 maps. bibliog.

This is perhaps the most accessible account of the various European traders, spies and eccentrics who first visited the area that now forms northern and north-western Pakistan. They include among others Moorcroft (q.v.), Vigne (q.v.) and Jacquemont (q.v.). Keay also published a sequel (*The Gilgit game: the explorers of the western Himalayas 1865–95*. London: John Murray, 1979) which concentrates on the period when exploration was more closely linked to the manoeuvres of the British and Russian empires along their common frontier.

62   **Where three empires meet: a narrative of recent travel in Kashmir, Western Tibet, Gilgit, and the adjoining countries.**
E. F. Knight.   London, New York: Longmans, Green & Co., 1893. 3rd ed. 582p. map.

Knight travelled extensively in Kashmir and what are now the northern areas of Pakistan in 1891, at a time when the Indian government was beginning to take a more active interest in the region. The volume contains his observations and an account of one episode of armed conflict between local tribesmen and Indian army troops. The background to this and the general political rivalry between Britain and Russia is covered by G. J. Alder in *British India's northern frontier 1865–95: a study in imperial policy* (q.v.).

63   **Travels of Fray Sebastien Manrique.**
Sebastien Manrique, translated and edited by C. Eckford Luard. Oxford, England: Hakluyt Society, 1927. 2 vols. 19 maps. bibliog. (Hakluyt Society 2nd Series, nos 59, 61).

Although he wrote in Spanish, Manrique was a Portuguese missionary of the 17th century who travelled widely in Asia. The second volume of his memoirs tells of his travels in India in 1640-41, during which time he visited Lahore and then travelled to Multan and thence via the Indus to Thatta.

17

Travellers' Accounts

64　**Where four worlds meet: Hindu Kush 1959.**
Fosco Mariani, translated by Peter Green.　London: Hamish Hamilton,
1964. 290p. 4 maps. bibliog.
A lively account of an Italian mountaineering expedition to the Hindu Kush region of
northern Pakistan in 1959. The larger part of the book is in fact taken up with the
journey there from Peshawar through Dir and Chitral, although there is also a detailed
description of the expedition's successful ascent of the hitherto unclimbed 24,000-feet
Mount Saraghrar.

65　**Abode of snow: a history of Himalayan exploration and mountaineering.**
Kenneth Mason.　London: Rupert Hart-Davis, 1955. 372p. bibliog.
The author was once Superintendent of the Survey of India and his book is a detailed,
sometimes rather dry account both of the geology of the Himalayas and of the stages
by which the region was explored and its high peaks climbed.

66　**Narrative of various journeys in Balochistan, Afghanistan and the
Panjab, including a residence in those countries from 1828 to 1838.**
Charles Masson, introduction by Gavin Hambly.　Karachi: Oxford
University Press, 1974. 3 vols. (Oxford in Asia Historical Reprints).
Charles Masson was one of the most remarkable figures in early British contact with
the areas that are now Pakistan. After deserting from the Indian army he wandered
alone, often penniless and dependent on the hospitality of people who had never
before encountered a European. He was among the first to recognize for what they
were the extensive Buddhist remains of north-west India and Afghanistan and
conducted the first archaeological investigations of them. Later on he was employed as
an intelligence agent by the government, although his relations with his superiors were
often tense. These volumes, first published in 1842, describe in detail his travels and
activities. His life is the subject of a sympathetic modern biography by Gordon
Whitteridge, *Charles Masson of Afghanistan* (Warminster, England: Aris & Phillips,
1986).

67　**Narrative of a journey to Kalat.**
Charles Masson, introduction by H. T. Lambrick.　Karachi: Oxford
University Press, 1977. 463p. map. (Oxford in Asia Historical Reprints).
Published slightly later, in 1844, and reprinted separately, this is also in some editions
the fourth volume of Masson's *Narrative*. In it, he relates his unintended involvement
in 1840 in the affairs of the state of Kalat in Baluchistan, which had been torn apart in
the aftermath of the first Afghan war. The events that he describes, and in which he
was an active participant, established the state in the form it retained up to 1947-48.
The volume includes a memoir of eastern Baluchistan.

68　**The narrow smile: a journey back to the North-West Frontier.**
Peter Mayne.　London: John Murray, 1955. 264p. 2 maps.
Peter Mayne had worked in India before independence and then briefly afterwards for
the Pakistan government. This book is an account, self-indulgent in places but lively
and interesting, of a return visit to the North-West Frontier in the early years of
independence. Mayne travelled on the Afghan side of the line as well as the Pakistani
and has some useful observations on the Pashtunistan issue which had been raised at
that time by the Afghan government.

18

69   **Continents in collision: the International Karakoram Project.**
Keith Miller, foreword by Lord Hunt.   London: George Philip, 1982.
212p. map.

This is the record of an expedition sponsored by the Royal Geographical Society of London in 1980 which brought together Pakistani, British and Chinese scientists to explore the Karakoram mountain range in northern Pakistan. The title of the book is to be taken literally, for this is an area of complex tectonic activity. The book itself, illustrated by dramatic colour photographs, is part travelogue and part report on the less specialized aspects of the scientific work of the expedition. There is a useful appendix on the history of European exploration of the area in the 19th and 20th centuries. A technical study of the same region is *Geology of Kohistan, Karakoram Himalaya, Northern Pakistan* (q.v.).

70   **Travels in the Himalayan provinces of Hindustan and the Panjab from 1819 to 1825.**
William Moorcroft, George Trebeck, introduction by G. J. Alder.
Karachi: Oxford University Press, 1979. 2 vols. map. (Oxford in Asia
Historical Reprints).

Although not the most famous, Moorcroft was the first British traveller to cross Afghanistan and reach Bokhara at a time when it was almost wholly unknown to Europeans. The purpose of his journey was to investigate trade possibilities between India and Central Asia, particularly in horses to improve the cavalry stock of the army. During his journey he passed through the kingdom of Ranjit Singh in the Punjab (and in fact met Ranjit Singh), as well as through what is now the North-West Frontier Province. Moorcroft died during his return journey from Bokhara, and the present work, first published in 1841, was assembled from his papers by H. H. Wilson. Alder, who wrote the introduction to the reprint, is also the author of a comprehensive biography of Moorcroft, *Beyond Bokhara: the life of William Moorcroft, Asian explorer and pioneer veterinary surgeon, 1767–1825* (London: Century, 1985).

71   **To the frontier.**
Geoffrey Moorhouse.   London; Sydney; Auckland; Toronto: Hodder
& Stoughton, 1984. 285p. map.

An account by a well-known travel writer describing a visit to Pakistan in 1983. From Karachi he travelled through Sindh and Baluchistan to Quetta and then to Lahore and Peshawar before moving on through the mountains to Chitral and Gilgit. Moorhouse comments on the passing scene and makes some perceptive observations of life during the height of the Zia period, although he does not follow any particular theme.

72   **Where the Indus is young.**
Dervla Murphy.   London: Century, 1983. 266p. map. bibliog.

A travelogue, originally published in 1977 by a well-known practitioner of the art of travelling rough, which covers a winter spent in 1974-75 in Baltistan, part of Pakistan's northern areas. As a woman accompanied by a young child, the author was able to see aspects of traditional Balti life that would not be open to a casual visitor. The author gives lively descriptions of the scenery and of the people that she encountered. Her earlier journey through Pakistan is described in *Full tilt* (London: John Murray, 1965).

73 **Passage to Peshawar: Pakistan between the Hindu Kush and the Arabian sea.**
Richard Reeves. New York: Simon & Schuster, 1984. 223p. map.

A lively and very readable account of Pakistan as it was in 1983 during the military régime of President Zia and at the time when the refugees from Afghanistan were making their initial impact on Pakistan society. The book is in the form of a travelogue, but there is a great deal of general information and analysis as well. The author is particularly interesting on Pakistan–US relations.

74 **That untravelled world: an autobiography.**
Eric Shipton. London: Hodder & Stoughton, 1969. 286p. 8 maps.

The autobiography of a renowned mountaineer who made some of the attempts in the 1920s and 1930s to climb Mount Everest. He made a major expedition to the Karakoram in 1937, to which a separate chapter of this book is devoted. He also described the expedition in *Blank on the map* (London: Hodder & Stoughton, 1938).

75 **Words for my brother: travels between the Hindu Kush and the Himalayas.**
John Staley. Karachi: Oxford University Press, 1982. 287p. 7 maps. bibliog.

The author is a professional geographer who visited the northern areas of Pakistan on a number of occasions to conduct research on glaciers but who at the same time became fascinated by the lives of the people who lived in these remote areas. This book tries, through the author's own experiences and his research, to convey the spirit of their lives, as well as to sketch in the development of relations between them and the wider world.

76 **Between Oxus and Jumna.**
Arnold J. Toynbee. London: Oxford University Press, 1961. 211p. map.

A travelogue by the distinguished historian and philosopher. Toynbee visited Pakistan (as well as India and Afghanistan) in 1960 and travelled widely within what was once the Kushan empire. Familiar with the literary and archaeological sources, he shares with the reader his excitement at visiting the historical sites, while at the same time commenting on the lives of the modern descendants of those who had lived there.

77 **Travels in Kashmir, Ladak, Iskardo ... and the Himalaya, north of the Panjab.**
G. T. Vigne. London: Henry Colburn, 1842. 2 vols. map.

Vigne travelled extensively in Kashmir and the Western Himalayas in the second half of the 1830s. Although Moorcroft (q.v.) had preceded him, he was the first European to visit Skardu and to explore the Baltistan region in any depth. He appears the archetypal English amateur, with his concern for hunting and for the local topography, although John Keay (q.v.) suggests he may also have worked as a British agent.

The vanishing jungle: the story of the World Wildlife Fund expeditions to Pakistan.
See item no. 49.

On Alexander's track to the Indus: personal narrative of explorations on the north-west frontier of India.
See item no. 99.

A glance at Sind before Napier or dry leaves from young Egypt.
See item no. 185.

Tourism

78 **A traveller's guide to Pakistan.**
Hilary Adamson, Isobel Shaw. Islamabad: Asian Study Group, 1981.
364p. 48 maps. bibliog.
Practically oriented if less glossily produced than many guidebooks, this volume is
intended for the foreigner resident in Pakistan for a year or two as much as for the
short-term visitor. There is much interesting information about smaller places on the
way between the main tourist sights.

79 **An insight and guide to Pakistan.**
Christine Osborne. Harlow, England; New York: Longmans, 1983.
268p. 6 maps. bibliog.
Written as a basic introduction to Pakistan for a prospective visitor or as a companion
for someone already there, the book seeks to capture the spirit of the country. Best
read in conjunction with a standard guidebook, it includes many photographs and a
small selection of recipes.

80 **Pakistan: a travel survival kit.**
Jose Roleo Santiago. South Yarra, Victoria: Lonely Planet, 1984. 2nd
ed. 213p. maps.
One of a series of guides intended mainly for the younger independent traveller. It
combines highly practical information on accommodation at all price levels and means
of transport with some suggestions on what to see. It is rather sketchy for some parts of
the country, but contains detailed information on trekking routes in the Himalayas.

81 **Pakistan: Collins illustrated guide.**
Isobel Shaw. London: Collins, 1989. 232p. 14 maps. bibliog.
Beautifully illustrated with drawings and colour photographs, this guide is a judicious
blend of enthusiasm and highly practical advice.

82 **The trekker's guide to the Himalaya and Karakoram.**
Hugh Swift.   San Francisco: Sierra Club Book, 1982. 342p. maps.
bibliog.

Covers the whole of the Himalayan region and contains three chapters describing in
detail treks that can be made in Chitral, Gilgit and Baltistan respectively. The
approach is sensible, and there are useful chapters giving a wide range of practical
information. There are also glossaries of several of the local languages and a chapter
on flora and fauna.

83 **A handbook for travellers in India, Pakistan, Nepal, Bangladesh and Sri
Lanka (Ceylon).**
L. F. Rushbrook Williams.   London: John Murray, 1975. 22nd ed.
(reprinted with amendments, 1982). 762p. maps. bibliog.

Often known as Murray's Guide, this is by far the oldest extant tourist guide for South
Asia, dating back to the 19th century. It is in some ways a historical curiosity. The
recommended routes follow the railways, and dak bungalows feature more frequently
than modern hotels, but it is more comprehensive than most in its listing of places to
see and does not just concentrate on the obvious sights. Some fifty pages are devoted
to Pakistan, besides a separate section on Kashmir.

Peshawar: historic city of the frontier.
See item no. 181.

Karachi.
See item no. 683.

Archaeology and Prehistory

84 **The rise of civilization in India and Pakistan.**
Bridget Allchin, Raymond Allchin. Cambridge, England: Cambridge
University Press, 1982. 379p. maps. bibliog. (Cambridge World
Archaeology).

This is a revised version of the same authors' *The birth of Indian civilization*
(Harmondsworth, England: Penguin, 1968) and covers the stone age, the Indus
civilization, and the arrival in the subcontinent of Indo-Aryan groups followed by the
re-emergence of cities in the middle of the first millennium BC. Intended for a non-
specialist readership, although very detailed in some parts, it is extensively illustrated.
It incorporates the new emphasis on non-traditional types of archaeological data, for
example from palaeoclimatology, to produce as integrated as possible a view of the
cultures concerned.

85 **Excavations at Mohenjo Daro, Pakistan: the pottery.**
George F. Dales, Jonathan Mark Kenoyer, with a contribution by Leslie
Alcock. Philadelphia, Pennsylvania: University of Pennsylvania,
University Museum, 1986. 586p. maps. bibliog. (University Museum
Monograph, no. 53).

This is the first of what are intended to be three final reports on excavations at
Mohenjo-daro in 1965. At that time Dales and his colleagues carried out an intensive
resurvey of a small area to extend the range of knowledge of the site and the Harappan
culture generally. Alcock's contribution makes available for the first time certain
material from Mortimer Wheeler's earlier excavations. When complete, these reports
will be the standard source for specialized information on Mohenjo-daro.

86 **The historic city of Taxila.**
Ahmad Hasan Dani. Tokyo: Centre for East Asian Cultural Studies;
Paris: UNESCO, 1986. 190p. maps. bibliog.

The author is a distinguished archaeologist but while he never loses sight of the archaeological dimension he seeks in this work to provide a more historically and anthropologically oriented account of this major city of ancient Punjab than that provided by Sir John Marshall's *A guide to Taxila* (q.v.).

87 **The roots of ancient India: the archaeology of early Indian civilization.**
Walter A. Fairservis, Jr., drawings by Jan Fairservis. London: George Allen & Unwin, 1971. 482p. 28 maps. bibliog.

A major synoptic work on Indian archaeology by a leading US scholar. Fairservis begins with the earliest evidence from the stone age dating back a quarter of a million years or more. He then deals with the transition to settled habitation before coming to the Harappan period. Because of the spatial distribution of human settlement in prehistoric India, much of the book derives its material from sites which are now in Pakistan.

88 **Studies in the archaeology of India and Pakistan.**
Edited by Jerome Jacobson. Warminster, England: Aris & Phillips; Delhi: Oxford & IBH, 1987. 327p. maps. bibliog.

A collection of scholarly papers designed to illustrate the work of US archaeologists working on South Asia in the 1980s. A number of the papers are concerned with the Harappan civilization both in terms of its social and cultural life and of its material culture.

89 **Antiquities of northern Pakistan: reports and studies.** vol. 1. *Rock inscriptions in the Indus valley.*
Edited by Karl Jettmar. Mainz am Rhein, West Germany: Verlag Philipp von Zabern, 1989 (1 vol. in 2 parts).

The petroglyphs or rock-carvings along the Indus valley in its upper reaches along the ancient trade routes have become fully known only in recent years. Dating back to at least the third millennium BC, they are a major source for the prehistoric and Buddhist periods. This volume of specialist essays has been brought together by the leading specialist on the subject. The second part of the volume, printed separately, is devoted to photographic illustrations of the carvings. A related volume of photographs and text, produced originally for an exhibition and intended for a general readership, is *Between Gandhāra and the silk road: rock-carvings along the Karakoram highway. Discoveries by German–Pakistani expeditions, 1979–1984*, edited by Karl Jettmar and Volker Thewalt (Mainz am Rhein, West Germany: Verlag Philipp von Zabern, 1987).

90 **Architecture and art treasures in Pakistan: prehistoric, protohistoric, Buddhist and Hindu periods.**
F. A. Khan. Karachi: Elite, 1969. 200p. bibliog.

This is a general book on the subject by a senior Pakistani archaeologist, divided equally between the architectural remains to be found at the country's major archaeological sites and the artefacts that have been found. There is only brief mention of the post-Gandhara period.

91   A comprehensive bibliography of Pakistan archaeology: paleolithic to
     historic times.
     Denise King.   East Lansing, Michigan: Michigan State University Asian
     Studies Center, 1975. 95p. 2 maps. (South Asian Series Occasional
     Paper, no. 24).

The bibliography includes 1,083 items published up to and including 1972. The entries
are not annotated and are arranged simply by author, but there is a subject index.
They include books, articles and unpublished dissertations. All items are in European
languages, mostly in English.

92   The people of South Asia: the biological anthropology of India, Pakistan,
     and Nepal.
     Edited by John R. Lukacs.   New York; London: Plenum, 1984. 465p.
     map. bibliog.

This is a specialized collection of papers in the field of physical anthropology. Two
distinct sections cover palaeoanthropology and the biological anthropology of the
contemporary population of the area. In the former section Pakistani material features
in a number of chapters, especially two on Harappa by Pratap C. Dutta and Jim G.
Shaffer respectively. A paper in the second section by Charles A. Weitz, 'The impact
of irrigation on the demographic structure of the Peshawar basin of northwest
Pakistan', argues that social factors need to be built into models relating material
resources and population growth.

93   A guide to Taxila.
     John Marshall.   London: Cambridge University Press, 1960. 4th ed.
     187p. maps. bibliog.

This is not so much a guidebook as a summary of Marshall's comprehensive account of
his archaeological discoveries at Taxila from 1913 to 1934 (*Taxila: an illustrated account
of archaeological excavations carried out at Taxila ... between the years 1913 and 1934.*
Delhi: Motilal Banarsidass, 1975 [first published by Cambridge University Press, 1951],
3 vols). It would however be useful to a student or an amateur archaeologist visiting
the sites of the successive cities of Taxila which were built by rulers of the area from at
least the 6th century BC onwards. These included among others the Bactrian Greeks
and the Kushans. Taxila was a major educational and cultural centre and there have
been many Buddhist finds.

94   Pakistan Archaeology.
     Karachi: Government of Pakistan, Ministry of Education, Department
     of Archaeology, 1964- . annual.

An annual publication designed for the archaeologist and carrying reports on current
excavations. Volumes appear several years after the nominal date given. Another
archaeological journal which also began publication in 1964 but has appeared
irregularly is *Ancient Pakistan*, from the Department of Archaeology at the University
of Peshawar.

95 **Harappan civilization: a contemporary perspective.**
Edited by Gregory Possehl. Warminster, England: Aris & Phillips,
1982. 440p. maps. bibliog.

The papers in this useful collection arose from a conference in 1979 of a group of mainly Indian and US archaeologists. They are arranged into sections dealing with the nature of Harappan urbanization, the results of recent fieldwork, ecology, technology and trade, biological anthropology, the later phases of the Harappan tradition, and history of research on the subject. There are single papers on the Indus script and on 'Paradigm changes in the study of the Indus civilization'. This last places the volume in perspective and emphasizes, in contrast to earlier approaches, how complex and interwoven were the processes of cultural change during the Harappan period. Another collection of papers which equally illustrate trends in archaeological research is *Studies in the archaeology and palaeoanthropology of South Asia*, edited by K. A. R. Kennedy and Gregory Possehl (New Delhi: Oxford & IBH Publishing Corporation, 1984). The papers with Pakistani relevance are mainly but not exclusively concerned with Harappan topics.

96 **The end of the ancient cities of the Indus.**
Robert L. Raikes. *American Anthropologist*, vol. 62, no. 2 (April 1964), p. 284-99. map. bibliog.

This is a provocative article which challenges existing interpretations of the decline of Harappa and Mohenjo-daro which see it essentially in terms of social factors. Instead, Raikes suggests that geomorphological changes and consequent flooding were primarily responsible. A critical review of Raikes's hypothesis is offered by Gregory Possehl ('The Mohenjo-daro floods: a reply', *American Anthropologist*, vol. 69, no. 1 (Feb. 1967), p. 32-40), who argues, following Wheeler, that the cities' decline was due primarily to over-utilization of the land.

97 **Asian axe two million years old.**
Helen Rendell, Robin Dennell. *The Geographical Magazine*, vol. 59, no. 6 (June 1987), p. 270-2. map.

This article reports the finding in 1983 in northern Pakistan of a stone axe which has been dated to at least two million years ago. If confirmed, this finding would revolutionize the whole study of hominids in Asia.

98 **The middle stone age cultures of northern Pakistan.**
Mohammad Salim. Islamabad: Quaid-i-Azam University, Centre for the Study of the Civilizations of Central Asia, 1986. 227p. map. bibliog.

This is a specialized study of stone age cultures in Pakistan based on intensive work at two sites, one in Mardan district, the other in the Soan valley in Rawalpindi. Salim is concerned to work out chronologies for the middle stone age sites of India and Pakistan.

99 **On Alexander's track to the Indus: personal narrative of explorations on the North-West Frontier of India.**
Aurel Stein. London: Macmillan, 1929. 182p. 2 maps. bibliog.

Sir Aurel Stein, one of the most scholarly of all the British Raj's officials, made his reputation by his work on Central Asia. His knowledge of the Chinese-language and

Buddhist sources made him particularly well qualified to write about the Buddhist period in North-West Frontier history. The present work combines travelogue with history and archaeology.

100 **Vergessene Städte am Indus: frühe Kulturen in Pakistan vom 8.–2. Jahrtausend v. Chr.** (Forgotten cities of the Indus: early cultures in Pakistan from the 8th to the 2nd millennium BC).
Günter Urban, Michael Jansen (et al.). Mainz am Rhein, West Germany: Verlag Philipp von Zabern, 1987. 312p. maps. bibliog.

Produced in connection with an exhibition on the 'Forgotten cities of the Indus' held first at Aachen in 1987, this volume is made up of a series of essays for the general reader. Well-known scholars write on different aspects of the Harappan culture. The quality of the printing and of the illustrations is of a high order.

101 **The Indus civilization.**
Mortimer Wheeler. London: Cambridge University Press, 1968. 3rd ed. 144p. maps. bibliog. (Supplementary Volume to the *Cambridge History of India*).

This is the most detailed and authoritative account available for the non-specialist reader on the Indus or Harappan civilization. Wheeler, who himself made one of the most significant contributions to its uncovering, discusses all aspects of the civilization from its artefacts to aspects of religion and language which can only dimly be perceived from the archaeological record.

102 **My archaeological mission to India and Pakistan.**
Mortimer Wheeler. London: Thames & Hudson, 1976. 96p. maps. bibliog.

A personal account by Sir Mortimer Wheeler of his time as Director-General of the Archaeological Survey of India from 1944 to 1947. After independence he was for a little while in charge of archaeology in Pakistan. During the six years after 1944 he carried out excavations at the major Pakistani sites at Charsadda, Harappa and Mohenjo-daro. These memoirs include both personal reflections and archaeological information.

Narrative of various journeys in Balochistan, Afghanistan and the Panjab including a residence in those countries from 1828 to 1838.
See item no. 66.

Between Oxus and Jumna.
See item no. 76.

Peshawar: historic city of the frontier.
See item no. 181.

Anthropology in Pakistan: recent socio-cultural and archaeological perspectives.
See item no. 399.

History

South Asia

103 **The AᶜīnÌ-i Akbarī.**
Abū'l Fazl ᶜAllāmī, translated by H. Blochmann, H. S. Jarrett, revised by D. C. Phillott, Jadunath Sarkar. Delhi: Atlantic Publishers, 1989.

This is in fact the final part of Abul Fazl's *Akbarnāmā* (q.v.) but is always referred to as a separate work. In it Abul Fazl describes in meticulous detail the mode of government of the Mughal empire during the reign of Akbar. The first section deals with the royal household and with military affairs, the second – which has been used to good effect by later economic historians such as Shireen Moosvi in her *The economy of the Mughal empire* (q.v.) – with the revenues of the empire, and the third with the social conditions of the population of India. There is also a section which lists the sayings and observations of the emperor. There is no single source that is so important for a study of Indian history in the Mughal period. A modern scholarly edition is badly needed but Blochmann's 19th-century translation, first published 1873–96, retains its value.

104 **The Akbarnāmā.**
Abu-l-Fazl, translated by H. Beveridge. Delhi: Atlantic Publishers, 1989. 3 vols.

This massive Persian work, which in translation runs to well over 2,000 pages, is the official life of the emperor Akbar by Abul Fazl, his principal administrator. While the literary form is that of a court biography, including for example minute astrological details, it remains one of the most important sources available for Mughal history. The edition, although first published 1902–39, is scholarly. There is a brief introduction to the third volume in which the translator offers his own assessment of Akbar, although it would strike most modern readers as unduly moralistic.

105 **The crisis of empire in Mughal North India: Awadh and the Punjab, 1707–48.**
Muzaffar Alam. Delhi: Oxford University Press, 1986. 365p. 7 maps. bibliog.

This major scholarly study of the 18th century moves beyond existing work on the period in its emphasis on the interaction of forces operating at the centre of the Mughal empire and those arising in the provinces, in this case the Punjab and Awadh. While Alam sees the period as one of decline of central control, he also emphasizes the extent of new growth at the provincial and local level. There is considerable material on the struggles between the Sikhs and Mughal officials in the Punjab. Another important work that covers a slightly later period but is also concerned with the post-Mughal situation in North India is C. A. Bayly, *Rulers, townsmen and bazaars: North Indian society in the age of British expansion, 1770–1870* (Cambridge, England: Cambridge University Press, 1983).

106 **Babur-nama (Memoirs of Babur).**
Translated by A. S. Beveridge. London: Luzac, 1922 (reprinted 1969). 880p.

This work was written by Babur, the first Mughal ruler of India and direct descendant of Taimur (Tamerlane), who brought his troops into India in the early 16th century and laid the foundations of the empire. His memoirs describe not only his campaigns but also the countryside and his interest in the arts. They were originally written in Turki but were soon translated into Persian. A number of translations into European languages exist. A particularly lavish edition which includes reproductions of miniatures from a manuscript copy of the Persian text is *Le livre de Babur: Mémoires du premier Grand Mogol des Indes (1494–1529)*, translated by Jean-Louis Bacqué-Grammont (Paris: L'Imprimerie Nationale, 1985).

107 **The patrimonial-bureaucratic empire of the Mughals.**
Stephen P. Blake. *Journal of Asian Studies*, vol. 39, no. 1 (Nov. 1979), p. 77-94.

An assessment of the Mughal empire in which the author argues that it is inappropriate to see it as a forerunner of the centralized British administration of the 19th century. It would be better, he suggests, to look at it in terms of a model derived from the Weberian concept of a patrimonial form of political organization focused on the person of the emperor wherever he happened to be.

108 **The Cambridge Economic History of India.**
Cambridge, England: Cambridge University Press, 1982. 2 vols. vol. 1, *c.1200-c.1750*, edited by Tapan Raychaudhuri, Irfan Habib. 543p. 10 maps. bibliog. vol. 2, *c.1757-c.1970*, edited by Dharma Kumar. 1073p. 12 maps. bibliog.

In the tradition of the Cambridge histories, these two volumes provide as far as possible a comprehensive and authoritative review of the subject by its leading academic exponents. What is now Pakistan is covered in the sections on Northern India (Punjab and the North-West Frontier Province) and Western India (Sindh and Baluchistan). In the second volume there is considerable material on the individual regions, rather less in the first. There is also much to be gleaned from the general chapters, especially those in the second volume on irrigation and the railways. A chapter in the final section reviews the performance of the Pakistan economy from independence to 1970.

109 The Cambridge History of India.
London: Cambridge University Press, 1922-37. 5 vols. maps. bibliog.

The *Cambridge History of India* was planned in six volumes, although the second volume on the later classical period was never written. The contributors and editors were a mixture of professional academics and scholar-administrators. While still valuable as a reference work in some areas, it has for the most part been overtaken by modern scholarship. Volume 1, published in 1922 and edited by E. J. Rapson, deals with ancient India; vol. 3 (1928, edited by Wolseley Haig) with the Turks and Afghans; vol. 4 (1937, edited by Richard Burn) with the Mughal period; vol. 5 (1929, edited by H. H. Dodwell) with British India, 1497-1858; and vol. 6 (1932, edited by H. H. Dodwell) with the Indian empire, 1858-1918. A supplement to volume 1 by Mortimer Wheeler, *The Indus valley civilization* (q.v.) was published separately at a later stage. A *New Cambridge History of India* has begun to appear, but this comprises a series of monographs on interconnected topics rather than the magisterial volumes of the earlier work. C. A. Bayly's *Indian society and the making of the British empire* (Cambridge, England: Cambridge University Press, 1988), is relevant to Pakistan.

110 The imperial impact: studies in the economic history of Africa and India.
Edited by Clive Dewey, A. G. Hopkins. London: Athlone Press, 1978. 409p.

The major essay in this collection of studies in economic history that bears on Pakistan is that by Clive Dewey, '*Patwari* and *Chaukidar*: subordinate officials and the reliability of India's official statistics' (p. 280-314), in which he argues that published statistics in South Asia depend critically on the village officials, who very often simply made them up. Many of his examples are taken from the Punjab. A more detailed article on the Punjab was published by Dewey in a specialist journal: 'The agricultural statistics of the Punjab, 1886–1947', *Bulletin of Quantitative and Computer Methods in South Asian Studies*, no. 2 (March 1974), p. 3-14.

111 The history of India as told by its own historians: the Muhammadan period.
H. M. Elliot, edited after his death by John Dowson. London: Trübner & Co, 1867-77. 8 vols.

Although designed, often in the crudest fashion, to glorify British rule and depict India's past as one only of tyranny and misery, this massive work is still a frequently used collection of translations of historical manuscripts mostly in Persian, many of which are not otherwise available. There are some editorial annotations and bibliographical comments.

112 The great Moghuls.
Bamber Gascoigne. London: Jonathan Cape, 1971. 264p. map. bibliog.

This is a beautifully illustrated popular account of the Mughal emperors. Separate chapters are devoted to Babur, Humayun, Akbar, Jahangir, Shah Jahan, and Aurangzeb.

31

113 **The agrarian system of Mughal India (1556–1707).**
Irfan Habib. Bombay: Asia Publishing House, 1963. 453p. map.
bibliog.

The publication of this book marked the beginning of a new phase in the study of Mughal economic and social history. Habib uses a wide range of Persian sources to describe and analyse the agrarian economy and social structure of Mughal India. He discusses the relationship between the land revenue system, the local economy, and the structure of the Mughal state, and identifies an agrarian crisis that gradually developed in the course of the 17th century.

114 **The technology and economy of Mughal India.**
Irfan Habib. *Indian Economic and Social History Review*, vol. 17,
no. 1 (Jan.-March 1980), p. 1-34.

A wide-ranging survey of the levels of technology reached during the Mughal period which indicates high levels in some areas and lesser achievements in others. Habib, a prominent scholar of the period, concludes that although there was no in-built resistance to technological change there was equally no overwhelming enthusiasm for it.

115 **Class structure and economic development: India and Pakistan since the Moghuls.**
Angus Maddison. London: George Allen & Unwin, 1971. 181p.
bibliog.

Maddison's essay in broad historical analysis discusses the links between the social structure of the Indian subcontinent and economic growth there. He looks particularly at the question of whether governments in India and Pakistan have been able to change underlying social structures to any substantial extent. He reviews critically the 'functional inequality' approach pursued in Pakistan in the 1960s.

116 **Mughals in India: a bibliographical survey of manuscripts.**
D. N. Marshall. London; New York: Mansell, 1985. 634p.

The compiler has attempted to include all manuscripts, whatever the language, which are relevant to the study of political, economic, and social conditions during the Mughal period. Items range therefore from the well known, for example the $A^c\bar{i}n$-*i Akbarī* (q.v.), to minor works which may nevertheless be highly relevant to one particular area or topic. Each of the 2,105 entries is annotated. The entries are arranged by author's name and there are title and subject indexes.

117 **The men who ruled India.**
Philip Woodruff (pseud. for Philip Mason). London: Jonathan Cape.
vol. 1. *The founders*, 1953. 402p. 8 maps. bibliog; vol. 2. *The guardians*, 1954. 385p. 4 maps. bibliog.

Mason's work has become the classic account of the British officials who succeeded first in conquering and then in ruling India. Through a series of biographical sketches he deftly weaves together historical incident with personal detail to recreate the world of the British officials and their changing perceptions of their role in India. Mason was himself a member of the Indian Civil Service in the last years of British rule, and his assessment of his colleagues and predecessors is sympathetic but informed by an acute awareness of the ambiguities and complexities of their position.

118   **The economy of the Mughal empire c.1595: a statistical survey.**
Shireen Moosvi.   Delhi: Oxford University Press, 1987. 442p. 11
maps. bibliog.
This is a careful attempt to establish as accurate a picture as possible of the state of the
Indian economy under the Mughals in 1595, a date which sees the empire at its high
point and for which there is available the uniquely valuable *A^{c}īn-i Akbarī* (q.v.).
Moosvi uses other documentary and numismatic evidence to discuss such topics as
agricultural productivity, money supply and foreign trade, population and the
distribution of the agrarian surplus at the local level and among the ruling class.

119   **India at the death of Akbar: an economic study.**
W. H. Moreland.   London: Macmillan, 1920. 328p. bibliog. 2 maps.
Although outmoded in many respects, this work remains an accessible and coherent
account of the economic and social conditions of India at the height of Mughal power.
Moreland foreshadows later research in his attempt to quantify wherever possible. He
was also the author of *The agrarian system of Moslem India* (Cambridge, England: W.
Heffer, 1929) and *From Akbar to Aurangzeb: a study in Indian economic history*
(London: Macmillan, 1923).

120   **Some aspects of religion and politics in India during the thirteenth
century.**
Khaliq Ahmad Nizami, foreword by C. C. Davies, introduction by
Mohammad Habib.   Aligarh: Aligarh Muslim University, Department
of History, 1961. 421p. bibliog. (Publications of the Department of
History, Aligarh Muslim University, no. 16).
This important study deals with India at the time of the Turkish invasions which led to
the establishment of the Delhi Sultanate in 1206. Nizami reviews the background and
then discusses the position of various groups in society, including the rulers, the *ulama*,
the sufis, and the Hindus. Appendices include relevant documents and discussion of
source material generally.

121   **The administration of the Sultanate of Delhi.**
Ishtiaq Husain Qureshi.   Karachi: Pakistan Historical Society, 1958.
4th rev. ed. 2 maps. bibliog. (Pakistan Historical Society Publication,
no. 10).
First published in 1942, this is a comprehensive review of the administrative system in
the area of the Sultanate of Delhi from its formation as an independent unit in 1206 till
its first defeat by the Mughals in 1526. The Sultanate's territories included the Punjab
and Sindh.

122   **The imperial monetary system of Mughal India.**
Edited by John F. Richards.   Delhi: Oxford University Press, 1987.
382p. maps.
This is a collection of specialized articles arising out of a conference which brought
together specialists in various aspects of the history of Mughal India to see how
numismatic studies could be brought to bear on wider issues in the economic history of
the period. Contributions cover, for example, the currency system in the time of

Akbar, the structure of monetary exchange in North India, and foreign merchants and the Mughal mints.

123 **Centre and periphery in the Mughal state: the case of seventeenth-century Panjab.**
Chetan Singh. *Modern Asian Studies*, vol. 22, no. 2 (May 1988), p. 299-318.
Singh uses the example of Punjab in the 17th century to challenge some current historiographical assumptions about the degree to which the Mughal state exercised control over peripheral areas. He draws attention to the existence of a strong regional landed élite in the Punjab with which the Mughal rulers had to come to terms.

124 **A history of the Indian people.**
D. P. Singhal. London: Methuen, 1983. 481p. 12 maps. bibliog.
Singhal provides a comprehensive narrative survey of Indian history from prehistoric times to the 1980s. After 1947 the focus is solely on what is now India, but for the rest the whole of the subcontinent is included. The classical and medieval periods are both well covered.

125 **A history of India: volume two.**
Percival Spear. Harmondsworth, England: Penguin Books, 1965. 284p. 2 maps. bibliog.
A standard history of the Indian subcontinent for the general reader written by a British historian of humanist and liberal persuasions. The second volume covers the Mughals and the colonial period. The final chapters deal with the post-independence period but are confined to India. The first volume of the history, by Romila Thapar (Harmondsworth, England: Penguin Books, 1966), covers the classical period and the early Muslim dynasties.

126 **The twilight of the Mughuls: studies in late Mughul Delhi.**
Percival Spear. London: Cambridge University Press, 1951. 270p. map. bibliog.
A beautifully written history of the city of Delhi from the late 18th century up to 1858 which evokes the intellectual and political atmosphere of the time. This was the Delhi both of the poet Ghalib and of Sir Sayyid Ahmad Khan. Another interesting study which overlaps with Spear in its treatment of the late Mughal period is Narayani Gupta, *Delhi between two empires 1803–1931: society, government and urban growth* (Delhi: Oxford University Press, 1981).

127 **A guide to Western manuscripts and documents in the British Isles relating to South and South East Asia.**
Compiled by M. D. Wainwright, Noel Matthews. London: Oxford University Press, 1965. 532p.
This is a major research tool for anyone working on any aspect of Pakistan in the colonial period. It lists in summary form the archival holdings of many different record offices and museums, from the Public Record Office down to small regimental museums and business firms. There is an extensive index by person and place. The records of the India Office Library and Records (well described in Martin Moir, *A*

general guide to the India Office Library and Records. London: British Library, 1988) are excluded, however. A limited amount of information on archives within Pakistan can be found in *Government archives in South Asia: a guide to national and state archives in Ceylon, India and Pakistan,* edited by D. A. Low, J. C. Iltis and M. D. Wainwright (London: Cambridge University Press, 1969).

An atlas of the Mughal empire: political and economic maps with detailed notes, bibliography and index.
See item no. 40.

A historical atlas of South Asia.
See item no. 45.

Early travels in India 1583–1619.
See item no. 59.

A matter of honour: an account of the Indian army, its officers and men.
See item no. 550.

South Asian history, 1750–1950: a guide to periodicals, dissertations and newspapers.
See item no. 787.

Muslims of South Asia

128 **Studies in Islamic culture in the Indian environment.**
Aziz Ahmad. Oxford, England: Clarendon Press, 1964. 311p. bibliog.
Aziz Ahmad sees the development of an Islamic culture in India both as a regional formulation of a general Islamic culture and as a process of interaction with the Hinduism that is indigenous to the region. He traces these two themes from the Delhi Sultanate of the pre-Mughal period to the 20th century. Topics include pan-Islamism in India, Islamic modernism, and sufism and syncretism.

129 **Muslim self-statement in India and Pakistan 1857–1968.**
Edited by Aziz Ahmad, G. E. von Grunebaum. Wiesbaden, West Germany: Otto Harrassowitz, 1970. 240p.
This is an anthology of extracts, mainly translated from Urdu, which illustrate some of the main themes in Islamic thought in the 19th and 20th centuries. Conservative and progressive tendencies are represented by such writers as Sayyid Ahmad Khan, Amir Ali, Abul Kalam Azad, Iqbal, and Maududi. The work is linked to Aziz Ahmad's *Islamic modernism in India and Pakistan 1857–1964* (q.v.).

130 **My life, a fragment.**
Mohamed Ali, edited by Afzal Iqbal. Lahore: Sh. Muhammad Ashraf, 1942. 363p.
Mohamed Ali, together with his older brother Shaukat, played a central role in

mobilizing support for the Khilafat campaign and was involved in all the major political developments of the 1910s and 1920s. This incomplete autobiography, written while he was in jail, deals primarily with his religious background and outlook. Three volumes of his political writings have appeared edited by Mushirul Hasan and covering the period 1907 to 1923 (*Mohamed Ali in Indian politics: selected writings.* Delhi: Atlantic Publishers, 1982, 1983, 1986), and two volumes of his articles from his newspaper *Comrade (Selections from Mohamed Ali's* Comrade, edited by R. A. Jafri. Lahore: Mohammad Ali Academy, 1965).

131 **Sources of Indian tradition.**
Compiled by W. Theodore de Bary (et al.). New York: Columbia University Press; London: Oxford University Press, 1958. 961p. 2 maps. bibliog. (Records of Civilization: Sources and Studies, no. 56).

This is an excellent collection of readings from South Asian authors of all periods in which Muslim writers are well represented. For the medieval writers in Persian or later in Urdu, the extracts translated here are often the only easily available English versions. The 19th and 20th centuries are represented by Sayyid Ahmad Khan, Iqbal, Muhammad Ali (i.e. Mohamed Ali), Rahmat Ali, Liaquat Ali Khan, Maududi, and I. H. Qureshi.

132 **Sharī'at and ambiguity in South Asian Islam.**
Edited by Katherine P. Ewing. Berkeley; Los Angeles; London: University of California Press, 1988. 321p. map. bibliog.

This volume, a successor to that on *adab* edited by Barbara Metcalf (q.v.), explores the codes of behaviour by which South Asian Muslims live their lives, and the interrelationship in those codes of the Islamic *sharia* and ideas drawn from other sources. The editor suggests that the relationship is often a deliberately ambiguous one. Contributors are historians and anthropologists.

133 **Islam in Asia.** vol. 1. *South Asia.*
Edited by Yohanan Friedmann. Jerusalem: Magnes Press, The Hebrew University, 1984. 289p.

This volume brings together a selection of papers from a conference held in 1977. Apart from a shared concern with Islam in South Asia, there is no common theme, and topics include both medieval and contemporary issues.

134 **Islam et société en Asie du Sud.** (Islam and society in South Asia.)
Edited by Marc Gaborieau. Paris: Editions de l'Ecole des Hautes Etudes en Sciences Sociales, 1986. (Collection Purusartha, no. 9).

A collection of essays in both French and English on various aspects of Muslim society in South Asia. The articles have brief summaries in both languages. Of particular interest are the five articles on pre-colonial Muslim society and culture, and the articles by Akbar S. Ahmed on Islam, ethnicity and the state and by Mariam Abu Zahab on the early history of the Pakistan People's Party from 1967 to 1971.

135   **The political theory of the Delhi sultanate (including a translation of Ziauddin Barani's *Fatawa-i Jahandari*, circa 1358–9 A.D.).**
Mohammad Habib, Afsar Umar Salim Khan.   Allahabad, India: Kitab Mahal, [1960]. 172p.

The bulk of this work is a translation into English of Barani's *Fatawa-i Jahandari*, which is regarded as the prime political text produced in the medieval period. A shorter section discusses Barani's thought. A related discussion of Barani can be found in P. Hardy, *Historians of medieval India: studies in Indo-Muslim historical writing* (London: Luzac, 1960). A general work on medieval Islamic political thought is E. I. J. Rosenthal, *Political thought in medieval Islam: an introductory outline* (London: Cambridge University Press, 1958).

136   **The Muslims of British India.**
Peter Hardy.   London: Cambridge University Press, 1972. 306p.
5 maps. bibliog. (Cambridge South Asian Studies, no. 13).

This masterly work surveys the historical experience of the Muslims of South Asia from the decline of Mughal power to what the author describes as the dual partition, the division of India into two sovereign states and of the Muslim population between them. He outlines the main intellectual trends both among those exposed to the colonial educational institutions and among those who remained with the traditional framework of the religious seminary, and discusses the ways in which Muslims entered politics, for what purposes, and with what success.

137   **Partners in freedom – and true Muslims: the political thought of some Muslim scholars in British India, 1912–1947.**
Peter Hardy.   Lund, Sweden: Studentlitteratur, 1971. 62p.
(Scandinavian Institute of Asian Studies Monograph Series, no. 5).

Not all Muslims supported the demand for Pakistan, and this is a study of the thought of some of those who opposed it. Hardy pays particular attention to the ideas of Abul Kalam Azad and the *ulama* who belonged to the Jamiat-ul-ulama-i-Hind, for example Maulana Madani. He establishes links between their ideas and those of earlier Muslim thinkers. There is a detailed study of Azad by Ian Henry Douglas, *Abul Kalam Azad: an intellectual and religious biography* (Delhi: Oxford University Press, 1988).

138   **Nationalism and communal politics in India, 1916–1928.**
Mushirul Hasan.   Delhi: Manohar, 1979. 372p. bibliog.

Originally a doctoral thesis, this is an important study of the subject. Hasan rejects simplistic notions of a politically homogeneous Muslim community in India and looks instead for the specific factors that were responsible for the development of a strong separatist movement in the 20th century. He attaches particular importance during the period under study to the relationships between national Hindu and Muslim leaders, although he recognizes that by the 1940s a grassroots separatist sentiment had developed.

139 **The Cambridge History of Islam.** vol. 2, *The Further Islamic Lands, Islamic society and civilization,* edited by P. M. Holt, Ann K. S. Lambton, Bernard Lewis. London: Cambridge University Press, 1970. 966p. 6 maps. bibliog.

The Cambridge histories aim at synoptic coverage of their subjects by acknowledged authorities, and this is no exception. Approximately 120 pages are devoted to South Asia. There are two chapters by I. H. Qureshi on the pre-Mughal and Mughal periods, and by S. A. A. Rizvi and Aziz Ahmad on the 18th century and the colonial periods respectively.

140 **The Indian Musalmans: are they bound in conscience to rebel against the Queen?**
William Wilson Hunter. London: Trübner, 1871. 215p.

Written at the request of the viceroy Lord Mayo, Hunter's book marked the beginning of a new British policy towards the Muslim community (despite Mayo's assassination shortly afterwards at the hands of a Muslim). Hunter argued that the considerable disaffection that existed was not entailed by Islam, although he was critical of many of the *ulama*, and that a policy of conciliation would pay considerable dividends. A famous review of Hunter's book was written by Sayyid Ahmad Khan (*Review of Dr. Hunter's* Indian Musalmans, by Syed Ahmad Khan Bahadur, Benares [Varanasi, India], the author, 1872), which argued strongly for government encouragement to the Muslim community.

141 **A history of the freedom movement (being the story of Muslim struggle for the freedom of Hind-Pakistan).**
Edited by Mahmud Husain, S. Moinul Haq (et al.). Karachi: Pakistan Historical Society, 1957-70. 4 vols. (Pakistan Historical Society Publications, nos 15, 19, 56).

Originally under government control, responsibility for this work was later transferred to the Pakistan Historical Society. Although the study was intended to go up to 1947, the last volume is incomplete and ends with the Simla conference of June 1945. Many of Pakistan's leading historians contributed to what was intended to be the authoritative work on the subject. The standard of the contributions is variable, however, and the tone often rather bland. The bibliographical details are somewhat confusing. Although it is divided into four volumes, volumes two and three are divided into two parts, published at different times. The first volume was not included in the Pakistan Historical Society Publications series.

142 **Islamic Culture.**
Hyderabad, India: Islamic Culture Board, 1927- . quarterly.

This longstanding journal published from Hyderabad, a major centre of Islamic culture in India, is devoted primarily to Islamic history and culture in South Asia, although a few articles tackle broader topics.

143 **Islamic society and culture: essays in honour of Professor Aziz Ahmad.**
Edited by Milton Israel, N. K. Wagle. New Delhi: Manohar, 1983. 383p. bibliog.

Twenty articles on a wide range of topics, but with one exception all concerned with

Muslims in South Asia. Contributors include many distinguished scholars in the fields of history, literature and religious studies.

144   **Journal of the Pakistan Historical Society.**
Karachi: Pakistan Historical Society, 1953- . quarterly.
This carries scholarly articles mainly on South Asian Muslims, but occasionally covers the pre-Islamic period and Muslim groups elsewhere in the world. Most articles are in English, with occasional contributions in Urdu.

145   **Muslim endowments and society in British India.**
Gregory C. Kozlowski.   Cambridge: Cambridge University Press, 1985. 211p. bibliog. (Cambridge South Asian Studies, no. 35).
Despite its apparently narrow focus this is a major contribution to the debate on the role of Islam among South Asian Muslims. The author's starting point is the controversy during the colonial period over the legal status of *waqfs* or religious endowments. Could they be used, as they had been in the pre-colonial period, to further private as well as public purposes, or could they, as the British courts came to insist in the late 19th century, be applied only to 'charitable purposes'? The status quo was restored by legislation in 1913, but the author argues that the debate between British administrators and Muslim political leaders had the effect of emphasizing a monolithic and narrow view of the Muslim community in India which has obscured its diversity both at the time and subsequently.

146   **Growth of Muslim population in medieval India (A.D. 1000–1800).**
K. S. Lal.   Delhi: Research Publications, 1973. 272p. bibliog.
A detailed demographic study which discusses the position of Muslims within the total Indian population. Lal reinforces the generally accepted view that most Muslims were initially local converts.

147   **Aligarh's first generation: Muslim solidarity in British India.**
David Lelyveld.   Princeton, New Jersey: Princeton University Press, 1978. 380p. 3 maps. bibliog.
A richly detailed account of the early years of the college founded at Aligarh in 1875 by Sir Sayyid Ahmad Khan. Lelyveld describes the intellectual and social milieu in which the college operated through an examination of *sharif* culture. He then examines the education which young men received at the college and the solidarity created among them as a result of their experiences there. This, he argues, was the setting for the development of new forms of Muslim self-awareness.

148   **Conversion to Islam.**
Edited by Nehemia Levtzion.   New York, London: Holmes & Meier, 1979. 272p. bibliog.
Apart from the general introduction, the main interest is an important article by P. Hardy, 'Modern European and Muslim explanations of conversion to Islam in South Asia: a preliminary survey of the literature', p. 68-99, which was first published in the *Journal of the Royal Asiatic Society*, 1977, no. 2, p. 177-206. Hardy discusses the early uncertainties about the size of the Muslim population, the conflicting theories based on

immigration and on conversion through sufi influence, and the meanings attached to these theories in ideological controversy.

149 Moslem nationalism in India and Pakistan.
Hafeez Malik.   Washington, DC: Public Affairs Press, 1963. 355p.

Malik offers a general survey of the subject beginning from the earliest period of Muslim contact with South Asia and ending with the creation of Pakistan. He examines the various strands, religious and secular, in the Pakistan movement, and describes its historical development. He also discusses those Muslim groups and individuals who opposed the Pakistan ideal.

150 Sir Sayyid Ahmad Khan and Muslim modernization in India and Pakistan.
Hafeez Malik.   New York: Columbia University Press, 1980. 340p.
bibliog. (Studies in Oriental Culture, no. 15).

A substantial historical study of Sayyid Ahmad Khan, a key figure in Muslim modernist thought in South Asia. Malik discusses his intellectual background in the Delhi of the first half of the 19th century and his experiences as an East India Company official, especially during the 1857 revolt, before describing his views on education and politics. Purely religious issues are covered more briefly.

151 Islamic revival in British India: Deoband, 1860–1900.
Barbara Daly Metcalf.   Princeton, New Jersey; Guildford, England: Princeton University Press, 1982. 386p. 7 maps. bibliog.

The focus of this absorbing if specialized study of Islamic revival in colonial India is the seminary that was established in 1867 at the small town of Deoband in northern India and which thereafter provided religious leadership for many of South Asia's Muslims. Metcalf describes the *ulama* associated with Deoband as reformers or renewers but working firmly within the established religious tradition of Islam compared to the modernists who reached out to newer sources of inspiration.

152 Moral conduct and authority: the place of *adab* in South Asian Islam.
Edited by Barbara Metcalf.   Berkeley, California; Los Angeles; London: University of California Press, 1984. 389p.

This very valuable collection of papers by leading scholars of South Asian Islam takes as its theme the concept of *adab*, an idea which is difficult to translate but which refers in a very broad sense to proper behaviour. Collectively, the authors of the papers seek to stress the continuity in South Asia of the basic ideal of *adab*, however much it may have been influenced by the Western world. The papers explore a range of different themes located in a number of different epochs to bring out the central meanings of the concept. There is much about sufism, but also about the life of officials, musicians and others.

153 The Khilafat movement: religious symbolism and political mobilization in India.
Gail Minault.   New York: Columbia University Press, 1982. 294p.
bibliog. (Studies in Oriental Culture, no. 16).

The Khilafat (Caliphate) movement which was at its peak in the 1919 to 1921 period was an attempt to bring pressure to bear on the British government not to destroy the defeated Ottoman empire after the First World War, and in particular to preserve its ruler's position as the Caliph of the Islamic world. It was a high point both of pan-Islamic feeling among Indian Muslims and, more surprisingly, of Hindu–Muslim cooperation. Minault's work, which draws on a wide range of Urdu and English sources, seeks to locate the movement in the framework of contemporary developments in India and to examine the multiple meanings the Caliphate had for different groups in the Muslim community. She concludes that the most significant aspect of the Khilafat movement was its symbolic value in the creation of a sense of a distinct Muslim identity within the broader Indian population. A collection of articles most of which are about the Khilafat period is *Communal and pan-Islamic trends in colonial India* (edited by Mushirul Hasan. Delhi: Manohar, 1981).

154 The Indian Muslims.

M. Mujeeb. London: George Allen & Unwin, 1967. 590p. bibliog.

This is perhaps the most authoritative account of the history of South Asia's Muslims from the 'nationalist Muslim' point of view. Mujeeb is concerned to depict the various ways in which over time Muslims have defined themselves and their distinctive position in Indian society. This takes him into the social, political, and artistic, as well as the religious fields.

155 The Khilafat movement in India, 1919–1924.

A. C. Niemeijer. The Hague: Martinus Nijhoff, 1972. 263p. bibliog. (Verhandeligen van het Koninlijk Instituut voor Taal-, Land- en Volkenkunde, no. 62).

This detailed study of the Khilafat movement relies heavily on official documents and the private papers of British officials. The frame of reference is general theories of nationalism rather than the specific history of South Asian Muslims.

156 Historians of India, Pakistan and Ceylon.

Edited by C. H. Philips. London: Oxford University Press, 1961. 504p. (Historical Writing on the Peoples of Asia, no. 1).

This is a unique survey of the historiography of South Asia which covers both Western and South Asian writers from the earliest times to the present. Three chapters are devoted to Muslim historians writing in the Mughal and pre-Mughal periods. Three chapters cover modern writing on aspects of Muslim history in South Asia, and there is relevant material in other chapters.

157 The Muslim community of the Indo-Pakistan subcontinent (610–1947): a brief historical analysis.

Ishtiaq Husain Qureshi. Karachi: Ma'aref, 1977. 2nd ed. 385p. bibliog.

First published in 1962, this work has become a standard account by a Pakistani of his country's history as part of the history of the Muslims of the subcontinent. Qureshi begins with the first Arab traders and moves on through the Muslim dynasties and the decline of Muslim political power to the rise of the Muslim League, the Khilafat movement, described by him as an 'adventure in altruism', and the Pakistan movement itself.

158 **A short history of Pakistan.**
Edited by Ishtiaq Husain Qureshi. Karachi: University of Karachi,
1967. 4 vols. maps. bibliog.

Intended for the student and the general reader alike, this work is a synoptic history which seeks, not always very successfully, to include all the relevant aspects of South Asian history within the perspective of Pakistan. The first volume, by A. H. Dani, covers the pre-Muslim period; the second, by M. Kabir, Muslim rule under the Sultans; the third, by A. Rashid, the Mughal empire; and the fourth, by a number of scholars, is devoted to 'alien rule and the rise of Muslim nationalism'.

159 **The ʿulamā of British India and the hijrat of 1920.**
M. Naeem Qureshi. *Modern Asian Studies*, vol. 13, no. 1 (Feb.
1979), p. 41-59.

During the Khilafat movement many Muslims in what is now Pakistan obeyed a call to migrate from India to Muslim-ruled Afghanistan, only to be forced to return in disarray. Qureshi describes the episode and discusses the divisions among the *ulama* on the appropriateness of the action. He concludes that the *hijrat* was an ill-advised move but that it reflected the frustrations of the period.

160 **The wonder that was India.** vol. II. *A survey of the history and culture
of the Indian sub-continent from the coming of the Muslims to the British
conquest.*
S. A. A. Rizvi. London: Sidgwick & Jackson, 1987. 416p. 7 maps.
bibliog.

Rizvi is a well-known writer on many aspects of medieval Indian Muslim history, and his account of medieval India draws extensively on his detailed knowledge of Islamic movements, especially the sufi orders, although it could be faulted for its lack of attention to areas that were not under Muslim rule. Rizvi portrays the period as one when Muslims retained their distinctive religious beliefs and practices but at the same time evolved a culture that was compatible with their Hindu neighbours. The book is a sequel to the same publisher's *The wonder that was India* by A. L. Basham (3rd ed., 1967), which dealt only with the classical period.

161 **Islam and Muslim society in South Asia.**
Francis Robinson. *Contributions to Indian Sociology* (n.s.), vol. 17,
no. 2 (July-Dec. 1983), p. 185-203.

This essay argues strongly in favour of a view of Muslim society in South Asia as defined by its constant tendency to move over time towards patterns of behaviour and belief that derive from the central core of Islam as transmitted by the *ulama*. He is critical of sociological approaches which portray an equilibrium between 'high Islamic' and custom-centred, more local traditions. Robinson's article provoked critical rejoinders from Veena Das (ibid., vol. 18, no. 2 [July-Dec. 1984] p. 293-300) and Gail Minault (ibid., p. 301-5). His reply (ibid., vol. 20, no. 1 [Jan.-June 1986], p. 97-104) reaffirms his original position.

162 **Modern Islam in India: a social analysis.**
Wilfred Cantwell Smith.   London: Victor Gollancz, 1946. rev. ed.
344p.

Although the author later changed his mind on many of the arguments put forward in this work, it remains a remarkable attempt at applying the categories of class analysis to the various ideological tendencies that were prominent in 20th-century Islam in South Asia. Smith deals first with individual writers and their followers, for example Sayyid Ahmad Khan, Amir Ali and Iqbal, and then with political groupings. These latter include a number of the small radical groups such as the Ahrars and Khaksars as well as the Muslim League, described by Smith as first a reactionary and then a bourgeois nationalist movement.

163 **The making of Pakistan.**
Richard Symonds.   London: Faber & Faber, 1950. 2nd ed. 227p.
bibliog.

Written very shortly after independence this book retains its value as a brief survey of the background to Pakistan. It is in two parts. The first, 'The growth of a nation', sketches in the history of the Muslims of South Asia from the earliest period. The second, 'The creation of a state' deals with partition and then describes the constituent parts of the new country and the initial lines of government policy. There is an appendix by Ahmed Ali on the culture of Pakistan.

164 **Political identity in South Asia.**
Edited by David Taylor, Malcolm Yapp.   London: Curzon Press;
Atlantic Highlands, New Jersey: Humanities Press, 1979. 266p.

The main interest of this work from the Pakistan perspective is in the two articles by Paul Brass and Francis Robinson where the issues raised by Brass in his *Language, religion and politics in North India* (q.v.) are debated in the specific context of the Muslim population of India. The major point at stake is the relative weight to be assigned to political competition compared to religious ideas in the emergence of Muslim separatism.

165 **The political triangle in India 1858–1924.**
Syed Razi Wasti.   Lahore: People's Publishing House, 1976. 240p.

This is a collection of the author's previously published articles, mainly in Pakistani journals, on the political history of India's Muslims in the period from immediately after the 1857 revolt to the Khilafat movement. Topics include British policy towards the Muslims and Muslim political organizations, especially the establishment of the Muslim League in 1906.

166 **Rise of Muslims in Indian politics: an analysis of developments from
1885 to 1906.**
Rafiq Zakaria, foreword by Y. B. Chavan.   Bombay: Somaiya, 1970.
427p. bibliog.

Originally a thesis, this is a useful study of the emergence of an all-India Muslim political leadership in the years up to the founding of the Muslim League in 1906. Zakaria traces the intellectual background, especially in the shape of the Aligarh movement, and discusses the immediate problems facing the Muslim community at that time. The focus is very much on figures like Sir Sayyid Ahmad Khan and others who were beginning to articulate the interests of the Muslim élite. Zakaria is sympathetic to the dilemmas they faced but regrets their lack of vision which he sees as having laid the foundations for Muslim separatism.

An historical atlas of Islam.
See item no. 38.

Atlas of the Islamic world since 1500.
See item no. 44.

Islamic modernism in India and Pakistan 1857–1964.
See item no. 347.

Islamic Studies.
See item no. 366.

The rose and the rock: mystical and rational elements in the intellectual history of South Asian Islam.
See item no. 368.

Essays on Islamic civilization presented to Niyazi Berkes.
See item no. 369.

South Asian intellectuals and social change: a study of the role of vernacular-speaking intelligentsia.
See item no. 397.

Islam in the political process.
See item no. 515.

Punjab Muslim press and the Muslim world, 1888–1911.
See item no. 772.

Constituent provinces of Pakistan

167 **From martial law to martial law: politics in the Punjab, 1919–1958.**
Syed Nur Ahmad. Edited by Craig Baxter, translated by Mahmud Ali. Boulder, Colorado; London: Westview Press, 1985. 455p. bibliog.

The author of this work, originally written in Urdu, was a journalist and civil servant who had been close to many of the leading political figures of the Punjab in the 20th century. It is on the one hand a rather routine account of political developments at the all-India and later all-Pakistan level but on the other a more interesting and valuable review of events and personalities in the Punjab, especially the leading landlord politicians. The editor has added an extensive and useful set of notes to the text, although the introduction itself is rather brief.

168 **Diary and notes of Mian Fazl-i-Husain.**
Edited by Waheed Ahmad. Lahore: Research Society of Pakistan,
1977. 363p. (Publication no. 47).

The first part of this work consists of the diary kept by Sir Fazl-i-Husain from 1930 to
his death in 1936, and the second of notes on various issues prepared for his colleagues
at the time when he was a member of the viceroy's executive council. The diary deals
with personal as well as political matters. Ahmad also produced an edition of Fazl-i-
Husain's letters: *Letters of Mian Fazl-i-Husain* (Lahore: Research Society of Pakistan,
1976 [Publication no. 39]).

169 **British India's northern frontier 1865–95: a study in imperial policy.**
G. J. Alder. London: Longmans, 1963. 392p. 3 maps. bibliog.
(Imperial Studies Series, no. 25).

This is a careful and detailed study of the northern rather than the north-west frontier
of India, stretching from the Pamirs to the eastern end of the Karakoram range, and of
the attempts during the 19th century to control the region by both Russians and
British. Eventually, after many alarms and excursions involving soldiers, diplomats and
explorers, an agreement was signed in 1895 which settled the spheres of influence of
the two sides. Alder also discusses the involvement of China in the area, as well as
relevant aspects of the history of Afghanistan.

170 **The Punjab under imperialism, 1885–1947.**
Imran Ali. Princeton, New Jersey; Guildford, England: Princeton
University Press, 1988. 264p. bibliog. 2 maps.

Ali's subject is the expansion of canal irrigation in the Punjab in the late 19th century,
in particular how it was that despite the major investment that the canals represented
the Punjab as a whole remained in most respects undeveloped and stagnant. He traces
the development of the canal system, its management, and the way the British used it
to tie the landed élite into support for colonial rule.

171 **Relations between the Muslim League and the Panjab National Unionist
Party, 1935–1947.**
Imran Ali. *South Asia*, no. 6 (Dec. 1976), p. 51-65.

The focus of this detailed article is the domination of Punjab politics in this period by
the landed interest. Its support was given first to the Unionist Party and then switched
to the Muslim League to serve purely provincial interests.

172 **The Chachnama, an ancient history of Sind.**
Ali Kufi, translated by Mirza Kalichbeg Fredunbeg. Lahore:
Vanguard Books, 1985. 207p. (Historical Reprints, no. 2).

This important source for the history of Sindh was written in the 13th century by one
Ali, originally from Syria but settled in India. The theme of the book is the conquest of
Sindh by the Arabs in the 8th century. Originally written in Arabic, it was then
translated into Persian. The Fredunbeg translation into English was first published in
1900. There is an article on the historical value of the *Chachnama* in Yohanan
Friedmann (ed.), *Islam in Asia*, vol. 1. *South Asia* (q.v.).

173 **N.-W.F.P. administration under British rule, 1901–1919.**
Lal Baha. Islamabad: National Commission on Historical and
Cultural Research, 1978. 297p. 3 maps. bibliog. (Historical Studies
(Muslim India) Series, no. 2).

This is a detailed account of its subject based on government records, private papers
and other material. The author discusses in turn the formation of the province out of
the Punjab in 1901, relations with the frontier tribes, and various aspects of
administration.

174 **The problem of "greater Baluchistan": a study of Baluch nationalism.**
I. Baloch. Stuttgart, West Germany: Steiner Verlag Wiesbaden, 1987.
299p. 4 maps. bibliog. (Beiträge zur Südasienforschung Südasien-
Institut Universität Heidelberg, vol. 116).

Originally a thesis, this work includes a considerable volume of general material on the
Baluch peoples and their culture, before dealing with Baluchistan in the 19th and 20th
centuries up to the time of independence and the failure of the Khanate of Kalat to
assert an independent status in 1947-48. The author argues that Baluchi nationalism
has been hindered in the past by the lack of a modern social basis but that this is
changing. Extensive appendices include a number of documents relevant to the
position of Kalat in 1947.

175 **Searchlights on Baloches and Balochistan.**
Mir Khuda Baksh Bijarani Marri Baloch. Karachi: Royal Book
Company, 1974. 387p. maps. bibliog.

A general history and survey of the Baluch people by a distinguished Baloch jurist.
While proud of his people's history, the author does not gloss over internal feuding and
strife.

176 **Inside Baluchistan: a political autobiography of His Highness Baiglar
Baigi, Khan-e-Azam – XIII.**
Mir Ahmad Yar Khan Baluch. Karachi: Royal Book Company, 1975.
352p. bibliog.

The author was ruler of Kalat, the major princely state of the Baluchistan area, from
1933 until March 1948 and thereafter played a controversial role in Pakistan politics.
The first half of the main text of this book summarizes Baluch history up to 1933. The
remainder is an attempt to justify the author's actions in 1947 and 1948 in delaying the
merger of his state with Pakistan and to demonstrate his loyalty to the country. He also
criticizes the actions of successive rulers of Pakistan up to 1971. The book also includes
the text of nineteen important documents from the initial agreement between Kalat
and the British in 1839 to the correspondence between the author and Jinnah at the
time of independence. An alternative account of the events described by Ahmad Yar
Khan can be found in W. A. Wilcox, *Pakistan: the consolidation of a nation* (q.v.).

177   **Lahore past and present (being an account of Lahore compiled from original sources).**
Muhammad Baqir.   Lahore: Panjab University Press, 1952. 556p.
map. bibliog. (Panjab University Oriental Publication, no. 34).
A scholarly and immensely detailed history of Lahore from its origin at some point in the first millennium AD to its height under the Mughals and thence to the 20th century. The author also includes descriptions of all the main mosques and other public buildings of the city, as well as lists of the rulers of Lahore and other relevant information.

178   **The Punjab Alienation of Land Bill of 1900.**
Norman G. Barrier.   Durham, North Carolina: Duke University, 1966. 125p. bibliog. (Monograph and Occasional Paper Series, no. 2).
This is a study of a colonial piece of legislation which succeeded in setting the political agenda for the whole period up to independence by giving special protection in matters of land ownership to so-called agricultural tribes and castes. Barrier discusses the complex policy processes of the government, which, he argues, were not at all monolithic, and the effect of the passage of the Bill on the balance of political forces in the province. A major contribution to the debate in government circles was published as *Musalmans and moneylenders* by S. S. Thorburn (q.v.).

179   **Punjab history in printed British documents: a bibliographic guide to parliamentary papers and select, nonserial publications, 1843–1947.**
N. Gerald Barrier.   Columbia, Missouri: University of Missouri Press, 1969. 108p. (University of Missouri Studies, vol. 50).
Includes 488 items on Punjab history in the colonial period and is a good guide to the wealth of material contained in printed documents.

180   **The wealth and welfare of the Punjab.**
H. Calvert.   Lahore: Civil & Military Gazette, 1936. 2nd ed. 421p.
First published in 1922, this is a good example of the colonial scholar-administrator at work. The author is primarily concerned with agriculture and the means by which it can be developed in such a way as to ensure stable prosperity. He is particularly concerned to argue the case for free trade rather than the protectionism then being demanded by industrial interests in India. The book is useful both for the data that it provides and as an example of colonial thinking on issues of economic development.

181   **Peshawar: historic city of the frontier.**
Ahmad Hasan Dani.   Peshawar: Khyber Mail Press, 1969. 253p.
3 maps.
The author, a distinguished archaeologist, here outlines the history of Peshawar from its earliest origins in the Kushan period to after independence. The major emphasis is on the people who lived in and around the city rather than on the physical fabric, but there are two chapters which describe the historic monuments of Peshawar city and the Peshawar valley respectively.

182   **The problem of the North-West Frontier, 1890–1908, with a survey of policy since 1849.**
C. Collin Davies.   London: Cambridge University Press, 1932. 220p. 3 maps. bibliog.

Based on official records, this work remains the starting point for later discussions of the subject. Davies reviews the history of British policy in the light of local and imperial considerations and notes that it was constantly in flux. He focuses in particular on the Curzon years, when the North-West Frontier Province was established and the 20th-century approach to the tribal areas was laid down.

183   **Punjab settlement manual.**
J. M. Douie.   Delhi: Daya Publishing House, 1985. 246p.

This apparently highly technical work on the way in which the British assessed (settled) and collected land revenue can usefully be read by anyone with a serious interest in the Punjab's history. It is divided into three parts. The first is a review of settlement policy from the annexation in 1849 until the time the work was written at the end of the 19th century. The second and third examine respectively the compilation of the 'record of rights', a key element in the British system, and the assessment of revenue itself. The edition cited here is reprinted from the first edition of 1899, although the work was several times reissued in updated form, most recently as the 4th edition in 1930. Douie was also the author of *The Panjab, North-west Frontier Province and Kashmir* (London: Cambridge University Press, 1916 [Provincial Geography of India]).

184   **The Punjab tradition: influence and authority in nineteenth-century India.**
P. H. M. van den Dungen.   London: George Allen & Unwin, 1972. 366p. map. bibliog.

The Punjab, both because it was the last province to be incorporated into British India and because of its military and strategic significance, was perceived by the British as needing special treatment. The 'Punjab tradition' that thus developed emphasized the importance of protecting the position of the rural population and excluding outside forces that might bring in subversive ideas. Van den Dungen's thorough study discusses in detail the emergence of official thinking on these issues, especially in the context of land ownership.

185   **A glance at Sind before Napier or dry leaves from young Egypt.**
E. B. Eastwick, introduction by H. T. Lambrick.   Karachi: Oxford University Press, 1973. 377p. map. (Oxford in Asia Historical Reprints).

This was originally published in 1849 as *Dry leaves from young Egypt or a glance at Sindhe before Napier*. The author was a government official posted in Sindh before its annexation by Napier in 1843. His account of his travels between 1839 and 1841 is delightful in its own right and is also of substantial historical interest. Eastwick was a strong proponent of the former rulers of Sindh, the *mirs*, and felt strongly that they had been cheated and duped by the British.

186 **A bibliography of economic literature relating to the Punjab.**
Cyril P. K. Fazal.   Lahore: Board of Economic Inquiry Punjab, 1941.
112p. (Board of Economic Inquiry Punjab, publication no. 73).
Most of the items included are government publications of one sort or another, ranging
from proceedings of official commissions and annual statistical publications to leaflets
of the Punjab Agricultural Department, although there are also lists of articles and
books on aspects of rural development related to the Punjab. The entries are
unnumbered and unannotated, but they are arranged by subject and there are author
and subject indexes. The same author compiled *Guide to Punjab government reports
and statistics*, 1939 (Board of Economic Inquiry Punjab, publication no. 10).

187 **Remarks on Baluchi history.**
Richard N. Frye.   *Central Asiatic Journal*, vol. 6 (1961), p. 44-50.
A specialist article which discusses the linguistic and other evidence bearing on the
origins of the Baluch people. The author considers they may well have come in the
11th and 12th centuries from the desert areas of Iran.

188 **The peoples of Pakistan: an ethnic history.**
Y. V. Gankovsky, translated by Igor Gavrilov.   Moscow: 'Nauka'
Publishing House, 1971. 247p. bibliog.
Using a Marxist categorization of history into slave-owning, feudal and bourgeois
periods, Gankovsky looks at the emergence and development of each of Pakistan's
main ethnic groups, viz. Punjabis, Sindhis, Baluch and Pukhtuns (and also Bengalis),
up to the 20th century. Religion and language were, he argues, the main factors
shaping the consciousness of the various groups as, with the emergence of capitalist
relations of production, ethnic consciousness evolved into national (in a specifically
Marxist sense) consciousness.

189 **Empire and nation: Punjab and the making of Pakistan.**
David Gilmartin.   London: I. B. Tauris, 1988. 258p. 2 maps. bibliog.
This important study looks at the tension within the Punjab in the 20th century
between the politics of colonialism, dominated by landlords and other intermediaries
between state and society, and the new ideal of Muslim community embodied in the
demand for Pakistan. Although in 1947 the Muslim League gained an apparent victory
over the forces of localism, it was not able to consolidate it. Gilmartin pays special
attention to the role of the *pirs*, religious leaders but also landlords in their own right.
In a separate article he has discussed in more detail the role they played in the critical
elections of 1946: 'Religious leadership and the Pakistan movement in the Punjab',
Modern Asian Studies, vol. 13, no. 3 (July 1979), p. 485-517.

190 **"Old Lahore": reminiscences of a resident.**
H. R. Goulding, with a historical and descriptive account by T. H.
Thornton.   Lahore: Universal Books, [1976]. 94p. 2 maps.
Published originally in book form in 1924, Goulding first wrote these reminiscences as
a series of articles for the *Civil and Military Gazette*. Most of the work is a mixture of
firsthand experience of the city in the late 19th century and snippets of information
gathered from many different sources on the earlier history of Lahore. The second part
of the book, by Thornton, was published as a pamphlet in 1860 and reviews the history
of the city from its origins to the British conquest.

191 **European adventurers of northern India, 1785 to 1849.**
C. Grey, edited by H. L. O. Garrett.   Lahore: Superintendent,
Government Printing, 1929. 361p. bibliog.

The subjects of this book are the motley crew of Europeans who sought their fortunes in the Punjab and Afghanistan in the late 18th and the first part of the 19th centuries. Some, like George Thomas, were adventurers pure and simple who exploited the disturbed conditions to carve out temporary fiefdoms for themselves. Others, like the famous or notorious Avitabile, were soldiers who were recruited into the army of Ranjit Singh. Most of the material is derived from Punjab government records or from previously published works. The book is popular in tone, although it naturally reflects the prejudices of the time it was written.

192 **Chiefs and families of note in the Punjab.**
Lepel H. Griffin, Charles Francis Massey, revised and corrected by
W. I. Conran, H. D. Craik.   Lahore: Government of the Punjab,
1909. 2 vols.

This large work was the final version of a series of British efforts, first begun in the 1860s, to put in writing the history of those prominent social figures whom they wished to make their loyal allies in the Punjab. Each prominent landlord family is given a chapter which begins with a genealogical table and goes on to describe the family history and fortunes. There are frequent comments on the moral qualities of individuals. The work has a period flavour and can be seen as a typical product of colonial rule, but it also contains some valuable source material.

193 **Sources on Punjab history.**
Edited by W. Eric Gustafson, Kenneth W. Jones.   Delhi: Manohar
Book Service, 1975. 454p.

As a whole this volume seeks to draw the attention of scholars to under-utilized sources for Punjab history, especially non-English language sources. Of special interest here are the chapters on Ahmadiyah history by Spencer Lavan, and on the printed literature of the Punjabi Muslims, 1860-1900, by Edward Churchill, although there are also relevant items in other chapters.

194 **A forgotten chapter of Indian history as described in the memoirs of
Seth Naomul Hotchand, C.S.I., of Karachi, 1804–1878.**
Naomul Hotchand, translated by Alumal Trikamdas Bhojwani, edited
by Evan M. James, introduction by Hamida Khuhro.   Karachi: Oxford
University Press, 1982. 222p. (Oxford in Asia Historical Reprints).

Seth Naomul Hotchand was an agent of the British both before and after the conquest of Sindh in 1843 and invaluable to them in many ways. These memoirs (first published in 1915) are a significant historical source to be set alongside the comparable works of Masson (q.v.) and others.

195 **Mizh: a monograph on government's relations with the Mahsud tribe.**
Evelyn Howell, foreword by Akbar S. Ahmed. Karachi: Oxford
University Press, 1979. 119p. map. (Oxford in Asia Historical
Reprints).

The Mahsuds are one of the most important of the Pukhtun tribal groups in the
unadministered areas on the North-West Frontier, and their conflicts with the British
formed a major chapter in frontier history. This short book, written originally for
British officials and published in 1931, contains a wealth of historical detail that
illuminates both British and tribal history. It is also, in the words of Akbar S. Ahmed,
'a masterly analysis of tribal structure and organization'.

196 **British relations with Sind, 1799–1843: an anatomy of imperialism.**
Robert A. Huttenback. Berkeley, California; Los Angeles:
University of California Press, 1962. 161p. map. bibliog.

This academic study reviews events in Sindh in the decades up to and including
annexation in 1843 and explores the paradox of its conquest at a time when in general
British policy was in a non-expansionist phase. Huttenback concludes that it can be
explained in terms of commercial and security considerations as interpreted by the
ambitious figure of Sir Charles Napier.

197 **Thirty seconds at Quetta.**
Robert Jackson. London: Evans Brothers, 1960. 248p. map.

A popular account of the devastating earthquake which almost completely destroyed
the city of Quetta, capital of Baluchistan, on 31 May 1935 and in which 30,000 people
died. The major emphasis of the book is on the part played in the rescue work by the
British troops quartered in the largely unaffected cantonment outside the city.

198 **India, Pakistan or Pakhtunistan: the nationalist movements in the
North-West Frontier Province, 1937–47.**
Erland Jansson. Uppsala: Acta Universitatis Upsaliensis (distributed
by Almqvist & Wiksell, Stockholm), 1981. 283p. 2 maps. bibliog.
(Studia Historica Upsaliensia, no. 119).

This is a doctoral dissertation which covers much the same ground as S. Rittenberg's
*Ethnicity, nationalism and the Pakhtuns: the independence movement in India's North-
West Frontier Province* (q.v.) and uses many of the same sources. The focus, however,
is more specifically on the 1937-47 period and Jansson differs to some extent from
Rittenberg in the relatively lesser weight he assigns to cultural aspects of Pukhtun
identity.

199 **Pakistan movement in Baluchistan.**
Inamul Haq Kausar. [n.p., n.d.]. 69p.

A brochure which gives a brief factual account of the main events and personalities in
Baluchistan during the years immediately preceding partition. The role of Jinnah is
given special prominence. It should be noted, however, that the Pakistan movement as
such made very little impact in Baluchistan before 1947.

200 **Multan: history and architecture.**
Ahmad Nabi Khan. Islamabad: Islamic University, Institute of
Islamic History, Culture and Civilization, 1983. 390p. maps. bibliog.
(A Fifteenth Century Hijra Publication).

Multan, the principal city of southern Punjab, was also a major centre of sufi activity in
the 13th and 14th centuries AD. The tombs of the saints form a major chapter in the
history of Indo-Islamic architecture. The first part of this volume is a scholarly study of
Multan's history, the second of its architecture, illustrated with plans of the buildings
and with black and white and colour photographs.

201 **Sind through the centuries: proceedings of an international seminar held
in Karachi in Spring 1975 by the Department of Culture, Government of
Sind.**
Hamida Khuhro. Karachi: Oxford University Press, 1981. 301p.

This volume contains 32 contributions from most of the leading scholars on Sindh in
Pakistan and abroad. They cover all periods of Sindhi history and aspects of Sindhi
culture.

202 **Sind before the Muslim conquest.**
H. T. Lambrick. Hyderabad: Sindhi Adabi Board, 1973 (distributed
by Oxford University Press, Pakistan). 218p. 4 maps. (History of Sind
Series, vol. 2).

A review by the leading foreign scholar of the history of Sindh from the Indus
civilization period to the downfall of the Brahman dynasty at the hands of Muslim
invaders in 712 AD. The work is based on a full review of all the relevant
archaeological and historical sources, but for large parts of the period even as late as
the 6th century evidence is altogether lacking. For much of the period Sindh belonged
as much to the Middle East as to South Asia.

203 **Sir Charles Napier and Sind.**
H. T. Lambrick. Oxford, England: Clarendon Press, 1952. 402p.
2 maps. bibliog.

The standard modern account of the British officer who conquered Sindh from the
Talpur *mirs* in 1843 and established the earliest British administration there.
Lambrick's work gives a brief account of Sindh before and after the conquest, but
concentrates on the 1842-47 period when Napier was in Sindh. Napier's activities
attracted criticism in England (e.g. E. B. Eastwick, *A glance at Sind before Napier*
[q.v.]) which Lambrick assesses.

204 **The terrorist.**
Translated and edited by H. T. Lambrick. London: Ernest Benn,
1972. 246p. 2 maps.

H. T. Lambrick was a senior official concerned with the repression of the rebellion
launched in 1942 by the Hurs, followers of a hereditary saint in the desert areas of
Sindh. The Sindhi text he has translated is a composite of a number of documents
which came into his hands after the end of the revolt and is in the form of an
autobiography of an otherwise unknown individual who took part in many attacks on
government forces and on others. The translation is lively and gives an insight into the

dynamics of the revolt and of the ties that bind the disciples of a saint to him, although very little background information on the rebellion is provided.

205 **Hindu–Muslim riots in the British Punjab (1849–1900).**
Ikram Ali Malik.   Lahore: Gosha-i-Adab, 1984. 50p.
A short monograph which uses contemporary newspapers and government records to discuss the factors involved in the communal riots which became increasingly frequent in this period. Malik sees them as primarily an urban phenomenon born of political competition between the main communities.

206 **The Sindh story.**
K. R. Malkani.   New Delhi: Allied, 1984. 192p. map. bibliog.
A Sindhi Hindu's view of Sindhi history. The book gives considerable emphasis to the Hindu contribution to Sindh's history and interprets the latter in terms of a specifically Sindhi, non-religious identity. The book is very critical of the way Sindh was dealt with at the time of partition.

207 **The Panjab Past and Present.**
Patiala, India: Punjabi University, 1967- . biannual.
Produced from India and with a bias towards Indian, especially Sikh subjects, this journal nevertheless frequently carries articles of relevance to Pakistani Punjab both in the modern and premodern periods.

208 **Personal observations on Sindh: the manners and customs of its inhabitants and its productive capabilities.**
T. Postans.   Karachi: Indus, 1973. 402p. map.
Originally published in 1843, this is a review by one of the officials involved of the general conditions and situation of Sindh at the time of the British conquest. Postans was concerned to describe the area's history and geography in order to assess the prospects of British commerce.

209 **Ethnicity, nationalism and the Pakhtuns: the independence movement in India's North-West Frontier Province.**
S. A. Rittenberg.   Durham, North Carolina: Carolina Academic Press, 1988. 286p. 2 maps. bibliog.
The most complete study so far of the 20th-century dominance of the politics of the NWFP by the Pukhtuns. The author sees the primary focus of Pukhtun political life as residing in their strongly developed sense of their own ethnic identity and character. Although this also leads to intense internal division, it gives the Pukhtun population the ability to dominate their own area and to resist outside encroachments except on their own terms. For a brief moment at the time of independence this led to a decision to join Pakistan. Before and after, however, the main theme was the maintenance of local autonomy. Although the author does not take his account beyond 1947, his work is of considerable relevance to the post-independence situation.

210 **Chitral: the story of a minor siege.**
George S. Robertson, introduction by M. E. Yapp. Karachi: Oxford
University Press, 1977. 363p. map. (Oxford in Asia Historical
Reprints).

The siege of Chitral in 1895 was an episode in the constant manoeuvrings by the British
to protect their frontiers against the possibility of Russian subversion. By the end of
the 19th century Dardistan, the remote area in the north of what is now Pakistan, had
acquired increased importance and ill-judged decisions by British officials led to the
siege of a small British force in Chitral by local tribesmen. A successful resistance by
the British inscribed the episode in imperial history, and Robertson's own account,
originally published in 1898, has become, in the words of the introduction, 'a minor
classic of the imperial frontier'. The historical background is covered at greater length
by G. J. Alder in *British India's northern frontier 1865–95: a study in imperial policy*
(q.v.).

211 **Makli hill: a center of Islamic culture in Sindh.**
Annemarie Schimmel. Karachi: University of Karachi, Institute of
Central and West Asian Studies, 1983. 45p. (First Syed Hussamuddin
Rashdi Memorial Lecture).

Makli hill, near the town of Thatta, is a religious centre of great importance where the
tombs of many saints are located. Schimmel places her account of these shrines and
saints against a broader canvas of Sindhi cultural history.

212 **North-West Frontier: people and events 1839–1947.**
Arthur Swinson. London: Hutchinson, 1967. 354p. 4 maps. bibliog.

A popular history of the Frontier, mainly from the British perspective. The body of the
work begins with the prelude to the first Afghan war in 1839 and ends a century or so
later with independence, although there are brief introductory and concluding
chapters. Much of the book deals in a racy way with the military side of things.

213 **Provincial politics and the Pakistan movement: the growth of the Muslim
League in north-west and north-east India, 1937–47.**
Ian Talbot. Karachi: Oxford University Press, 1988. 155p. bibliog.

This is a brief survey of the provinces – excluding Baluchistan – that became Pakistan
in 1947. Talbot looks at the interplay of popular enthusiasm for Islam and Islamic
brotherhood and factional conflicts among the élite. The Muslim League used both in
its final push for Pakistan but failed, the author argues, to build an adequate
organization to sustain itself beyond 1947. Talbot has also written a detailed study of
the Punjab, focusing especially on the role of the Unionist Party, *Punjab and the Raj,
1849–1947* (Delhi: Manohar, 1988).

214 **Musalmans and money-lenders in the Punjab.**
S. S. Thorburn. Delhi: Mittal, 1983. 198p.

First published in 1886, this is a passionate plea by a government official for measures
to protect the Muslim agriculturists of the Punjab from becoming serfs to the Hindu
moneylenders (by the side of whom, Thorburn says, Shylock was a gentleman).
Although many of Thorburn's assertions would no longer be accepted by scholars, his

book initiated the debate which eventually resulted in the 1901 Alienation of Land Act (covered by Barrier's book [q.v.]).

215 **Strategies of British India: Britain, Iran and Afghanistan, 1798–1850.**
M. E. Yapp. Oxford, England: Clarendon Press, 1980. 682p. 8 maps.
bibliog.

This important and meticulously researched study covers the early 19th-century period in British imperial policy before the establishment of a definite north-west frontier, although the Russian factor already loomed large. Towards the end of it the British annexed both Sindh and the Punjab and began to take a direct interest in Baluchistan.

The Pathans 550 BC – AD 1957.
See item no. 5.

Sind: a general introduction.
See item no. 10.

Lords of the Khyber: the story of the North-West Frontier.
See item no. 21.

Scinde; or the unhappy valley.
See item no. 55.

Narrative of a journey to Kalat.
See item no. 67.

Sailors and the crowd: popular protest in Karachi, 1946.
See item no. 236.

Facts are facts: the untold story of India's partition.
See item no. 238.

Divide and quit.
See item no. 241.

Pakistan: the consolidation of a nation.
See item no. 261.

Fazl-i-Husain: a political biography.
See item no. 270.

Sikandar Hayat Khan (1892–1942): a political biography.
See item no. 277.

India as I knew it, 1885–1925.
See item no. 280.

Father and daughter: a political autobiography.
See item no. 284.

Abdul Ghaffar Khan: faith is a battle.
See item no. 288.

Colonel Sir Robert Sandeman: his life and work on our Indian frontier. A

memoir, with selections from his correspondence and official writings.
See item no. 289.

Rusticus loquitur, or the old light and the new in the Punjab village.
See item no. 407.

Focus on Baluchistan and Pushtoon question.
See item no. 489.

Bugles and a tiger: a personal adventure.
See item no. 551.

Pakistan movement

216 **Pakistan or the partition of India.**
B. R. Ambedkar. Bombay: Thacker & Co., 1946. 3rd ed. 481p.
3 maps.
Dr Ambedkar was a distinguished constitutional lawyer as well as the preeminent
figure of his time from India's untouchable or scheduled castes. As a political leader
who was in some ways on the edge of both Hindu society as well as mainstream
Congress politics, he was in a special position to analyse the demands being put
forward by the Muslim League and possible ways in which they could be met without
necessarily involving a permanent partition. In this major work he makes a sustained
effort to understand the aspirations of the Muslim population. Although constitutional
arrangements matter, he argues, a united state has to be based on a shared sense of
national identity. If that cannot be achieved, he says, it would be better for a division
to take place.

217 **The historical background of Pakistan 1857–1947: an annotated digest of
source material.**
K. K. Aziz. Karachi: Pakistan Institute of International Affairs, 1970.
626p.
This is a listing of over 9,000 printed items relating to the subject, with brief
annotations which serve to indicate the subject of the entry. Despite the number of
entries, the work is not comprehensive, but its strength lies in its extensive coverage of
newspaper and periodical articles from the period under study.

218 **The making of Pakistan: a study in nationalism.**
K. K. Aziz. London: Chatto & Windus, 1967. 223p. bibliog.
An essentially historical approach to the rise of Muslim nationalism in India. The
author sees feelings of nationalist sentiment as the product of a range of historical,
religious and cultural factors. To an extent, therefore, Muslim nationalism in South
Asia was a contingent development in that it was a subjective state of mind. Once it
began to develop, however, it thrived on the opposition it encountered from the Indian
National Congress.

219 **Language, religion and politics in North India.**
Paul R. Brass. London: Cambridge University Press, 1974. 467p.
maps. bibliog.

This major contribution to the theoretical debate on nationalism and nationality formation uses as one of its principal case-studies the emergence among north Indian Muslims of the demand for Pakistan. Brass stresses throughout the work the importance of political and social change in creating political expressions of religious and linguistic differences. This thesis is challenged in the specific case of South Asian Islam by Francis Robinson in D. Taylor and M. Yapp (eds), *Political Identity in South Asia* (q.v.).

220 **Muslim separatism in India: a brief survey 1858–1947.**
Abdul Hamid. Lahore: Oxford University Press, 1967. 263p. bibliog.

A general narrative by a Pakistani scholar of the emergence of the Pakistan movement which sees it as the product of a complex of factors, but principally the Muslim urge for freedom. The author examines the work of Sayyid Ahmad Khan and the impact of the partition of Bengal before telling the story of the Khilafat movement and then the rise of the Muslim League.

221 **Letters of Iqbal to Jinnah: a collection of Iqbal's letters to the Qaid-i-Azam conveying his views on the political future of Muslim India.**
Muhammad Iqbal, with foreword by M. A. Jinnah. Lahore:
Sh. Muhammad Ashraf, 1942. 32p.

These letters sent by Iqbal between May 1936 and November 1937, shortly before his death, give his views on the immediate political situation in India, and express his belief in the importance of separate Muslim states in those areas where they were in a majority. Unfortunately, Jinnah's replies have not been preserved. The two most important letters can also be found in the collection of Jinnah's correspondence edited by S. S. Pirzada, *Quaid-e-Azam Jinnah's correspondence* (q.v.).

222 **The sole spokesman: Jinnah, the Muslim League and the demand for Pakistan.**
Ayesha Jalal. Cambridge, England: Cambridge University Press,
1985. 310p. 6 maps. bibliog. (Cambridge South Asian Studies, no. 31).

A major reassessment of Jinnah's aims that has evoked strong criticism in some quarters in Pakistan. Jalal argues on the basis of close scrutiny of Jinnah's actions and a search for the 'inwardness' of his strategy that Jinnah's real aim was to preserve some form of unity for the whole subcontinent while guaranteeing Muslim access to political power and that he was outmanoeuvred in the end-game of empire by an alliance of Congress leaders and the last viceroy, Mountbatten.

223 **Iqbal, Jinnah, and Pakistan: the vision and the reality.**
Edited by C. M. Naim. Syracuse, New York: Syracuse University,
Maxwell School of Citizenship and Public Affairs, 1979. 216p. (Foreign and Comparative Studies/South Asian Series, no. 5).

This volume brings together six useful studies of Iqbal and Jinnah, some of which look at them separately, others jointly. Those by Saleem Qureshi, Manzooruddin Ahmed, Sheila McDonough, Barbara Metcalf, and Lawrence Ziring (whose contribution deals primarily with the post-independence situation), were originally presented to a conference in 1977 to mark the birth centenaries; that by Anwar H. Syed was added later.

224 **Prelude to partition: the Indian Muslims and the imperial system of control 1920–1932.**
David Page. Delhi: Oxford University Press, 1982. 288p. 3 maps. bibliog.

This is a careful study by a historian of the political background in the 1920s, especially in north India, against which Jinnah and the Muslim League eventually came to articulate the demand for Pakistan. Page is particularly concerned with the effect on the structure of politics of the introduction of provincial autonomy under the Government of India Act of 1919. It was the working of these reforms, he argues, which alienated many Muslims from the Congress and heightened communal tensions. They also led to the development of important political interests in the Punjab, whose support had to be obtained before Pakistan could become a reality.

225 **The collected works of Quaid-e-Azam Mohammad Ali Jinnah.**
Edited by Syed Sharifuddin Pirzada. Karachi: East and West Publishing Company, 1984- . In progress.

Although Jinnah is revered as Pakistan's founder, he has not been as well served by Pakistan's historians and archivists as, for example, Mahatma Gandhi has been in India. Although his private papers are held by the Pakistan government and are available to scholars, there are no plans to publish them. What is included in these volumes are Jinnah's public pronouncements. The first three volumes, which run from his first entry into public life in 1906 up to his participation in the first Round Table Conference in London in 1930, include in particular his speeches as a leading member of the Central Legislative Assembly but also other public speeches and letters to the press. Each volume has a historical introduction. When complete, the project will be an important source of information for Jinnah's political career.

226 **Foundations of Pakistan: All-India Muslim League documents, 1906–1947.**
Edited by Syed Sharifuddin Pirzada. Karachi; Dacca: National Publishing House, 1981, 1982. 2 vols.

These volumes bring together the previously difficult to find resolutions and addresses at the annual sessions of the Muslim League from its foundation in 1906 until independence in 1947. For certain years the League was split and both factions' meetings are covered. The volumes also include documentation for League Council meetings in the critical years immediately before independence and key statements of Jinnah. Vol. 1 covers the period 1906-42, vol. 2 the remainder.

227 **Quaid-e-Azam Jinnah's correspondence.**
Edited by Syed Sharifuddin Pirzada. Karachi: East and West Publishing Company, 1977. 3rd rev. and enlarged ed. 425p.

This collection aims at coverage of all Jinnah's important political correspondence between 1918 and his death in 1948. There are facsimiles of a few items.

228 **Separatism among Indian Muslims: the politics of the United Provinces' Muslims, 1860–1923.**
Francis Robinson. London: Cambridge University Press, 1974. 469p. 4 maps. bibliog. (Cambridge South Asian Studies, no. 16).

This is one of the earliest academic studies to look at the emergence of political demands for separate political representation in terms of the dynamics of local and regional politics. Robinson takes as his subject the key area of northern India, from which sprang most of the original leaders of the Muslim League and where the Urdu-speaking élite among the Muslim community was most entrenched. He traces the emergence of so-called old and young parties among the Muslim élite and the struggle between them for leadership as they had to come to terms with threats to their privileged positions.

229 **Pakistan: the formative phase.**
Khalid bin Sayeed. Karachi: Pakistan Publishing House, 1960. 492p. bibliog.

This is an old but still valuable study of the origins of the Pakistan movement from the mid-19th century and of the initial years of independence from 1947 to 1951. Sayeed was able to interview many leading political figures and senior officials who had participated in the events he describes.

230 **Muslims and political representation in colonial India: the making of Pakistan.**
Farzana Shaikh. *Modern Asian Studies*, vol. 20, no. 3 (July 1986), p. 539-57.

A study of the way Indian Muslims expressed their views on how they should be represented politically. The author argues that Western concepts based on liberal individualism were rejected not merely because they were contrary to the short-term interests of the community's leadership but because they offended against Islamic concepts of community. She suggests that this point is central to an understanding of the expression of Muslim demands from the beginning of the 20th century to the attainment of Pakistan in 1947. The Indian National Congress and the Muslim League put forward 'wholly irreconcilable sets of political norms'. The argument is extended to the post-independence period in 'Islam and the quest for democracy in Pakistan', *Journal of Commonwealth and Comparative Politics*, vol. 24, no. 1 (March 1986), p. 74-92.

231 **Pakistan: old country new nation.**
Ian Stephens. Harmondsworth, England: Penguin Books, 1964. 352p. 3 maps. bibliog.

First published in 1963 simply as *Pakistan*, this is a now rather dated and old-fashioned but sympathetic and informed account of Pakistan's history by someone who was an official in British India, a newspaper editor, and finally for a short period official historian to the Pakistan army. Rather more attention is given than would be today to the circumstances of the Pakistan movement and the foundation of the state and less to Pakistan's post-1947 history.

232 **M. A. Jinnah – Ispahani correspondence 1936–1948.**
Edited by Z. H. Zaidi. Karachi: Forward Publication Trust, 1976.
718p.

M. A. H. Ispahani was a member of a distinguished Muslim business family based in
Calcutta who became one of Jinnah's most devoted lieutenants in the Pakistan
movement and after independence Pakistan's ambassador to the United States. His
correspondence with Jinnah is one of the few opportunities we have to see Jinnah at
work as a politician, although he always has his cards close to his chest. There are also
glimpses of the private individual. The volume, which includes all the items extant in
the Ispahani papers, includes a useful introduction and notes by the editor.

233 **Students' role in the Pakistan movement.**
Mukhtar Zaman, with supplementary articles by Abdus Salam
Khurshid, M. A. Mekhari. Karachi: Quaid-i-Azam Academy, 1978.
242p. (Historical Studies (Pakistan) – 1).

The author was a leading figure in the All-India Muslim Students' Federation
immediately before independence. He draws on his own recollections as well as
documentary sources to describe the role played by Muslim students as propagandists
and activists for the Pakistan movement, especially at the time of the 1945-46 elections.
The situation in each province is described in detail, as is the part played by Jinnah in
inspiring student activity.

The Muslims of British India.
See item no. 136.

Nationalism and communal politics in India, 1916–1928.
See item no. 138.

A history of the freedom movement (being the story of Muslim struggle for the freedom of Hind-Pakistan).
See item no. 141.

Moslem nationalism in India and Pakistan.
See item no. 149.

The Khilafat movement: religious symbolism and political mobilization in India.
See item no. 153.

The Muslim community of the Indo-Pakistan subcontinent (610–1947): a brief historical analysis.
See item no. 157.

Modern Islam in India: a social analysis.
See item no. 162.

Political identity in South Asia.
See item no. 164.

From martial law to martial law: politics in the Punjab, 1919–1958.
See item no. 167.

Independence and partition

234 **The emergence of Pakistan.**
Chaudhri Muhammad Ali.   New York; London: Columbia University Press, 1967. 418p. 5 maps.
Chaudhri Muhammad Ali, who later became prime minister of Pakistan in the mid-1950s, was a senior civil servant at the time of independence and became Pakistan's representative on the steering committee of the Partition Council. This carefully

written memoir, which depends on written sources as well as the author's own recollections, deals with the situation immediately before and after 14 August 1947. He describes in particular the mechanics of partition.

235 **Freedom at midnight.**
Larry Collins, Dominique Lapierre. London: Collins, 1975. 500p. 5 maps. bibliog.
An often highly coloured account of independence and partition which has achieved considerable prominence in the popular literature. Jinnah, whose personal contribution to the achievement of Pakistan is made much of, is described as a man of towering vanity.

236 **Sailors and the crowd: popular protest in Karachi, 1946.**
Anirudh Deshpande. *Indian Economic and Social History Review*, vol. 26, no. 1 (Jan.-March 1989), p. 1-28. map.
The naval uprisings of February 1946 in Bombay and Karachi were significant events in creating the climate in which the transfer of power took place. This article looks not only at the mutiny itself, but at the parallel activities in the city of Karachi. Deshpande is particularly concerned with the dynamics of crowd behaviour.

237 **The great divide: Britain – India – Pakistan.**
H. V. Hodson. Karachi: Oxford University Press, 1985. 2nd ed. 590p. bibliog.
Although first published in 1969 without access to all the documentation that subsequently became available, this book is valuable both because of its considerable merits as a literary work and because its author had free access to the papers of Lord Mountbatten, the last viceroy. Half the book is devoted to the period up to Mountbatten's arrival in March 1947, half to the negotiations that produced the partition plan and to its implementation. Mountbatten is very much the central figure and Hodson rates his achievements very highly. The second edition is unchanged except for a 25-page epilogue which looks at India and Pakistan after independence.

238 **Facts are facts: the untold story of India's partition.**
Wali Khan, translated by Syeda Saiyidain Hameed. Delhi: Vikas, [1987]. 182p.
Son of Abdul Ghaffar Khan and himself a major political figure in Pakistan who has been at odds with successive governments, Wali Khan writes here of his views of the political history of India from the First World War up to partition, and in particular of his own frontier region. He is concerned, on the basis of British official records, to document the claim that the colonial government followed a policy of 'divide and rule' on religious lines so as to limit the power of the nationalist movement, especially that part represented in the Frontier by the Khudai Khidmatgars. Although his immediate target is the British rulers of India, it is clear that he is also challenging the legitimacy of the view that only the Muslim League and its leaders represented the real interests of Muslims in India.

239 **Constitutional relations between Britain and India: the transfer of power 1942–7.**
Editor-in-Chief, Nicholas Mansergh, editors and assistant editors (vols 1-4) E. W. R. Lumby; (vols 5-12) Penderel Moon. London: Her Majesty's Stationery Office, 1970-83. 12 vols. maps.
This truly monumental project is on a scale never likely to be repeated in the field of South Asian studies. The twelve volumes, each around 900 pages and impeccably edited, contain all the documents of any significance from the British archives which bear on the question of how and why policy was framed as it was. From the telegrams, minutes, notes, etc. which are included it is possible to build up an immensely rich and detailed picture of the progress of events on the British side. Even though a complete story would require equal documentation from the Congress and Muslim League leaders, which does not exist, by itself the *Transfer of Power* series is an invaluable source for any serious scholar of the subject.

240 **The transfer of power in India.**
V. P. Menon. Bombay: Orient Longmans, 1957. 542p.
Written by an Indian official who was closely involved in the negotiations preceding the transfer of power and who was on intimate terms with the Indian leadership, this detailed work naturally reflects an Indian view on events and personalities. It nevertheless strives for and in large measure achieves perspective and balance.

241 **Divide and quit.**
Penderel Moon. London: Chatto & Windus, 1961. 302p. 2 maps.
The author was a senior official in Bahawalpur state in the Punjab during the partition period and witnessed at first hand the communal killings that took place in and around the state. His memoir of this period describes carefully and compassionately the dreadful events that he witnessed, although the scale of the killing in the state was relatively less than in other parts of the Punjab. Moon also includes some more general analysis of the political background to partition.

242 **Escape from empire: the Attlee government and the Indian problem.**
R. J. Moore. Oxford, England: Clarendon Press, 1983. 376p. bibliog.
This meticulously researched and written work deals with the 'high politics' of the period from Attlee's appointment as prime minister in July 1945 to the transfer of power in August 1947. Relying principally on government documents and the private papers of those most closely involved, Moore reconstructs as far as is possible the negotiations and manoeuvrings that took place as it became clear after the war that the British wished to leave but that there were fundamental disagreements as to how power should be transferred. Moore has written two other volumes dealing in similar vein with the earlier period, *The crisis of Indian unity, 1917–1940* (Oxford, England: Clarendon Press, 1974) and *Churchill, Cripps, and India, 1939–1945* (ibid., 1979), and a collection of essays, *Endgames of empire: studies of Britain's Indian problem* (Delhi: Oxford University Press, 1988).

243 **Making the new Commonwealth.**
R. J. Moore. Oxford, England: Clarendon Press, 1987. 218p. bibliog.
Although the focus of this detailed and authoritative monograph is inevitably on India and in particular on Nehru, Pakistan was also centrally involved in the efforts of

Mountbatten and others to keep the two post-partition states in the Commonwealth. Moore pays due attention to the position of Jinnah and his successor Liaquat Ali Khan and to the importance of the Kashmir dispute of 1947-48. The book concludes with the Commonwealth Conference of April 1949 which established the Commonwealth on a new footing, although earlier hopes for joint defence arrangements between Britain, India and Pakistan for the Indian Ocean region proved illusory.

244 **The last days of the British Raj.**
Leonard Mosley. London: Weidenfeld & Nicholson, 1961. 263p. 2 maps. bibliog.

A racily written account, based on personal research as well as on the standard sources then available, of the partition of India. The author does his best to be fair to all concerned, although he is convinced that if things had been done in less of a hurry much of the suffering could have been avoided, and that Mountbatten in particular must bear some of the responsibility for the undue haste.

245 **The partition of India: policies and perspectives 1935–1947.**
Edited by C. H. Philips, Mary Doreen Wainwright. London: George Allen & Unwin, 1970. 607p. bibliog.

The valuable papers included in this volume were originally presented to a conference in London in 1967 which brought together Pakistani, Indian and British participants in the events of 1947 as well as scholars from the three countries. Thirteen papers, mainly but not exclusively by academics, are included in the first section on policies and parties, and sixteen in the second on perspectives and reflections. Although not a comprehensive history of the subject, this is a major contribution to its study.

246 **The partition of the Punjab 1947: a compilation of official documents.**
Compiled by Mian Muhammad Sadullah. Lahore: National Documentation Centre, 1983. 4 vols. 7 maps.

These four volumes provide comprehensive documentation of the work of the Punjab Boundary Commission which, under the chairmanship of Sir Cyril Radcliffe, drew the boundary line in the Punjab in 1947. Much of the material included has hitherto been available only in archive collections. Volume 1 contains material relating to the establishment of the commission and the initial representations submitted to it; volume 2 is a verbatim record of the public sessions at which each party argued its case; volume 3 brings together the reports of the individual members of the commission, who were unable to reach a consensus, and the final award by the chairman; volume 4 consists of a selection of maps submitted to the commission and an illustrative map added by the editors.

247 **Experiment with freedom: India and Pakistan 1947.**
Hugh Tinker. London; Bombay; Karachi: Oxford University Press, 1967. 165p. (Chatham House Essays, no. 16).

Although written before the official archives were open, this remains one of the most lucid and balanced introductions to the tangled web of negotiations that produced the transfer of power in 1947 but at the same time the partition of the country. Tinker, a distinguished historian and political scientist, compresses a great quantity of detail into his narrative but never loses sight of the main points.

248 **The Viceroy's journal.**
Archibald Wavell, edited by Penderel Moon. London: Oxford
University Press, 1973. 528p.
Lord Wavell was viceroy of India during the closing stages of the war and in 1945 and
1946, when increasingly frantic efforts were being made by the British to find a formula
that would maintain the unity of India after the transfer of power. Wavell himself tried
at the Simla conference in June 1945, and was deeply involved in the Cabinet Mission
Plan the ramifications of which provided the focus for Congress–League manoeuvring
during most of 1946. His private diary, well edited by Moon, is a prime source for the
period and tells the reader both about the day-to-day negotiations and about the way
the Viceroy himself perceived the impasse. Wavell was eventually replaced by Lord
Mountbatten, who was able to push through the partition. As Moon remarks,
however, it was Wavell's failure which paved the way for Mountbatten's success.

The making of Pakistan.
See item no. 163.

The Sindh story.
See item no. 206.

Pakistan: the formative phase.
See item no. 229.

Pakistan: old country new nation.
See item no. 231.

**The economic consequences of divided India: a study of the economy of India
and Pakistan.**
See item no. 619.

Pakistan 1947-

249 **Can Pakistan survive? The death of a state.**
Tariq Ali. Harmondsworth, England: Penguin, 1983. 237p. 2 maps.
A journalistic survey of Pakistan from the beginning of the Pakistan movement to the
early 1980s, in which the author, a well-known journalist and left-wing political
activist, develops his thesis that the country in its present shape is held together only by
the coercive power of the army and the bureaucratic apparatus with the support of the
United States. The style is vigorous and no previous knowledge is assumed.

250 **Pakistan: military rule or people's power.**
Tariq Ali. London: Jonathan Cape, 1970. 270p.
The writer describes his history of Pakistan since 1947 as 'an unabashed and
straightforward polemic against the feudal and capitalist class of Pakistan'. He is
particularly concerned to describe and analyse the mass movement against the Ayub
Khan régime from November 1968 to March 1969, and calls for a revolutionary party
to lead further struggles.

251 **Party politics in Pakistan, 1947–1958.**
K. K. Aziz. Islamabad: National Commission on Historical and Cultural Research, 1976. 302p. bibliog. (Historical Studies (Pakistan) Series, no. 1).

Party politics in the period from independence up to the coup of 1958 were often chaotic and confused. Aziz gives a meticulous account of the parties and their activities, and of the attempts to find a constitutional settlement. Appendices list the members of successive governments at the national level and chief ministers at the provincial, and give biographical notes for the principal political figures.

252 **The great tragedy.**
Zulfikar Ali Bhutto. Karachi: Pakistan People's Party, 1971. 107p

Bhutto has often been accused of at least partial responsibility for the 1971 civil war. This pamphlet, written in the middle of the crisis, puts his case and argues that the Pakistan People's Party (PPP) was always prepared to meet the Awami League's essential demands and that a grand coalition of the two parties could have solved the problem.

253 **Pakistan under Bhutto 1971–1977.**
Shahid Javed Burki. London: Macmillan, 1988. 2nd ed. 285p. bibliog.

First published in 1980, this is a major contribution to the study of the Bhutto period and to the study of Pakistan politics more generally. Burki analyses in detail the social groups that made up Bhutto's initial constituency and the effect on those and other groups of the policies he pursued when in power. By 1977, he says, the PPP had lost its middle-class support and had to rely on 'landed interests, rural poor and urban marginals'. The second edition reproduces the first more or less unchanged and adds further material on the 1977 elections and a new chapter assessing the Bhutto legacy.

254 **The last days of united Pakistan.**
G. W. Choudhury. London: C. Hurst, 1974. 239p.

This is a detailed account of the 1969-71 period in Pakistan by a Bengali academic political scientist who was at the same time directly involved as a member for a time of Yahya Khan's cabinet. Choudhury argues that the dismemberment of Pakistan was not the answer to any of South Asia's regional problems. The book sets out to justify some at least of the actions taken by the Pakistan government towards the Bangladesh demand. Choudhury's account of the period, and his own bona fides, were fiercely atacked by Altaf Gauhar in 'The last days of united Pakistan: a review article', *Third World Quarterly*, vol. 1, no. 1 (Jan. 1979), p. 91-104.

255 **Revolution in Pakistan: a study of the Martial Law administration.**
Herbert Feldman. London: Oxford University Press, 1967. 242p.

This is a detailed and useful account of the history of Pakistan from the coup of October 1958 which brought General Ayub Khan to power to the framing of the new constitution in 1962. Feldman discusses the social and legal reforms introduced by the Martial Law government as well as the economic policies pursued by it. A number of relevant documents are included in appendices. Feldman wrote two subsequent volumes which carried the story forward to the end of united Pakistan: *From crisis to crisis: Pakistan in 1962–69* (London: Oxford University Press, 1970) and *The end and the beginning: Pakistan, 1968–71* (London: Oxford University Press, 1975).

256   **A history of Pakistan (1947–1958).**
Y. V. Gankovsky, L. R. Gordon-Polonskaya.   Lahore: People's
Publishing House, 1964. 335p. bibliog.
Translated from a Russian original, this is an example of well-informed work in an
orthodox Marxist mode. The first quarter of the book in fact deals with the origins of
Pakistan rather than the period from independence to the Ayub Khan coup of 1958.
The authors interpret the history of Pakistan in terms of the development of class and
regional (national) contradictions.

257   **Pakistan: failure in national integration.**
Rounaq Jahan.   New York, London: Columbia University Press,
1972. 248p. bibliog.
Written before the break-up of Pakistan in 1971, although published afterwards, this
major study by a Bangladeshi political scientist discusses issues of interwing disparity in
economic, administrative and military terms. The main emphasis, however, is on the
period after 1958 and the consequences of the policies pursued by Ayub Khan. The
author traces the rise in East Pakistan of what she terms the 'vernacular elite' and
studies its rivalry with the national élite based in West Pakistan.

258   **Economic history of Pakistan.**
Anwar Iqbal Qureshi.   Lahore: Islamic Book Service, 1978. 466p.
The writer was the first Economic Advisor to the Government of Pakistan after
independence, and his work draws heavily on his personal experience. His direct
involvement is also reflected in the rather polemical tone adopted in the treatment of
Pakistan's economic relations with India and of trade relations between East and West
Pakistan. The work is a valuable source of information, especially for the economic
aspects of partition and for the physical development of the economy after
independence. There is a brief and now rather dated account of pre-1947 economic
history.

259   **Persistent praetorianism: Pakistan's third military regime.**
William L. Richter.   *Pacific Affairs*, vol. 51, no. 3 (Fall 1978),
p. 406-26.
This is a detailed account of the months immediately following General Zia's coup of
July 1977. Richter discounts the view that the coup itself was part of a carefully
designed grand strategy but argues presciently that the weakness of the country's
democratic traditions would lead the military régime to cling to power.

260   **Witness to surrender.**
Siddiq Salik.   Karachi: Oxford University Press, 1977. 245p. 7 maps.
This is an eyewitness account, with the emphasis on the military side of events, by a
senior Pakistani officer who was present in East Bengal throughout the civil war in
1971. Salik also comments on the earlier stages of the crisis. While he seeks to rebut
the more devastating of the charges against the Pakistan army, he provides a balanced
account of events and personalities. Appendices include the text of the Awami
League's six points, the operational document for 'Operation Searchlight', and the
instrument of surrender.

261 **Pakistan: the consolidation of a nation.**
Wayne Ayres Wilcox. New York; London: Columbia University
Press, 1963. 276p. 4 maps. bibliog.

The title of this book is somewhat misleading in that the actual focus is the way in
which the government of the newly independent Pakistan dealt with the princely states
that fell within its undisputed territory (i.e. excluding Jammu and Kashmir). These
included Bahawalpur and Khairpur, adjacent to and easily absorbed into Punjab and
Sindh respectively, the barren states of Baluchistan and the small and isolated units in
the northern areas. Wilcox deals with each state in turn, detailing the often tortuous
negotiations which led to their integration into Pakistan, a process completed for all
but the northern states in 1956. There is a brief chapter reviewing developments
thereafter, including the tribal revolt in Baluchistan. Wilcox is sympathetic to the
Pakistan government's policy of eliminating princely power but critical of what he sees
as excessive centralization of government in the 1950s.

262 **The Ayub Khan era: politics in Pakistan, 1958–1969.**
Lawrence Ziring. Syracuse, New York: Syracuse University Press,
1971. 234p. 2 maps. bibliog.

This work is divided into two parts. The first is a historical survey of the period of
Ayub Khan's power from 1958 to his downfall in March 1969; the second examines
themes in the politics of the period, notably the bureaucratic legacy and the attempt to
accelerate rural change through the institution of basic democracies. Ziring argues that
Ayub achieved political stability but at the cost of stagnation. The key to progress, he
argues, is the growing middle class.

263 **Pakistan: the long view.**
Edited by Lawrence Ziring, Ralph Braibanti, W. Howard Wriggins.
Durham, North Carolina: Duke University Press, 1977. 485p. bibliog.
(Duke University, Commonwealth Studies Center Publication, no. 43).

A set of papers originally prepared for a symposium in 1974 in memory of a leading
American scholar of Pakistan, Wayne A. Wilcox. The purpose of the collection was to
place Bhutto's Pakistan in a wider perspective and the subjects covered range across
the fields of history, economics and foreign policy. Although some of the papers are
now rather dated, others are of lasting value.

From martial law to martial law: politics in the Punjab, 1919–1958.
See item no. 167.

Pakistan: old country new nation.
See item no. 231.

Contemporary Pakistan: politics, economy and society.
See item no. 447.

The political economy of Pakistan 1947–85.
See item no. 473.

Biographies and Autobiographies

264 **The memoirs of Aga Khan: world enough and time.**
The Aga Khan, foreword by W. Somerset Maugham. London:
Cassell, 1954. 350p.

The Aga Khans, hereditary leaders of the Ismaili sect among Shia Muslims, came originally from Iran but settled in India in the 19th century. The third Aga Khan played an intermittent part in Muslim politics in the years before independence and his autobiography touches on these matters, although much of the book is devoted to more personal affairs. A racy history of the Aga Khans is Mihir Bose's *The Aga Khans* (Kingswood, England: World's Work, 1984).

265 **Quaid-i-Azam Mohammad Ali Jinnah: the formative years 1892–1920.**
Riaz Ahmad. Islamabad: National Institute of Historical and Cultural
Research, 1986. 254p. bibliog. (Biographical Series, no. 10).

A detailed account of Jinnah's early political career, when his links were more with the Congress than the League, as also of his professional career as a barrister in Bombay. 1892 was the year when Jinnah left for London to train as a lawyer, although the author also reviews the rather scanty evidence that exists relating to his childhood. From 1920 on, with the rise of Gandhi and a new style of political action, Jinnah broke his links with the Congress. Ahmad wishes to demonstrate that although Jinnah never sympathized with Gandhian tactics and preferred the legislative arena, he was no less a radical in his approach to politics.

266 **Daughter of the East: an autobiography.**
Benazir Bhutto. London: Hamish Hamilton, 1988. 333p.

Written just before the death of President Zia and Benazir Bhutto's own assumption of the office of prime minister, this book clearly has a political purpose. Much of it is an account of her father's trial and execution and her own detention at the hands of the military régime as well as developments after her release first to go into exile in London and then to return to the political fray in 1986. There is also, however, some personal material on which to build up a picture of the first woman to become leader of a Muslim country. In Pakistan the book was published as *Daughter of destiny*.

267 **Interview with history.**
Oriana Fallaci, translated by John Shepley.   London: Michael Joseph, 1976. 376p.

Oriana Fallaci, whose collection of interviews with world leaders was first published in Italian in 1974, is a well-known journalist and writer who met Zulfikar Ali Bhutto in April 1972, just after his accession to power. Much of the discussion that she records in this book is about the Bangladesh war and Bhutto's account of his own role in it, although he also talks about his personal beliefs and aims.

268 **Eight lives: a study of the Hindu–Muslim encounter.**
Rajmohan Gandhi.   Albany, New York: State University of New York Press, 1986. 359p. bibliog.

Even if it does not live up to the promise of its subtitle to examine the Hindu–Muslim encounter this book provides very readable and reliable accounts of its subjects: Jinnah, Iqbal, Sayyid Ahmad Khan, Jinnah's principal lieutenant Liaquat Ali Khan, Fazlul Huq, who was a major figure in Bengal politics before and after independence, and Muhammad Ali, Abul Kalam Azad and Zakir Husain, three figures who in rather different ways were associated with the Indian National Congress and Mahatma Gandhi (the author's grandfather). Rajmohan Gandhi's own outlook is based on a tolerant humanism which comprehends the Muslim dilemmas in pre-independence India while regretting that they had to be resolved through partition. The book was published in India under the title *Understanding the Muslim mind* (Delhi: Penguin, 1987).

269 **Life of Iqbal: general account of his life.**
Masud-ul-Hasan.   Lahore: Ferozsons, 1978. 506p.

Masud-ul-Hasan's biography of Iqbal is a straightforward chronological account of his life which takes the reader from his early days in Sialkot and Lahore to his death in 1938. Considerable use is made of Iqbal's correspondence. Compared to other works on Iqbal there is much more stress on his political activities as an exponent of Muslim interests. According to the introduction, the work is to be the first in a series of four books on Iqbal. Collections of Iqbal's English letters and speeches have been made by B. A. Dar, *Letters and writings of Iqbal* (Karachi: Iqbal Academy, 1967), and by Shamloo, *Speeches and statements of Iqbal* (Lahore: Al-Manar Academy, 1948, 2nd ed.).

270 **Fazl-i-Husain: a political biography.**
Azim Husain, foreword by C. Rajagopalachariar.   Bombay: Longmans, Green & Co, 1946. 388p.

Fazl-i-Husain was a major figure in the politics of the Punjab in the earlier part of the 20th century. Founder of the Unionist Party which held power until the eve of independence, he became a provincial minister and at the time of his death in 1936 was a member of the viceroy's council. He awaits a good modern biography which takes account of new historiographical developments from the 1960s on but this account by his son is reliable and useful in its recounting both of Fazl-i-Husain's own life and of the Unionist Party.

271   **Modern Muslim India and the birth of Pakistan (1858–1951).**
S. M. Ikram.   Lahore: Sheikh Muhammad Ashraf, 1970. 2nd rev. ed.
506p.

This work has gone through a number of previous versions. Based on an earlier book
in Urdu, it was first published in English under the pseudonym A. H. Albiruni in 1950
as *Makers of Pakistan and modern Muslim India*. The present version was first
published in 1965. Originally, it was composed of a set of straightforward biographical
sketches of the principal political and intellectual figures in the Pakistan movement and
its predecessors. The current version is approximately twice as long and includes
substantial sections dealing with the emergence of Muslim political activity in the areas
that were to become Pakistan. The approach remains primarily biographical, however.

272   **From purdah to parliament.**
Shaista S. Ikramullah.   London: Cresset Press, 1963. 168p.

An autobiographical memoir of a woman from a traditional Muslim family. Daughter
of Hassan Suhrawardy, and therefore from one of the principal upper-class families of
Muslim India, she was born in Calcutta in 1915. With encouragement from her
husband, a member of the Indian Civil Service, she moved with ease into the wider
world. Her family connections brought her close to Jinnah and into a political role in
the years just before 1947. After independence she became a member of Pakistan's
constituent assembly, although she writes little of her activities there.

273   **The last Wali of Swat: an autobiography as told to Fredrik Barth.**
Miangul Jahanzeb.   Oslo: Norwegian University Press
(Universitetsforlaget); New York: Columbia University Press, 1985.
199p. bibliog.

Swat, in Pakistan's North-West Frontier Province, was initially a princely state and
then an autonomous unit within Pakistan with which it merged finally in 1969. The last
ruler, Miangul Jahanzeb, gives a detailed account of his political career and of the
negotiations in which he was involved, but the book would be useful to anyone
interested in the anthropological or historical background to this Pukhtun society.

274   **Pathway to Pakistan.**
Choudhry Khaliquzzaman.   Lahore: Longmans Pakistan Branch,
1961. 432p.

Choudhry Khaliquzzaman was an important figure in the politics of the United
Provinces and significant within all-India Muslim politics as well. From a distinguished
family, he had close links with the Congress leaders, Nehru in particular, but
eventually committed himself fully to the Muslim League. At independence he was
asked by Jinnah to remain in India as leader of the Muslim community there, although
in the end he came to Pakistan. His autobiography is essentially a record of the
political events in which he participated.

275   **Friends not masters: a political autobiography.**
Mohammad Ayub Khan.   London: Oxford University Press, 1967.
275p. 2 maps.

The first of Pakistan's military rulers, Ayub Khan was also in the line of those who saw
the country as embodying a progressive and modernist conception of Islam. His

autobiography, written while he was in power and clearly intended to make an impact domestically and internationally, describes his life from his days as one of the first Indian cadets at Sandhurst to the presidential election of 1965, although most of the attention is given to events after the coup of October 1958. A clearly worked-out set of views on the appropriate constitutional forms for Pakistan and on the future of Pakistan as a Third World country is presented.

276 **Mohammed Ali Jinnah: maker of modern Pakistan.**
Edited by Sheila McDonough. Lexington, Massachusetts: D. C. Heath, 1970. 101p. bibliog. (Problems in Asian Civilizations).

Intended primarily for students, this work brings together readings on Jinnah from a wide variety of scholars, and political leaders who interacted with him. These are intended to allow the reader to assess both Jinnah's character and his political strategy. There is a brief introduction to set the readings in context.

277 **Sikandar Hayat Khan (1892–1942): a political biography.**
Iftikhar Haider Malik. Islamabad: National Institute of Historical and Cultural Research, 1985. 211p. bibliog.

Sikandar Hayat Khan was, after Fazl-i-Husain, the dominant Muslim political figure in the Punjab before independence. This study discusses his political career as a leader of the Unionist party and as prime minister of the Punjab from 1937 until his death, and his complex relationship with Jinnah and the Muslim League. A number of appendices cover relevant correspondence and other documents, including Sikandar's own 1939 scheme for an Indian federation.

278 **Sir George Cunningham: a memoir.**
Norval Mitchell. Edinburgh; London: William Blackwood, 1968. 183p. map.

Governor of the North-West Frontier Province at the time of independence, Cunningham remained in post until April 1948 during the early stages of the Kashmir crisis. This is a largely personal account of his long career as a British official on the frontier.

279 **Quaid-i-Azam: studies in interpretation.**
Sharif al Mujahid. Karachi: Quaid-i-Azam Academy, 1981. 2nd ed. 806p. bibliog.

This account of Jinnah takes a sympathetic but not a blinkered view of him. The focus is more on Jinnah's political career than on his personality. Approximately half of the work is given over to a useful selection of documents. A briefer and simpler study of Jinnah which follows the same basic approach as Mujahid is Waheed-uz-Zaman, *Quaid-i-Azam Mohammad Ali Jinnah: myth and reality* (Islamabad: National Institute of Historical and Cultural Research, 2nd ed., 1985).

280 **India as I knew it, 1885–1925.**
Michael O'Dwyer. London: Constable, 1925. 453p. 2 maps.

O'Dwyer was governor of the Punjab at the time of the Jallianwala Bagh massacre in April 1919, a turning point in Indian history. His memoirs seek to justify his actions at that time, but they are also a document of the views of a staunch imperialist who believed in the appropriateness for Punjab of a paternalist government. The earlier chapters recount his life as an official in various parts of the Punjab and elsewhere in India.

281 **The story of soldiering and politics in India and Pakistan.**
Sher Ali Khan Pataudi. Lahore: Wajidalis, 1978. 430p. map.

This is the autobiography of a member of a princely family in India who joined the army in 1933 and in 1947 opted for Pakistan. Apart from his military service the author held diplomatic assignments and was a minister during the Yahya Khan period. Although there is little that is new in the book on the inner story of politics, the memoirs are an interesting record of the experience of a senior member of the Pakistan élite. Another military autobiography by someone who rose from the ranks to become first commander-in-chief and then governor of West Pakistan under Ayub Khan is Mohammad Musa, *Jawan to general: recollections of a Pakistani soldier* (Karachi: East & West Publishing Company, 1984).

282 **Mohammad Ali Jinnah: a political study.**
Matlubul Hasan Saiyid. Lahore: Sh. Muhammad Ashraf, 1953. 2nd ed. 529p.

An early biography of Jinnah which still has value as the first attempt to provide a comprehensive political account of his life. Saiyid concentrates mainly on Jinnah's activities as a principal leader of the Muslims and their representative in talks with the British and the Congress. The first edition of the work was published in 1945, before the final round of negotiations.

283 **Bhutto: trial and execution.**
Victoria Schofield. London: Cassell, 1979. 250p.

The author was a university friend of Benazir Bhutto and she writes here a detailed acount of the period from the arrest of Zulfikar Ali Bhutto in September 1977 through the trial to his execution in April 1979.

284 **Father and daughter: a political autobiography.**
Jahan Ara Shahnawaz. Lahore: Nigarishat, 1971. 304p.

Jahan Ara Shahnawaz was the daughter of Sir Muhammad Shafi, a distinguished Punjabi politician of the pre-independence period. She herself played some political role, especially as a representative of women's interests within the Muslim League. After independence she became a member of the Constituent Assembly. In this autobiography she describes both her personal life and the political activities of her father and herself at the Punjab and national levels.

285 **The garden of fidelity, being the autobiography of Flora Annie Steel 1847–1929.**
Flora Annie Steel. London: Macmillan, 1929. 293p.

Flora Annie Steel, the novelist and collector of Punjab folktales, lived for some years in the Punjab as the wife of a British official. She was herself appointed Inspectress of Schools for the Punjab with responsibility for female education. Her autobiography, which devotes much space to her years in India, particularly in the districts of Kasur and Sialkot, shows her as indomitably Victorian in her moral concerns, for example over the position of women in India, as also in her immense energy and forthrightness. She died in 1929 and the last chapter of the book was in fact written by her daughter. There is a modern biography: *Flora Annie Steel: novelist of India* by Violet Powell (London: Heinemann, 1981).

286 Punjabi saga (1857–1987).
Prakash Tandon. Delhi: Penguin, 1988. 664p.

An omnibus edition of three volumes of autobiography written by Prakash Tandon, who grew up in West Punjab in the early years of the 20th century. Son of an engineer in the irrigation department, he describes in the first part, published originally as *Punjabi century* (London: Chatto & Windus, 1961), the rural life of the areas where his father was posted, as well as the traditions and social customs of his middle-class community at a time of rapid change. The second and third parts of the book, originally titled *Beyond Punjab* (Berkeley and Los Angeles: University of California Press, 1971) and *Return to Punjab* (New Delhi: Vikas, 1980) deal with the author's life as a senior business executive in India and elsewhere, and deal only in passing with Pakistan Punjab. Ved Mehta, whose family belonged to the same milieu, has written a comparable trilogy: *Daddyji* (London: Secker & Warburg, 1972); *Mamaji* (New York and Oxford, England: Oxford University Press, 1979); and *The ledge between the streams* (London: Harvill Press, 1984). The last includes Mehta's memories of the partition period in Lahore until the point in June 1947 when his family left for India as refugees.

287 Bhutto: a political biography.
Salmaan Taseer. London: Ithaca Press, 1979. 216p. bibliog.

Although the author is an admirer and supporter of the late Mr Bhutto, this is by no means a hagiography. The book, completed shortly after Mr Bhutto's execution in April 1979, contains a considerable amount of information and comment about its subject as an individual, a politician and a statesman. Taseer's basic view of Bhutto is that he was above all a politician for whom loyalty rather than ideology was the key factor.

288 Abdul Ghaffar Khan: faith is a battle.
D. G. Tendulkar. Bombay: Popular Prakashan, 1967. 550p. map.

Often known as the 'Frontier Gandhi' or Badshah Khan, Abdul Ghaffar Khan played a leading role in the politics of the North-West Frontier in the 20th century. Organizer of the Khudai Khidmatgars or servants of God, he succeeded in leading a largely non-violent movement against colonialism among a notoriously warlike population. His views first on the desirability of a united India and then on an autonomous Pakhtunistan did not endear him to successive Pakistan rulers and he was imprisoned and spent time in exile. This very detailed biography, by someone who wrote also on Mahatma Gandhi, sees him primarily as a participant in the Congress movement and touches only briefly on the post-independence period.

289 **Colonel Sir Robert Sandeman: his life and work on our Indian frontier.**
     A memoir, with selections from his correspondence and official writings.
     Thomas Henry Thornton, with foreword by Ronald Wingate.
     Karachi: Oxford University Press, 1979. 392p. map. (Oxford in Asia
     Historical Reprints).

First published in 1895, this is the standard life of Sir Robert Sandeman who in the
1870s first established British control or suzerainty over Baluchistan, where he was
agent for a number of years. Thornton discusses the particular qualities that allowed
Sandeman to win the trust of the tribal leaders of the area.

290 **Jinnah of Pakistan.**
     Stanley Wolpert. New York; Oxford, England: Oxford University
     Press, 1984. 421p. 2 maps. bibliog.

This is a full-dress biography of Jinnah by an American historian. Wolpert takes the
reader meticulously through Jinnah's personal and political life from his early days as a
successful lawyer in Bombay through the years of relative isolation from 1921 to 1934
to the intense activity thereafter. Half the book is devoted in fact to the period from
the passing of the Pakistan Resolution in 1940 to Jinnah's death in 1948.

Babur-naìma (Memoirs of Babur).
See item no. 106.

Diary and notes of Mian Fazl-i-Husain.
See item no. 168.

The sole spokesman: Jinnah, the Muslim League and the demand for
Pakistan.
See item no. 222.

Iqbal, Jinnah, and Pakistan: the vision and the reality.
See item no. 223.

The collected works of Quaid-e-Azam Mohammad Ali Jinnah.
See item no. 225.

Quaid-e-Azam Jinnah's correspondence.
See item no. 227.

M. A. Jinnah – Ispahani correspondence 1936–1948.
See item no. 232.

An analysis of contemporary Pakistani politics: Bhutto versus the military.
See item no. 474.

Ghalib: the poet and his age.
See item no. 719.

Population

291 Census of Pakistan 1951.
Karachi: Government of Pakistan, Manager of Publications, [n.d.].
9 vols. maps.

The first census for Pakistan after independence was conducted in February 1951 and the results published after a couple of years (with earlier *Bulletins* giving interim results). The first volume gives the results for the whole country (excluding Jammu and Kashmir and certain other areas) for basic demographic data, literacy, language and economic activity, while volumes 2-7 present the same categories on a provincial basis. Volumes 8 and 9 report the results of separate labour force inquiries.

292 Census of Pakistan 1961.
Karachi: Government of Pakistan, Ministry of Home and Kashmir Affairs, 1963-64. 10 vols. maps.

The second census followed very much the pattern of that held in 1951, with data collected in January 1961 on the principal demographic variables of age, marital status, religion etc., on literacy and on economic activity. Volumes 8-10 report the results of a separate housing census carried out in 1960. Volume 7 was a report on the administration of the census and was not available for public circulation. As well as *Bulletins* reporting the initial results, the census organization also produced *District census reports* based on the census material. These resemble the earlier district gazetteers produced during the British period.

293 Housing, economic and demographic survey, 1973.
Islamabad: Government of Pakistan, Interior Division, Census Organization, [n.d.]. 2 vols. (vol. 2 published in 5 parts).

Unlike the earlier censuses the 1972–73 operation was carried out in two parts. A 'big count', as it was officially termed, was conducted in September 1972, and its results published in the form of separate volumes for each province, in which the simple population totals for each unit right down to the village level were given (*Census bulletin*, no. 2, Islamabad: Government of Pakistan, Interior Division, Census

Organization, 1974–75. 5 vols). The following year a sample of approximately a quarter of a million households was interviewed in greater depth and the results published in two volumes. The first covered methodological issues and reviewed the main findings. The second, in five parts, presented detailed statistical tabulations for each province for demographic, employment and housing variables.

294 **1981 census report of Pakistan.**
Islamabad: Government of Pakistan, Statistics Division, Population Census Organization, 1984. 200p. 2 maps. (Census Report, no. 69).
The fourth census in Pakistan was conducted in March 1981 and collected data for the usual categories. An additional section includes information on migration both within Pakistan and abroad. The report for the whole country is made up of a short introductory text followed by 24 summary tables. Separate volumes published simultaneously give the same information on a disaggregated basis for each of the four provinces.

295 **The population of Pakistan.**
Mohammad Afzal with the cooperation of Mazhar Hussain.
Islamabad: Pakistan Institute of Development Economics, 1974. 112p. bibliog. (C.I.C.R.E.D. Series).
This is a general review of the subject undertaken in connection with the World Population Year 1974. The author examines population growth in Pakistan and its components. Appendices discuss the history of census-taking in Pakistan.

296 **Fertility in Pakistan: a review of findings from the Pakistan fertility survey.**
Edited by Iqbal Alam, with assistance from Betzy Dinesen.
Voorburg, The Netherlands: International Statistical Institute, 1984. 259p. bibliog.
The Pakistan Fertility Survey was carried out from 1974 to 1975 as part of the World Fertility Survey organized by the International Statistical Institute and has become the baseline for further demographic research in this area. In all, 5,246 households were interviewed on a random basis to collect data on nuptiality, fertility, family size preferences, and use of contraception. The papers included in this volume, most of which were initially presented at a conference in 1980 and subsequently revised, are a major contribution to the second-stage analysis of the data. Topics covered include fertility levels and trends, fertility differentials, age at marriage, use of contraception, breastfeeding practices, community variables, and infant and child mortality. The initial findings of the survey were published in 1976 by the International Statistical Institute but would be of interest only to specialists. The main conclusions can be found in *The Pakistan fertility survey 1976: a summary of findings* (Voorburg, The Netherlands: International Statistical Institute, 1977 [World Fertility Survey Summary of Findings, no. 3]). A comment on the methodology of the survey with special reference to Pakistan is M. Nizamuddin, 'Collecting WFS community data: the Pakistan experience', in John B. Casterline (ed.), *The collection and analysis of community data* (Voorburg, The Netherlands: International Statistical Institute, 1985).

Population

297 **The population of India and Pakistan.**
Kingsley Davis.   Princeton, New Jersey: Princeton University Press,
1951. 263p. 22 maps. bibliog.

Davis's book has been the starting point for all subsequent demographic work on the
Indian subcontinent. In it he first reviews the nature and reliability of the historical
evidence for population levels and for trends in birth and death rates and discusses
social structure and change from a demographic perspective. He then discusses
possible population policies based on a mixture of rapid industrialization and birth
control, although presciently he predicted a worsening of the demographic situation
before it stabilized.

298 **Sozio-ökonomische Determinanten der Fertilität der Landbevölkerung**
im Nord-Punjab. Fallbeispiel: Muradi Janjil (Pakistan).
(Socio-economic determinants of fertility in the rural population of
northern Punjab. Case study: Muradi Janjil (Pakistan).)
Eva-Maria Herms.   Stuttgart, West Germany: Franz Steiner Verlag,
1987. 256p. bibliog. (Beiträge zur Südasienforschung Südasien-Institut
Universität Heidelberg, vol. 119).

A study of the comparative importance of the various factors affecting fertility levels
based on a detailed study of a village a little to the south of Rawalpindi. The author
concludes that the cultural importance to a family of having sons in order to increase
its status is such as to outweigh official efforts to encourage effective family planning.

299 **Education, income, and fertility in Pakistan.**
Mohammad Ali Khan, Ismail Sirageldin.   *Economic Development and*
Cultural Change, vol. 27, no. 3 (April 1979), p. 519-47.

Using data derived from a 1968-69 sample survey, the authors construct an
econometric model to analyse factors affecting family size in Pakistan. Education,
whether of husband or wife, is shown to be positively associated with small families;
the effect of income levels varies across urban and rural areas.

300 **Population redistribution and development in South Asia.**
Edited by Leszek A. Kosinski, K. Maudood Elahi.   Dordrecht, The
Netherlands; Boston; Lancaster, England: D. Reidel, 1985. 243p.
maps. bibliog.

This volume emerged out of a symposium on the subject of population redistribution
organized in Karachi in 1980 by the International Commission on Population
Geography. The first two papers provide valuable comparative data for the whole of
South Asia on migration flows from and within the region. Two papers are devoted
solely to Pakistan, one on the redistribution of population in the aftermath of the 1947
partition and the effects of urbanization, the other on North-West Frontier Province
where the impact of the Afghan refugees after December 1979 has been a major
factor.

301 **Population and social organization.**
Edited by Moni Nag. The Hague; Paris: Mouton, 1975. 367p. bibliog.
(World Anthropology series).

This volume of conference papers includes an essay by Karam Elahi entitled 'Some aspects of socioeconomic change and fertility control among the emerging elite of the Pathans' (p. 93-125) which argues that there is a marked shift among the small but growing group of Pathans in modern élite occupations towards a preference for small families.

302 **Pakistan Demographic Survey.**
Karachi: Federal Bureau of Statistics, 1984- . annual.

These volumes are an attempt to remedy the absence in Pakistan of an efficient registration system for births, deaths and marriages, and also to provide a corrective for census figures which are regarded as unreliable as sources of fertility and mortality statistics. Each volume, published some time after the year to which it relates, is based on a sample survey (in 1986 22,715 households were covered) and provides data by province on standard demographic variables.

303 **Women's status and fertility change in Pakistan.**
Zeba Sathar, Nigel Crook, Christine Callum, Shahnaz Kazi.
Population and Development Review, vol. 14, no. 3 (Sept. 1988),
p. 415-32.

A general discussion of the low status of women in Pakistan relative to men, and the consequences of this for fertility levels. Drawing on survey data for the 1970s and early 1980s the authors argue that there is so far no conclusive evidence of sustained declines in fertility levels but that signs of change may be detected in the larger urban areas.

304 **Migration in Pakistan: theories and facts.**
Edited by Frits Selier, Mehtab S. Karim. Lahore: Vanguard Books, 1986. 193p. map. bibliog.

Quite apart from the huge movements of population which occurred at the time of independence and subsequently the phenomenon of substantial overseas migration, there has been considerable internal migration of population within Pakistan since 1947. Much of it has been from rural to urban areas, especially but not exclusively to Karachi. The articles in this volume make use of data from the population censuses and migration surveys carried out in 1979-80 and 1983-84 to examine various aspects of the process.

305 **Pakistan's economic problems and demographic policy.**
Alexander Zablotsky. *Journal of South Asian and Middle Eastern Studies*, vol. 7, no. 1 (Fall 1983), p. 57-76.

An analysis by a Soviet scholar of the search for solutions to problems of unemployment, low production and rapidly increasing population. The author reviews Pakistan's efforts to introduce family planning programmes and concludes that they will not succeed unless they are made part of a comprehensive programme of economic and social change, including radical land reform, state-controlled industrialization and changes in the status of women.

Population

Growth of Muslim population in medieval India (A.D. 1000–1800).
See item no. 146.

Age and social status at marriage, Karachi, Pakistan, 1961–64 and 1980: a comparative study.
See item no. 395.

Pakistani women: a socioeconomic and demographic profile.
See item no. 444.

Pakistan Development Review.
See item no. 612.

Minorities

306 **The city in South Asia: premodern and modern.**
Edited by Kenneth Ballhatchet, John Harrison. London: Curzon
Press; Atlantic Highlands, New Jersey: Humanities Press, 1980. 342p.
maps.
This contains an article by Raffat Khan Haward, 'An urban minority: the Goan
Christian community in Karachi', p. 299-323, in which the author uses an anthropological
perspective to discuss the position of the Goan Christians in Karachi in the mid-1970s.

307 **Afghan refugees in Pakistan: from emergency towards self-reliance.**
A report on the food situation and related socio-economic aspects.
Hanne Christensen. Geneva: United Nations Research Institute for
Social Development, 1984. 87p. (UNRISD Refugee Settlement Series,
84.2).
Despite the narrowness of the title, this report in fact ranges quite widely across issues
to do with the situation of the Afghan refugee population in Pakistan. The author
argues that after the initial period the refugee community achieved a degree of self-
reliance in food supply and in some other aspects of its material existence. Another
piece on the same subject is Nancy Hatch Dupree, 'Demographic reporting on Afghan
refugees in Pakistan', *Modern Asian Studies*, vol. 22, no. 4 (Oct. 1988), p. 845-65. The
economic aspects are covered in more detail by Asif Ashraf, *Economic impact of
Afghan refugees in NWFP* (Peshawar: Pakistan Academy for Rural Development,
1988).

308 **The Ahmadiyah movement: a history and perspective.**
Spencer Lavan. Delhi: Manohar Book Service, 1974. 220p. bibliog.
The Ahmadiyah movement, whose adherents are also sometimes known as Qadianis,
was founded by Mirza Ghulam Ahmed and is a religious reform movement within
Islam which had its origins in late 19th-century Punjab. Since independence the
Ahmadis have been the target of attack from orthodox Muslims and in 1974 they were

declared to be a non-Muslim minority. A number of Ahmadis have nevertheless achieved prominence within Pakistan, most notably Muhammad Zafrullah Khan, Foreign Minister in the 1950s and subsequently a judge of the International Court. Lavan's study, originally a doctoral thesis, discusses the history of the Ahmadiyah movement up to the 1930s and sets it against the religious background of the late 19th century where reformists of all the main religions were contending against each other as well as against conservatives within their own communities. The teachings of the Ahmadiyah movement are most conveniently found in English in Bashir-ud-din Mahmud Ahmad, *Invitation to Ahmadiyyat* (London; Boston; Henley, England: Routledge & Kegan Paul, 1980 [orig. published 1961], 328p.). There is an article on the recent position of the group by Charles H. Kennedy: 'Towards the definition of a Muslim in an Islamic state: the case of Ahmadiyya in Pakistan', in Dhirendra Vajpeyi and Yogendra K. Malik (eds), *Religious and ethnic minorities in South Asia* (Delhi: Manohar, 1989), p. 71-108.

309 **Al-Mushir.**
Rawalpindi: Christian Study Centre, c.1959- . quarterly.
This well-produced quarterly from an interdenominational centre in Pakistan describes itself as a theological journal, but the range of articles carried is much wider than this might imply. While some are research-based historical pieces on the various Christian groups in Pakistan and their history, others are concerned with questions of dialogue with Islam or with the situation of Christianity in Pakistan. Each issue contains news items on religious matters in Pakistan. The title of the journal is Arabic for 'counsellor', and each issue is divided more or less equally into English and Urdu sections.

310 **Eine sozio-ethno-religiöse Minderheit: die Christen West-Pakistans.**
(A socio-ethno-religious minority: the Christians of West Pakistan.)
Karl Heinz Pfeffer. *Sociologus* (n.s.), vol. 12, no. 2 (1962),
p. 113-27.
This general description by a sociologist looks, on the one hand, at high-status sections among the Christian population who since independence have mostly kept a low public profile and, on the other, at the much more numerous low-status Christians, mostly belonging to the sweeper community, for whom, the author argues, there is little opportunity for real social mobility.

311 **The hesitant dawn (Christianity in Pakistan 1579–1760).**
John Rooney. Rawalpindi: Christian Study Centre, 1984. 120p. map.
bibliog. (Pakistan Christian History Monograph, no. 2).
This short but carefully researched book looks at the work of the Jesuits and other Catholic missionaries who visited and worked in Mughal India. He describes in detail their activities in what is now Pakistan. Rooney is also the author of *Shadows in the dark (a history of Christianity in Pakistan up to the 10th century)* (Rawalpindi: Christian Study Centre, 1984 [Pakistan Christian History Monograph, no. 1]).

312 **The Christian community and change in nineteenth century North India.**
John C. B. Webster. Delhi: Macmillan, 1976. 293p. 2 maps. bibliog.
The author is himself a missionary as well as a scholar, and the dissertation on which this book is based looks at the work of the American Presbyterian missionaries in the

Punjab and the neighbouring United Provinces in the 19th century. Their impact on Indian society is depicted against a background of intellectual and political questioning. Webster concludes that their influence is to be measured not in terms of converts but of their educational and religious work.

The crow eaters.
See item no. 743.

Overseas Populations

313 **The myth of return: Pakistanis in Britain.**
Muhammad Anwar. London: Heinemann, 1979. 278p. bibliog.
This is an anthropological study of Pakistanis, mostly from the Punjab, in Rochdale in the north of England. Anwar discusses how they recreated kin-based networks and the links between these networks and economic activity. He shows more generally how Pakistan continues to be used as a point of reference for people's lives.

314 **Urban ethnicity.**
Edited by Abner Cohen. London: Tavistock, 1974. 391p. map.
bibliog.
This volume of conference papers includes (p. 77-118) 'The nature of Pakistani ethnicity in industrial cities in Britain' by Badr Dahya. Dahya, basing himself on fieldwork in Birmingham and Bradford mainly in the mid-1960s, is particularly concerned with the economic motives for migration and with the maintenance by the communities of a set of values distinct from that of the indigenous population. He criticizes earlier studies of Pakistani migrants for lack of perspective on these points.

315 **Migrants, workers and the social order.**
Edited by Jeremy Eades. London; New York: Tavistock, 1987. 281p.
bibliog. (ASA Monographs, no. 26).
This is a collection of papers from an academic conference of British anthropologists held in 1986 around the theme of migration. Two papers deal with Pakistani migrants. Roger Ballard's 'The political economy of migration: Pakistan, Britain, and the Middle East' focuses on migrants from the Mirpur district of Kashmir and the economic and social context in which they make decisions on migration. Pnina Werbner entitles her discussion of businessmen in Manchester and their place in the community 'Enclave economies and family firms: Pakistani traders in a British city'.

316 **Citizens, slaves, guest-workers: the dynamics of labour migration from South Asia.**
Ijaz Shafi Gilani, with Jonathan S. Addelton (*sic*, Addleton).
Islamabad: Institute of Policy Studies, 1985. 84p. bibliog.

This is a summation of a number of studies carried out by Gilani on the subject of labour migration from Pakistan mainly to the Middle East. He looks at the process from the points of view of both sending and receiving countries and from that of the migrants themselves. He discusses the uses made of remittances from workers abroad and looks at other economic consequences of labour migration. The most important of the specialized studies referred to is Ijaz Gilani, M. Fahim Khan and Munawar Iqbal, *Labour migration from Pakistan to the Middle East and its impact on the domestic economy* (Islamabad: Pakistan Institute of Development Economics, 1981 [Research Report Series, no. 126]).

317 **Migrants and refugees: Muslim and Christian Pakistani families in Bristol.**
Patricia Jeffery. Cambridge, England: Cambridge University Press, 1976. 221p. 3 maps. bibliog.

This is a detailed study by an anthropologist of a number of families of Pakistani origin living in the large English city of Bristol. In theoretical terms the study is marked by its awareness of the Pakistani background; empirically it is unusual in its inclusion of both Christians and Muslims (the 'refugees' and 'migrants' of the title). The families studied came from urban rather than rural backgrounds in Pakistan. The fieldwork was conducted in 1970-71.

318 **Minority families in Britain: support and stress.**
Edited by Verity Saifullah Khan. London: Macmillan, 1979. 203p.
bibliog. (Studies in Ethnicity, no. 2).

The contributors to this collection, much of which originated in a conference in 1976, are concerned to challenge popular misconceptions about the relationship between minority families and the social services, particularly those which see the former simply as generating 'problems' for the latter. Papers specifically or substantially on groups of Pakistani origin are by Catherine Ballard on second-generation Asians in Britain and by the editor on Mirpuris (from Azad Jammu and Kashmir) in Bradford. There is a paper on the same topic by Verity Saifullah Khan, 'The Pakistanis: Mirpuri villagers at home and in Bradford', in James L. Watson (ed.), *Between two cultures: migrants and minorities in Britain* (Oxford, England: Basil Blackwell, 1977, p. 57-89).

319 **My beautiful launderette *and* the rainbow sign.**
Hanif Kureishi. London; Boston: Faber & Faber, 1986. 111p.

Born in London of a Pakistani father and an English mother, Hanif Kureishi is a well-known playwright and scriptwriter. *My beautiful launderette* was his first major success. In it he explores the pressures on young people in Britain of Pakistani origin. *The rainbow sign* is an autobiographical essay which covers the same topics on the basis of Kureishi's own experience both of Britain and of Pakistan.

320 Pakistanis in Europe.

London Centre for Pakistan Studies.   London: New Century
Publishers, 1982. 188p.

The proceedings of a conference held by community leaders in Manchester in 1982.
The volume includes background papers on Pakistani communities in Britain and
elsewhere in Europe and the particular issues facing them, together with appendices
which give much practical information on Pakistani organizations.

321 A Pakistani community in Britain.

Alison Shaw.   Oxford, England: Basil Blackwell, 1988. 187p. 3 maps.

This is an anthropological study based on fieldwork in Britain and Pakistan of the
relatively small Pakistani community in Oxford. The author emphasizes its links with
Pakistan and the continuity of values, for example the importance of kinship and of
mutual obligation.

322 The export of manpower from Pakistan to the Middle East, 1975–1985.

Isabelle Tsakok.   *World Development*, vol. 10, no. 4 (April 1982),
p. 319-25.

A brief review of the subject which assesses the value to individual households and to
the economy as a whole of high flows of remitted funds from overseas workers and
balances them against the cost to the economy of the export of skills in short supply
domestically. Tsakok concludes that the balance at the point of writing had been
favourable. She contributed a chapter on a similar theme to the volume on Pakistan's
development priorities edited by Burki and LaPorte (q.v.).

323 Ethnic communities in business: strategies for economic survival.

Edited by Robin Ward, Richard Jenkins.   Cambridge, England:
Cambridge University Press, 1984. 270p. bibliog.

This well-focused collection of essays looks at the business activities of various
immigrant groups into Britain. It includes case-studies and more general analyses of
the complex interrelationship of ideology, racism and social factors that influence the
extent to which migrants become businessmen. A separate section deals with Asian
groups and all four chapters in it deal wholly or in part with Pakistani groups.

324 Manchester Pakistanis: lifestyles, ritual and the making of social distinctions.

Pnina Werbner.   *New Community*, vol. 9, no. 2 (Autumn 1981),
p. 216-29.

Reprinted in Eric Butterworth and David Weir (eds), *The new sociology of modern
Britain* (London: Fontana, 1984), this is a theoretically oriented piece by an
anthropologist who sees 'lifestyle' as a means of conveying messages to others and uses
the concept to distinguish social categories among the Pakistani community in
Manchester. Two earlier articles by Werbner in *New Community* are also relevant:
'Avoiding the ghetto: Pakistani migrants and settlement shifts in Manchester', vol. 7,
no. 3 (Winter 1979), p. 376-89; 'From rags to riches: Manchester Pakistanis in the
textile trade'. vol. 8, nos 1&2 (Spring-Summer 1980), p. 84-95.

The impact of international migration on economic development in Pakistan.
See item no. 594.

Languages and Dialects

325 An English–Panjabi dictionary.
T. Grahame Bailey.   Delhi: Ess Ess Publications, 1976. 159p.
First published in 1919, this dictionary has been included for want of anything more up to date. The Punjabi equivalents of nearly 6,000 English words are given transliterated into Roman.

326 Panjabi grammar: a brief grammar of Panjabi as spoken in the then Wazirabad district.
Thomas Grahame Bailey.   Lahore: Saaddi Panjabi Academy, 1977. 60p.
First published in 1904, this is a brief and straightforward grammatical sketch. All material is transliterated into Roman.

327 A course in Baluchi.
Muhammad Abd-al-Rahman Barker, Aqil Khan Mengal.   Montreal: McGill University, Institute of Islamic Studies, 1969. 2 vols. 2 maps.
This is the most comprehensive modern course available for Baluchi and is based on extensive original research. The dialect chosen as the basis is Rakhshani, spoken extensively in central Baluchistan. The course is designed primarily for use in the classroom. A Roman-based phonemic script is used in the initial sections, with the Arabic script being introduced in the second volume.

328 A course in Urdu.
Muhammad Abd-al-Rahman Barker (et al).   Montreal: McGill University, Institute of Islamic Studies, 1967. 3 vols. map.
This is a comprehensive and well-researched textbook designed for intensive classroom use (the authors recommend at least five hours a week with a teacher). The first two volumes introduce the student to grammar, vocabulary, idiom, and, in the later

sections, the Persian script. The third volume is devoted to vocabulary lists. Barker and his associates have published several companion works, including *A reader of classical Urdu poetry* (Ithaca, New York: Spoken Languages Services, 1977, 3 vols); *Urdu–English vocabulary: student's pronouncing dictionary* (Ithaca, New York: Spoken Languages Services, 1980); *An Urdu newspaper reader* (Montreal: McGill University, Institute of Islamic Studies, 1968).

329   **The Baluchi language: a dialectology with texts.**
      J. H. Elfenbein.   London: Royal Asiatic Society, 1966, 48p. 2 maps.
      (Royal Asiatic Society Monographs, vol. 27).
The purpose of this work is to distinguish the features of the various dialects of Baluchi, and to provide a modern classification of them, based primarily on phonological and morphological features. Elfenbein suggests that six main dialects can be identified, with some further subclassification.

330   **Linguistic survey of India.**
      George Abraham Grierson.   Calcutta: Government of India, Central Publications Branch, 1903–28. 11 vols (some in multiple parts). maps. bibliog.
Although out of date in many important respects, Grierson's work, carried out in the late 19th and early 20th centuries, is still the starting point for linguistic research on South Asia. The first volume (in three parts) provides a general and comparative survey of the subject and establishes the classificatory scheme. Each volume in turn then deals with the languages in each of the groups identified. Altogether 179 languages and 544 dialects are covered. For each one there are carefully recorded and analysed specimens and brief accounts of grammar, syntax and a limited vocabulary. Languages spoken in Pakistan today are mainly covered in volumes 8, 9 and 10.

331   **The standard English–Urdu dictionary.**
      Abdul Haq.   Aurangabad, India: Anjuman-e-Urdu Press, 1937. 1513p. (Anjuman-e-Taraqqi-e-Urdu (India) Series, no. 106).
Despite its age, this large volume has often been reprinted and is also the basis for many more recent dictionaries. *Ferozsons English–Urdu dictionary* (Lahore: Ferozsons, n.d.), for example, is little more than an abbreviated version. The compiler was a great Urdu scholar who acquired the title of Baba-i-Urdu, father of Urdu. It should be noted that the Urdu entries are only in Persian script.

332   **The standard Urdu–English dictionary.**
      Abdul Haq.   Delhi: Chaman Book Depot, [?1938]. 831p.
Like Abdul Haq's English-Urdu dictionary (see previous entry), this has become the basis for other dictionaries. Despite its claim to originality, *Ferozsons Urdu–English dictionary* (Lahore: Ferozsons, 1960) is only a copy.

333   **Lehrbuch des Pashto (Afghanisch).** (Pashto teaching book (Afghan).)
      Manfred Lorenz.   Leipzig, East Germany: VEB Verlag Enzyklopädie, 1979. 303p.
Arranged into 44 sections, this work provides an introduction to Pashto grammar and would be suitable for the student working on his or her own as well as for those in the

classroom. Each lesson includes grammar, vocabulary and exercises. The script is introduced from the beginning, but except in the translation exercises each word is also transliterated.

334 Report on a linguistic mission to north-western India.
Georg Morgenstierne. Oslo: H. Aschehoug, 1932. 76p. 2 maps.
(Instituttet for Sammenlignende Kulturforskning, series C III-1).

Morgenstierne was a distinguished scholar of Indo-Iranian languages. The present work is a brief field report on a visit that he made to the isolated areas of what is now northern Pakistan, especially Chitral, in order to study the languages spoken there. He was interested in the character of the languages spoken on the frontier between the Iranian and Indo-Aryan branches of the larger Indo-European family.

335 Development and use of writing system across culture: the case of Arabic-Persian Urdu orthographic model.
Gopi Chand Narang. *Journal of South Asian and Middle Eastern Studies*, vol. 10, no. 2 (Winter 1986), p. 64-77.

Urdu is derived phonologically and grammatically from Indian sources but uses a script adapted from Arabic and Persian. Narang discusses the practical difficulties this has caused and the expedients that were developed to overcome them. He concludes that the result is a complex but nevertheless functional system with substantial cultural resonance.

336 Newsletter of Baluchistan Studies.
Naples, Italy: Istituto Universitario Orientale, Dipartimento di Studi Asiatici; Rome: Istituto Italiano per Medio ed Estremo Oriente, 1982- irreg.

Although this newsletter is concerned with Baluchistan studies in all its aspects, articles on language form the largest category. Most contributions are in the form of fairly short research notes.

337 A dictionary of Urdu, classical Hindi, and English.
John T. Platts. London: Oxford University Press, 1930. 1259p.

Although in most respects Platts' dictionary dates back more than a hundred years, it is an essential tool for any serious student of the Urdu language. The Urdu word is in each case given first, followed where the word is also used in Hindi, by its transliteration in *devanagari* (the Hindi script), and then by an English definition.

338 A new course in Urdu and spoken Hindi for learners in Britain.
Ralph Russell. London: School of Oriental and African Studies, External Services Division, 1986. 2nd ed. 4 vols.

First published in 1980 as *A new course in Hindustani*, this is designed specifically as a teach yourself course for adult learners in Britain, especially those in contact with Urdu-speaking members of the South Asian community there. It would be useful for anyone with limited time available. The first part is the basic course, the second an outline of the grammar, the third readings; the fourth part is devoted to the script.

Languages and Dialects

339 **Punjabi in Lahore.**
Christopher Shackle. *Modern Asian Studies*, vol. 4, no. 3 (July 1970), p. 239-67.

A fascinating study by a sociologically aware linguist of the position of Punjabi in post-independence Lahore. Squeezed between English and Urdu, Punjabi nevertheless has its own position, especially as a spoken language. At the time the article was written, a significant literary movement existed to promote Punjabi.

340 **The Siraiki language of central Pakistan: a reference grammar.**
Christopher Shackle. London: School of Oriental and African Studies, 1976. 198p. 2 maps. bibliog.

Sometimes called Multani or Southern Lahnda, Siraiki is the language of a large number of people in southern Punjab and Sindh, although it is not recognized as a separate language by the Census of Pakistan. It is nevertheless, although it is difficult to disentangle it entirely from Punjabi and Sindhi, a separate language with its own literature. The present work is a descriptive grammar by a modern philologist intended for academic use. There is a similar work by a Soviet scholar, U. A. Smirnov: *The Lahndi language* (Moscow, 'Nauka' Publishing House, 1975 [Languages of Asia and Africa]).

341 **South Asian languages: a handbook.**
Edited by Christopher Shackle. London: School of Oriental and African Studies, External Services Division, 1985. 62p. 6 maps. bibliog. (External Services Division Occasional Papers, no. 10).

Staff at the University of London's School of Oriental and African Studies collaborated to produce this short guide to South Asian languages designed to give the layman basic information. Written in an easily accessible style, the book gives a brief history and description of each language and its script, as well as of its literature and present position in the region. The chapter on Urdu is by D. J. Matthews and on Punjabi by C. Shackle.

342 **The Sindhi–English dictionary.**
Anandram T. Shahaney. Bombay: School and College Bookstall, [n.d.]. 5th ed. 560p.

Shahaney's work has often been reprinted and can be used as a basic dictionary for the language. Each Sindhi word is given only in Arabic script. There is a companion English to Sindhi version (*The English–Sindhi dictionary*. Bombay: School and College Bookstall, 1966, new ed.).

343 **Sindhi self-instructor.**
A. T. Shahaney. Bombay: School and College Bookstall, 1967. 3rd ed. 200p.

Originally published in 1905, this is still one of the few available textbooks for Sindhi, although it gives only a basic grounding and does not measure up to modern standards. The author, who taught British officials and their families, provides notes on grammar and vocabulary. Sindhi is spoken by Hindu Sindhis who migrated to India at independence, and the present edition published from Bombay uses *devanagari* as well as Arabic script. It also uses Roman transcriptions. Another, shorter version of

Shahaney's work has also been reprinted in Pakistan, *The Sindhi instructor [a useful book to acquire working knowledge of Sindhi language]* by Munshi Anandram, revised and edited by Mohammed Ibrahim M. Joyo (Hyderabad: Sindhi Adabi Board, 1971, 130p.). Although the text is in English, Sindhi words are given only in Arabic script, a knowledge of which would therefore be a prerequisite for using the book.

344 **The Sindhi language.**
R. P. Yegorova, translated by E. H. Tsipan.   Moscow: 'Nauka' Publishing House, 1971. 162p. bibliog. (Languages of Asia and Africa).

Originally published in Russian in 1966, this is a reference grammar for the specialist linguist. After a brief introduction which describes the historical and current position of the language, there are sections on phonetics, morphology and syntax.

345 **Languages of South Asia: a guide.**
G. A. Zograph, translated by G. L. Campbell.   London: Routledge & Kegan Paul, 1982. 231p. 2 maps. bibliog. (Languages of Asia and Africa, vol. 3).

This is a brief but systematic description, based initially on Grierson's *Linguistic Survey of India*, of the languages spoken in what philologists now think of as the 'Indian linguistic area'. Urdu is subsumed in the Indo-Aryan group, along with Punjabi and Sindhi and related languages. Other languages covered are Pashtu, Baluchi, Brahui and the Dardic group. For each language there is a description of its phonology and morphology. The book was originally published in Russian in 1960 as *Yazyki Indii, Pakistana, Tseilona i Nepala* (Moscow: Oriental Publishing House).

Religion

346 **An intellectual history of Islam in India.**
Aziz Ahmad. Edinburgh: Edinburgh University Press, 1969. 226p.
bibliog. (Islamic Surveys, no. 7).

Despite the title this work by one of the most distinguished students of the subject is really a survey of Indian Islam and the religious and spiritual tendencies within it. The major sub-groups and the sufi orders are each described in a few pages. There are also chapters on literature and the fine arts.

347 **Islamic modernism in India and Pakistan 1857–1964.**
Aziz Ahmad. London: Oxford University Press, 1967. 294p. bibliog.

A major work of scholarship but accessible to anyone with an interest in the subject. Aziz Ahmad looks at Sayyid Ahmad Khan and Muhammad Iqbal as the key figures in the 19th and 20th centuries respectively, and then at other complementary and contrasting writers. He is alert to both the religious and the political aspects of his subject. All of the writers considered are of relevance to contemporary thought in Pakistan, although only Maulana Maududi and G. A. Parwiz wrote in the post-1947 context.

348 **Islamic perspectives: studies in honour of Mawlānā Sayyid Abul A'lā Mawdūdī.**
Edited by Khurshid Ahmad, Zafar Ishaq Ansari. Leicester, England:
Islamic Foundation, 1979. 394p. bibliog.

Mawdudi (often spelt Maududi) was the most prominent South Asian 'fundamentalist' Muslim writer of the 20th century who had tremendous influence internationally as well. These essays by Muslim scholars and intellectuals cover a wide range of topics in the general field of Islamic studies. Maududi himself is the subject of three papers and there is a full bibliography of his writings, totalling 138 items, and 62 items in English, Urdu and other languages about his work. There are passing references to Pakistan in several of the other papers.

349 **A late nineteenth century Muslim response to the Western criticism of Islam – an analysis of Amir Ali's life and works.**
Abdullah Ahsan. *American Journal of Islamic Social Sciences*, vol. 2, no. 2 (Dec. 1985), p. 179-206.

An overview of the work and writings of Amir Ali, a prominent 19th-century Indian Muslim who led a counter-attack against dismissive views of Islam in the West, especially the influential work of Sir William Muir. His insistence on the superiority of Islam to Christianity, especially in his book *The Spirit of Islam*, gave him a considerable reputation, although his interpretation of Islam owed much to European rationalism and his political views were in favour of the continuation of British rule.

350 **Analytical catalogue of books on Allama Muhammad Iqbal (1877–1977).**
Compiled and edited by Abdul Hafeez Akhtar. Karachi: Government of Pakistan, Ministry of Education, Department of Libraries, 1978. 97p. 182p.

Produced at the time of the Iqbal centenary in 1977, this lists 306 items in English, 464 in Urdu and smaller numbers in other Asian languages. For each entry there is a content analysis under standardized headings.

351 **Religion and thought of Shāh Walī Allāh Dihlawī 1703–1762.**
J. M. S. Baljon. Leiden, The Netherlands: E. J. Brill, 1986. 221p. bibliog. (Studies in the History of Religions [Supplements to *Numen*], no. 48).

A major study of this key figure in the South Asian Islamic tradition whose influence has always been recognized but whose work has not been given specialized attention in the English literature. Baljon writes primarily for the scholar and some prior background knowledge would be necessary for the general reader. The work concentrates on Wali Allah's religious rather than political views.

352 **Islam in the modern world.**
A. K. Brohi, edited by Khurshid Ahmad. Lahore: Publishers United, 1975. 2nd ed. 323p.

A. K. Brohi was a distinguished lawyer who served for a time as President Zia's law minister and was an ardent advocate of orthodox Islam. This collection of speeches and essays addresses such themes as Islam and socialism, the historical role of Pakistan, and Islam and material progress. A parallel collection, *Testament of faith* (Lahore: Publishers United, 1975) brings together thoughts on more purely religious themes.

353 **Iqbal und Europa: vier Vorträge.** (Iqbal and Europe: four lectures.)
Edited by J. C. Bürgel. Bern; Frankfurt; Las Vegas, Nevada: Peter Lang, 1980. 85p. (Schweizer Asiatische Studien/Etudes Asiatiques Suisses, Studienhefte/Cahiers, no. 5).

Four lectures delivered to mark the centenary of Iqbal's birth which compare his characteristic emphasis on the self or *khudi* with the ideas of Goethe and other European philosophers and writers. A Czech scholar, Jan Marek, covers Iqbal's social thought.

354 A study in Iqbal's philosophy.
Bashir Ahmad Dar, foreword by Mumtaz Hasan. Lahore:
Sh. Ghulam Ali & Sons, 1971. rev. ed. 329p. bibliog.

First published in 1944, this is a sympathetic treatment of Iqbal's philosophical position and its relation to Islamic and Western ideas. Iqbal's ideas on the self and on society occupy the main chapters of the book. Dar also wrote *Iqbal and post-Kantian voluntarism* (Lahore: Bazm-i-Iqbal, 1956).

355 Religious thought of Sayyid Ahmad Khan.
Bashir Ahmad Dar. Lahore: Institute of Islamic Culture, 1957. 304p.

This is an older but still valuable study of Sayyid Ahmad Khan which discusses his religious thought in the context of the challenges Islam faced in 19th-century South Asia from Christian missionaries and from Hindu revivalism. He describes in detail Sayyid Ahmad's reconciliation of human reason and divine omnipotence, and its implications for the sources of religious authority. Dar's sympathetic account of Sayyid Ahmad sees him as the originator of contemporary progressive and liberal Islamic thought. An appendix includes extracts from his *The causes of the Indian revolt.*

356 The profile of popular Islam in the Pakistani Punjab.
Richard M. Eaton. *Journal of South Asian and Middle Eastern Studies*, vol. 2, no. 1 (Fall 1978), p. 74-92.

The author has used the register of disciples of a major sufi shrine in the Punjab, going back with breaks to its foundation in the 17th century, to demonstrate the potentiality of such a source not only for the study of sufi shrines as social institutions but also for the study of social and economic structures over an extended period of time.

357 The encyclopaedia of Islam.
Leiden, The Netherlands: E. J. Brill; London: Luzac (vols 1-3 only), 1960- . 2nd ed. In progress.

This multi-volumed work is a major example of worldwide scholarly cooperation. Some hundreds of scholars, Muslim and non-Muslim (although the latter predominate), have contributed articles over the years to a work which covers all major events, personalities, places and themes in Islamic religion and history. There is also some coverage of economic and social issues. There are many entries which relate specifically to Pakistan and to South Asian Muslims. The first edition, in five volumes, was published by E. J. Brill between 1913 and 1942. The second edition had reached five volumes by 1986 but the final work is likely to be double that number. A parallel French edition is published by E. J. Brill in partnership with G. P. Maisonneuve (Paris).

358 Shaykh Aḥmad Sirhindī: an outline of his thought and a study of his image in the eyes of posterity.
Yohanan Friedmann. Montreal; London: McGill-Queen's University Press, 1971. 130p. bibliog. (McGill Islamic Studies, vol. 2).

A specialist study of Sheikh Ahmad Sirhindi, an early 17th-century sufi and a major figure in Indo-Muslim thought. Friedmann suggests that most current interpretations of Sirhindi see him through a prism of 20th-century concerns and present him therefore as a strictly orthodox revivalist. We should look at him, he argues, as a more complex figure whose concerns remained primarily the mystical ones of the typical sufi.

359 The faith movement of Mawlānā Muḥammad Ilyās.
M. Anwarul Haq.   London: George Allen & Unwin, 1972. 210p. bibliog.

A committed but also scholarly study of the life and work of a 20th-century religious leader who came from a sufi background and worked until his death in 1944 to revive the personal faith of Muslims rather than concerning himself with issues of political power. Haq's book is one of the few works in English to give access to this side of Islam in South Asia. Ilyas himself worked in the region round Delhi but his followers are also to be found in Pakistan.

360 The Shi'a of India.
John Norman Hollister.   London: Luzac, 1953. 440p. bibliog.

This is a work typical of the scholar-missionary. Written in fact before 1947, it is a useful and authoritative compendium of information on the various groups described, but it does not attempt to provide an interpretative understanding of the spirit of Shia Islam. Hollister discusses the 'mainstream' Ithna 'Ashariya, who recognize twelve actual Imams, and the Ismailis and their subsects, the Nizari branch of which regard the Aga Khan as their spiritual head. The total Shia population of Pakistan today is uncertain but it is at least 10 per cent and may be substantially more.

361 Javid-nama.
Muhammad Iqbal, translated by Arthur J. Arberry.   London, George Allen & Unwin, 1966. 151p. bibliog. (UNESCO Collection of Representative Works, Pakistan Series).

Regarded as Iqbal's most important single poetic work, the *Javid-nama* or Book of Eternity was written in Persian and first published in 1932. By telling of a spiritual journey to the presence of God, Iqbal is able to convey his views on philosophy and on Islamic history. The *Javid-nama* has been translated into German (*Das Buch der Ewigkeit*, by Annemarie Schimmel. Munich: Max Hueber Verlag, 1957), French (*Le livre de l'éternité*, by Eva Meyerovitch and Mohammed Mokri. Paris: Albin Michel, 1962) and many other languages.

362 The secrets of the self (Asrar-i-Khudi): a philosophical poem.
Muhammad Iqbal, translated by Reynold A. Nicholson.   London: Macmillan, 1920. 148p.

In his Persian poem *Secrets of the self* and its companion *Mysteries of selflessness* (original title *Rumuz-i-Bekhudi*, translated by Arthur J. Arberry. London: John Murray, 1953) Iqbal puts forth his distinctive theory of the individual ego (*khudi*) and its relation to God. 'The moral and religious ideal of man', Iqbal wrote in a letter to Nicholson, 'is not self-negation but self-affirmation, and he attains to this ideal by becoming more and more individual, more and more unique.'

363 **The reconstruction of religious thought in Islam.**
Muhammad Iqbal. London: Oxford University Press, 1934. 192p.

Reprinted and translated many times, this is the most systematic statement by Iqbal of
the religious and philosophical ideas which he otherwise expressed in poetry. With
reference both to the traditions of Muslim thought and to contemporary European
philosophers such as Henri Bergson, Iqbal develops his view of the creative and
dynamic individual within Islam. He writes also of the principle of movement in Islam.

364 *Shikwa* and *Jawab-i-Shikwa*: **complaint and answer. Iqbal's dialogue
with Allah.**
Muhammad Iqbal, translated and with an introduction by Khushwant
Singh. Delhi: Oxford University Press, 1981. 96p.

These two poems, written in 1909 and 1913 respectively, represent Iqbal as a poet at
his most audacious and brilliant. In the first he asks God why he has allowed Muslim
power to decline; the second gives the answer that the Muslims have declined because
they have abandoned a truly Muslim way of life. The present edition includes the Urdu
text in parallel with the English translation, and also a *devanagari* transliteration.
There is an earlier translation of the poems by A. J. Arberry, *Complaint and Answer*
(Lahore: Sh. Muhammad Ashraf, [n.d.]).

365 **Iqbal Review.**
Lahore: Iqbal Academy Lahore, 1960- . biannual.

A journal devoted to articles in English primarily on the life and thought of Iqbal but
also on related Islamic topics. A volume containing a representative selection of
articles from it in English was published by the Academy in 1983, edited by Waheed
Qureshi: *Selections from the Iqbal Review*.

366 **Islamic Studies.**
Islamabad: International Islamic University, 1962– . quarterly.

Published by a government-sponsored institution, this journal reflects Pakistan's
concern to promote Islamic studies in general. Articles cover historical, theological and
cultural aspects of Islam. The majority of the contributors are Pakistani, but some are
from abroad, in some cases non-Muslim scholars.

367 **Die Religionen des Hindukusch.** (The religions of the Hindukush).
K. Jettmar, with contributions by Schuyler Jones, Max Klimburg.
Stuttgart, West Germany: Verlag W. Kohlhammer, 1975. 525p.
2 maps. bibliog. (Die Religionen der Menschheit, vol. 4, no. 1).

This is a massive, anthropologically oriented account of the religious beliefs of the non-
Muslim tribal groups in the Hindu Kush mountains. For each major group of peoples,
there is a description of gods, rites and festivals. The first portion of the book has been
translated into English by Adam Nayyar as *The religions of the Hindukush*, vol. 1 *The
religion of the Kafirs: the pre-Islamic heritage of Afghan Nuristan* (Warminster,
England: Aris & Phillips, 1986), and contains some additional material, especially a
glossary by Peter S. C. Parkes. Publication in English of the remaining parts, which
deal with Pakistani areas, is promised.

368 **The rose and the rock: mystical and rational elements in the intellectual history of South Asian Islam.**
Edited by Bruce B. Lawrence. Durham, North Carolina: Duke University Programs in Comparative Studies on Southern Asia and in Islamic and Arabian Development Studies, 1979. 200p. (Comparative Studies on Southern Asia, no. 15).

Originally given to a conference in 1975, the papers in this valuable collection focus on the situation of élite Muslims in North India in the 19th and 20th centuries as they confronted the challenge of European colonialism to the mystical and poetical roots of their culture. The major figures considered are Ghalib, Sayyid Ahmad Khan and Iqbal, but there are studies also of the 17th-century poet Bedil, strictly speaking outside the scope of the volume, and of 18th-century sufi saints.

369 **Essays on Islamic civilization presented to Niyazi Berkes.**
Edited by Donald P. Little. Leiden, The Netherlands; E. J. Brill, 1976. 364p.

This *Festschrift* for a scholar of Turkey includes the following items of relevance to Pakistan: Charles J. Adams, 'The authority of the prophetic *Ḥadīth* in the eyes of some modern Muslims' (in fact Maududi); Sajida Alvi, 'The historians of Awrangzēb: a comparative study of three primary sources'; Sheila McDonough, 'Iqbāl, Gāndhī, and Muhammad 'Alī: religious charisma and the nationalist Muslims, 1920–1928'; Fazlur Rahman, 'Some Islamic issues in the Ayyūb Khān era'.

370 **Muslim ethics and modernity: a comparative study of the ethical thought of Sayyid Ahmad Khan and Mawlana Mawdudi.**
Sheila McDonough. Waterloo, Ontario: Wilfrid Laurier University Press for the Canadian Corporation for Studies in Religion, 1984. 128p. (Comparative Ethics Series, vol. 1).

A monograph on the thinking on ethical questions of two major Muslim writers in South Asia who are often seen as the foremost proponents of respectively modernist and fundamentalist positions. McDonough sees both as looking for ways in which Muslims can live in the contemporary world without abandoning their past. The book is intended for serious students of comparative ethics as well as of South Asian Islam. An earlier work by McDonough (*The authority of the past: a study of three Muslim modernists*. Chambersburg, Pennsylvania: American Academy of Religion, 1970. 56p. bibliog. [AAR Studies in Religion, 1970:1]) considers Sayyid Ahmad Khan alongside Muhammad Iqbal and Ghulam Ahmad Parwez.

371 **Iqbal: poet-philosopher of Pakistan.**
Edited by Hafeez Malik. New York; London: Columbia University Press, 1971. 441p. bibliog. (Studies in Oriental Culture, no. 7).

An important collection of specially written studies on Iqbal designed to make him better known in the United States. The editor has brought together scholars from the USA, Pakistan, India, Europe and the Soviet Union to provide an informed assessment of Iqbal's political, philosophical, religious and poetical contributions.

372 **Towards understanding the Qur'ān. English version of Tafhīm al-Qur'ān.** vol. 1. *Sūrahs 1–3.*
Sayyid Abul Aʿlā Mawdūdī, translated and edited by Zafar Ishaq Ansari.   Leicester, England: Islamic Foundation, 1988. 370p. 3 maps. bibliog.

A verse-by-verse commentary on the Quran in the *tafsir* tradition, this expresses the mature religious thought of Maududi. It was first written in Urdu and published in 1950. The translation will eventually be a multi-volume work. It is edited in such a way as to be accessible to the non-Muslim reader.

373 **Islam.**
Fazlur Rahman.   London: Weidenfeld & Nicholson, 1966. 271p. bibliog.

Rahman gives an excellent general description of Islam as a religious system, its history and theological tendencies within it. He writes as an Islamic scholar with a modernist slant. The publication of the book led to protests in Pakistan against Rahman and to his dismissal from his official position.

374 **Islam and modernity: transformation of an intellectual tradition.**
Fazlur Rahman.   Chicago; London: University of Chicago Press, 1982. 172p. (Publication of the Center for Middle Eastern Studies, no. 15).

A general work on the Islamic intellectual and educational tradition, particularly its attitude to the interpretation of the Quran, where Rahman argues for a modernist approach. Considerable space is given to a number of Pakistani writers and their Indian forerunners, including Maududi, Iqbal and I. H. Qureshi.

375 **Iqbal's concept of God.**
M. S. Raschid.   London; Boston: Kegan Paul International, 1981. 124p. bibliog.

This is a careful and philosophically informed study which argues that Iqbal is mistaken in his concept of God and puts forward a case for the traditional Quranic view. Raschid suggests that Iqbal's concept of God is actually a superficial extrapolation from Western philosophers such as Hegel and Bergson.

376 **A history of sufism in India.**
Saiyid Athar Abbas Rizvi.   Delhi: Munshiram Manoharlal, 1978, 1983. vol. 1. *Early sufism and its history in India to 1600 AD.* 2 maps. bibliog. vol. 2. *From sixteenth century to modern century.* bibliog.

The bulk of this work is made up of an immensely detailed, often anecdotal, but scholarly account, based on Persian sources, of the saints who belonged to the *silsilas* or orders of sufis who were active in India up to the 19th century. As far as possible, each major figure and his teachings are described. There are also chapters on the sufis' relationship to the Hindu tradition of mysticism, on sufi concepts of politics, and on sufi poetry.

377 **The legacy of Islam.**
Edited by Joseph Schacht, with C. E. Bosworth. Oxford, England: Clarendon Press, 1974. 2nd ed. 530p.

This collective work replaces an earlier volume published in 1931. The authors see Islam as defining a civilization rather than simply a set of religious values. There are chapters therefore not just on religion and philosophy but on law, science, medicine, art, etc. Many of the contributions are very oriented towards the 'central lands' of Islam but there is a contribution specifically on South Asia by Aziz Ahmad.

378 **Gabriel's wing: a study into the religious ideas of Sir Muhammad Iqbal.**
Annemarie Schimmel. Leiden, The Netherlands: E. J. Brill, 1963. 428p. bibliog. (Studies in the History of Religions [Supplements to *Numen*], no. 6).

This large work remains one of the most important studies of Iqbal's thought. After an initial chapter dealing with his life and work, Schimmel shows how Iqbal approached the essentials of the Islamic faith and discusses his relationship to Eastern and Western influences. She explores the meaning of his key concept of *khudi* or self.

379 **Islam in the Indian subcontinent.**
Annemarie Schimmel. Leiden, The Netherlands; Cologne: E. J. Brill, 1980. 303p. map. bibliog. (Handbuch der Orientalistik. Abteilung 2, Band 4, Abschnitt 3).

A general review of the subject by one of its leading scholars. The framework is chronological but throughout the emphasis is on the development of religious ideas and expression, particularly mystical thought.

380 **Pain and grace: a study of two mystical writers of eighteenth-century India.**
Annemarie Schimmel. Leiden, The Netherlands: E. J. Brill, 1976. 310p. bibliog. (Studies in the History of Religions [Supplements to *Numen*], no. 36).

A major work by one of the leading figures in the study of Indian Islam on two sufi poets of the 18th century. Khwaja Mir Dard, who lived in Delhi and wrote in Urdu and Persian, has been relatively little studied in the past, while Shah Abdul Latif, who wrote in Sindhi, has attracted considerable attention as a figure in Sindhi literature and as a mystic. Schimmel discusses both as members of the sufi tradition concerned to see the true unity of existence beyond the immediate diversity, while depicting Mir Dard as a more urban, sophisticated figure than the rural Shah Abdul Latif. The book ends with a number of translations by the author into German of the poetry both writers.

381 **The ardent pilgrim: an introduction to the life and work of Mohammed Iqbal.**
Iqbal Singh. London; New York; Toronto: Longmans, Green, 1951. 247p. bibliog.

This is an early biography of Iqbal by an Indian writer, which sets out the main features of Iqbal's life. Singh is an admirer of Iqbal not as a prophet or inspirer of

Pakistan but as a poet. He sees him as bridging the past and present worlds of Persian and Urdu poetry.

382   **Islam in India and Pakistan: a religious history of Islam in India and Pakistan.**
Murray T. Titus.   Madras: Christian Literature Society, 1959. 328p. bibliog. (Christian Students' Library, no. 20).

Originally published in 1930 as *Indian Islam: a religious history of Islam in India*, this is an attempt by an American missionary to describe as objectively as possible the development of Islam in India and Pakistan from its earliest contact with the subcontinent. Although some areas of the book have been overtaken by more recent research, it is still valuable as a synopsis of the subject.

383   **The sufi orders in Islam.**
J. Spencer Trimingham.   Oxford, England: Clarendon Press, 1971. 333p. bibliog.

A general history of the sufi orders, including those which have been important in South Asia, especially the Chishtiyya, the Qadiriyya, the Naqshbandiyya and the Suhrawardiyya. Trimingham traces the descent of the leaders, and discusses each order's distinctive beliefs and practices.

384   **Sayyid Ahmad Khan: a reinterpretation of Muslim theology.**
Christian W. Troll.   New Delhi: Vikas, 1978. 384p. bibliog.

Originally a PhD thesis, this is a major study of the religious thought of Sayyid Ahmad Khan. Troll discusses Sayyid Ahmad Khan's intellectual formation, with special emphasis on his early life, and then presents his mature position on the relationship of reason and faith. The second half of the book consists of translations from Urdu of sixteen important texts of Sayyid Ahmad Khan on religious topics.

Saints of Sind.
See item no. 15.

Studies in Islamic culture in the Indian environment.
See item no. 128.

Muslim self-statement in India and Pakistan 1857–1968.
See item no. 129.

Shariat **and ambiguity in South Asian Islam.**
See item no. 132.

Islam in Asia. vol. 1. *South Asia.*
See item no. 133.

Islam et société en Asie du Sud. (Islam and society in South Asia.)
See item no. 134.

Partners in freedom – and true Muslims: the political thought of some Muslim scholars in British India, 1912–1947.
See item no. 137.

The Cambridge History of Islam.
See item no. 139.

Islamic Culture.
See item no. 142.

Islamic society and culture: essays in honour of Professor Aziz Ahmad.
See item no. 143.

Conversion to Islam.
See item no. 148.

Islamic revival in British India: Deoband, 1860–1900.
See item no. 151.

Moral conduct and authority: the place of *adab* in South Asian Islam.
See item no. 152.

Islam and Muslim society in South Asia.
See item no. 161.

Makli hill: a center of Islamic culture in Sindh.
See item no. 211.

The sufi as saint, curer, and exorcist in modern Pakistan.
See item no. 393.

Pir and murshid: an aspect of religious leadership in West Pakistan.
See item no. 398

Astor: eine Ethnographie. (Astor: an ethnography.)
See item no. 415.

Panjabi sufi poets, A.D. 1460–1900.
See item no. 732.

Social Structure

General

385 Class and power in a Punjabi village.
Saghir Ahmad, introduction by Kathleen Gough. New York;
London: Monthly Review Press, 1977. 174p. bibliog.

This book is, to quote the introduction by Kathleen Gough, 'a valuable and pioneering study of class, economy, power and status in a Punjabi village', by a scholar who was killed in an accident before he could develop his initial work into a full-fledged sociological study. The fieldwork was carried out in 1964-65 in a village in the canal-colony district of Sargodha. The study outlines the system of economic and political power in the village at the time when the government of Ayub Khan was trying to initiate social change through institutional innovation. Besides the central village study, the volume also includes the introduction by Kathleen Gough which makes useful comparisons with India, and two essays by the author based on the same body of data which raise questions about 'modernization' and population policy.

386 Pakistan society: Islam, ethnicity and leadership in South Asia.
Akbar S. Ahmed. Karachi: Oxford University Press, 1986. 264p.

This is a collection of previously published essays by one of Pakistan's leading anthropologists and intellectuals. All date from the 1980s and are grouped into three sections, 'Islam in society', 'Ethnicity and leadership', and Contemporary issues'. The majority of the essays deal with the North-West Frontier, Ahmed's own area of specialization, but others range more widely. The first essay analyses South Asian Islam in terms of types of leadership linked respectively to orthodox, eclectic and modernist forms of Islam and argues that Pakistan needs a healthy synthesis of all three.

387 **Kinship in West Punjab villages.**
Hamza A. Alavi. *Contributions to Indian Sociology* (n.s.), no. 6
(Dec. 1972), p. 1-27.
The subject of this article is the anthropological question of what provides the basic principle of social organization in the villages studied by Alavi in West Punjab. He concludes that it is not caste, as suggested by some writers, but the more tightly defined *biraderi* which is important. He discusses patrilateral parallel cousin marriage and *vartan bhanji* as aspects of this institution.

388 **The politics of dependency: a village in West Punjab.**
Hamza A. Alavi. *South Asian Review*, vol. 4, no. 2 (Jan. 1971),
p. 111-28.
Alavi examines the structures and processes of village-level politics in a village in a canal-colony area of the Punjab. He discusses traditional social institutions such as the *biraderi*, the formal structure of the state, and the economic structure within which political conflict takes place. He draws attention to cattle-stealing as an important form of political activity.

389 **No five fingers are alike: cognitive amplifiers in social context.**
Joseph C. Berland. Cambridge, Massachusetts; London: Harvard
University Press, 1982. 246p. bibliog.
A study of a group of nomadic entertainers (Qalandar) by an anthropologist who is also interested in comparative psychology. While much of the book is theoretical in orientation, focusing for example on the ideas of Piaget on cognitive ontogeny, it contains much fascinating material on the lives of groups who live outside the settled framework of Pakistan life.

390 **Pakistan society (a sociological perspective).**
M. Iqbal Chaudhry. Lahore: Aziz, 1980. 4th rev. and enlarged ed.
728p. bibliog.
First published in 1964, this is a textbook designed for Pakistani students in the social sciences. Rather didactic in tone, it contains a considerable volume of information not just on aspects of Pakistan's social structure but on rural development issues. It lacks the necessary footnotes and critical bibliography to facilitate further inquiry.

391 **The structure of marriage preferences: an account from Pakistani fiction.**
Veena Das. *Man* (n.s.), vol. 8, no. 1 (March 1973), p. 30-45.
A study from an anthropological perspective of preferred marriage patterns in Pakistan, especially the preference for patrilateral parallel cousin marriage. The author uses as her data material from a number of popular Urdu novels published between 1947 and 1969 and discusses the rules which seem to be followed in the arrangement of marriages. The *khandan* or lineage is seen as forming a unit the preservation of whose integrity the rules are meant to maintain.

392 **Marriage among Muslims: preference and choice in northern Pakistan.**
Hastings Donnan. Delhi: Hindustan Publishing Corporation; Leiden,
The Netherlands: E. J. Brill, 1988. 231p. 3 maps. bibliog.

This is a technical study by an anthropologist which addresses the question of the basis
on which Muslim families express preference in choosing marriage partners. Basing
himself on fieldwork in Rawalpindi district, Donnan argues that although there is an
expressed preference for patrilateral cousin marriage in reality many non-kin factors
enter into the picture and that these must be incorporated into the analysis.

393 **The sufi as saint, curer, and exorcist in modern Pakistan.**
Katherine Ewing. *Contributions to Asian Studies*, vol. 18 (1984),
p. 106-14.

On the basis of fieldwork carried out in the mid-1970s, the author discusses the role of
the sufi saint or *pir* as a healer. She describes the healing techniques employed and
shows how the *pir* makes no distinction between the physical and the spiritual domains
in his diagnoses and cures.

394 **Caste, patti and faction in the life of a Punjab village.**
Inayat Ullah. *Sociologus* (n.s.), vol. 8, no. 2 (1958), p. 170-86.

The author describes the social organization of a Jat-dominated village in northern
Punjab. He regards caste as the basic unit of social life, and after that the *patti* or
group of landowning families originally created for revenue collection purposes. He
also discusses the emergence during the twenty years preceding the study of factional
conflict in the village.

395 **Age and social status at marriage, Karachi, Pakistan, 1961–64 and 1980:
a comparative study.**
J. Henry Korson, M. A. Sabzwari. *Journal of Comparative Family
Studies*, vol. 15, no. 2 (Summer 1984), p. 257-79.

Since 1961 marriages have been supposed to be registered with the local authorities.
The authors compare sample registrations for 1961-64 and 1980 in the urban
environment of Karachi and conclude that the age of marriage increased significantly
for females but hardly at all for males. These findings are correlated with levels of
education and employment. Other aspects of marriage are also discussed.

396 **Endogamous marriage in a traditional Muslim society: West Pakistan. a
study in intergenerational change.**
J. Henry Korson. *Journal of Comparative Family Studies*, vol. 2,
no. 2 (Autumn 1971), p. 145-55.

A study of the incidence of cousin marriage among a limited sample of university
students and their parents in Karachi and Lahore. The results show a decline across
generations from around 40 per cent to half that level.

397   **South Asian intellectuals and social change: a study of the role of vernacular-speaking intelligentsia.**
Edited by Yogendra K. Malik.   New Delhi: Heritage, 1982. 352p. bibliog.
This volume contains a study by Bilal Hashmi and Hasan Nawaz Gardezi of Urdu-speaking intellectuals and their structural and cultural context. The authors concentrate particularly on Shah Wali Allah, Iqbal and Faiz Ahmed Faiz in their discussion of the social origins of ideas.

398   **Pir and murshid: an aspect of religious leadership in West Pakistan.**
Adrian Mayer.   *Middle Eastern Studies*, vol. 3, no. 2 (Jan. 1967), p. 160-9.
A brief but suggestive article by an anthropologist on one of the central institutions of rural life in Pakistan, that of the often hereditary spiritual guide or leader. The author distinguishes two roles which are often combined in the same individual but which nevertheless have separate places, that of the spiritual guide or *murshid* on the one hand and that of the healer or *pir* on the other. He also discusses their relations with their disciples or *murids* and their political role.

399   **Anthropology in Pakistan: recent socio-cultural and archaeological perspectives.**
Edited by Stephen Pastner, Louis Flam.   Cornell University, South Asia Program, 1982. 230p. (South Asia Occasional Papers and Theses, no. 8).
This is a collection of seventeen short papers mostly based on fieldwork in the 1970s by the younger generation of US anthropologists and archaeologists working on Pakistan, some of whom have not published extensively so far. The work of several Pakistani scholars is also included. The book is divided approximately equally between the two disciplines. Change and adaptation are common themes to both anthropological and archaeological sections.

400   **The sweepers of Slaughterhouse: conflict and survival in a Karachi neighbourhood.**
Pieter Streefland.   Assen, The Netherlands: Van Gorcum, 1979. 150p. map. bibliog.
Originally a dissertation and as such published in Dutch in 1975, this is an anthropological study based on extensive field research in 1970-71 of a group of Christian Punjabi sweepers in a crowded slum area of Karachi. Streefland describes the setting for their lives, the role of kinship, the way conflicts emerge and are handled, and the types of leadership that exist. Although regular work ensures a degree of economic security for the time being, Streefland describes their situation as subordinate and marginal.

401   *Zat* **and** *qoum* **in Punjabi society: a contribution to the problem of caste.**
Parvez A. Wakil.   *Sociologus* (n.s.), vol. 22, nos 1-2 (1972), p. 38-48.
Wakil argues in this theoretical article that the concept of caste is not appropriate when trying to conceptualize in sociological terms the terms *zat* and *qoum* which are used in Pakistan Punjab to describe various types of status and occupational groupings, as well

as the network of reciprocal obligations called *seyp*. He suggests that the possibility of individual mobility and the looseness of endogamy indicate that the notion of caste is not appropriate. He thus reaches similar conclusions, although by a different route, to those of Alavi in his article on 'Kinship in West Punjab villages' (q.v.). Another article by Wakil discusses *biraderi*, which in some respects is the basis of an alternative approach to the understanding of social organization: 'Explorations into the kin-networks of the Punjabi society: a preliminary statement', *Journal of Marriage and the Family*, vol. 32, no. 4 (Nov. 1970), p. 700-7.

Peoples of South Asia.
See item no. 12.

Pakistan: society and culture.
See item no. 13.

Muslim peoples: a world ethnographic survey.
See item no. 23.

Eine sozio-ethno-religiöse Minderheit: die Christen West-Pakistans. (A socio-ethno-religious minority: the Christians in West Pakistan.)
See item no. 310.

A Punjabi village in Pakistan.
See item no. 408.

Women's seclusion and men's honor: sex roles in north India, Bangladesh, and Pakistan.
See item no. 437.

Rural women and the family: a study of a Punjabi village in Pakistan.
See item no. 442.

Elite politics in an ideological state.
See item no. 464.

Lebensverhältnisse ländlicher Familien in Westpakistan: eine Typisierung ländlicher Haushalte als Grundlage für entwicklungspolitische Maßnahmen, dargestellt am Beispiel von sechs Dörfern im Distrikt Peshawar, Westpakistan. (Conditions of life of rural families in West Pakistan: a typology of rural households as a foundation for political development measures, based on the example of six villages in Peshawar district, West Pakistan.)
See item no. 637.

Rural–urban migration and the urban poor in Pakistan.
See item no. 638.

Regional

402 **Millennium and charisma among Pathans: a critical essay in social anthropology.**
Akbar S. Ahmed. London; Henley, England; Boston: Routledge & Kegan Paul, 1976. 173p. bibliog.

The first of Ahmed's major anthropological studies, this is an extended theoretical critique of Barth's work on the Pathans, *Political leadership among Swat Pathans* (q.v.). Ahmed argues against the static and individualist thrust which he sees as typifying Barth's approach, and argues instead for one which gives weight to a dynamic view of Pukhtun society. The Wali of Swat's emergence as a leader is used as the major example to indicate the advantages of this alternative approach.

403 **Pukhtun economy and society: traditional structure and economic development in a tribal society.**
Akbar S. Ahmed. London: Routledge & Kegan Paul, 1980. 406p. 9 maps. bibliog.

The author of this major study of Pukhtun society is both an academic and a senior official of the Pakistan government. His work is an attempt to look at the relationship between the lives of members of a particular Pukhtun tribe, the Mohmand, and the ideal code of Pukhtun society, *pukhtunwali*. The study was carried out in two villages, one in a remote tribal area, the other in the so-called settled areas of the Peshawar valley. The author concludes that at the time of his fieldwork in 1975-76 the values of Pukhtun society were still effective in both places but that they were likely to change sharply in the years to come as the villages were penetrated economically by the wider world.

404 **Religion and politics in Muslim society: order and conflict in Pakistan.**
Akbar S. Ahmed. Cambridge, England: Cambridge University Press, 1983. 215p. 4 maps. bibliog.

Ahmed pursues his long-standing concern with the interaction of religious ideas, the structure of tribal society and the impact of the wider political environment through an extended case-study of events in the South Waziristan tribal agency, where a tribal revolt occurred in the 1970s. Particular attention is paid to the position of the government-appointed political agent, a role in fact fulfilled by the author during part of the period under study.

405 **Features of person and society in Swat: collected essays on Pathans.**
Fredrik Barth. London; Boston; Henley, England: Routledge & Kegan Paul, 1981. 190p. 4 maps. bibliog. (Selected essays of Fredrik Barth, vol. 2).

Barth, well known for his work on the social structure of the Pukhtuns, brings together in this volume essays on the subject published between 1956 and 1971. An extended final chapter, 'Swat Pathans reconsidered', previously unpublished, includes his reply to critics of his earlier work, notably Akbar S. Ahmed (*Millennium and charisma among Pathans: a critical essay in social anthropology* [q.v.]) and Talal Asad.

406 **Political leadership among Swat Pathans.**
Fredrik Barth.   London: Athlone Press; New York: Humanities Press,
1959. 143p. 2 maps. bibliog. (London School of Economics
Monographs on Social Anthropology, no. 19).

Barth's seminal study of the Swat Pukhtuns concerns itself with the question of how the political system of the area he studied in northern Pakistan operated in a atmosphere where the prevalent values were those of 'freedom and rebellion'. An extended critique can be found in *Millennium and charisma among Pathans: a critical essay in social anthropology*, by Akbar S. Ahmed (q.v.).

407 **Rusticus loquitur, or the old light and the new in the Punjab village.**
Malcolm Lyall Darling.   London: Oxford University Press, 1930.
400p. map.

Darling was a British official who spent much of his career in the 1920s working in the rural areas of the Punjab to encourage rural development through cooperation and in other ways. His books were designed, as he writes in the preface, 'to ascertain what the peasant does and what he thinks on each question, believing that this is an indispensable preliminary to all schemes for his betterment.' Most of this book records his impressions as he went the length and breadth of the Punjab on horseback in 1928-29. Little escapes his attention, whether it be the price of jewellery or the changes in the power of the moneylender. As the title of the book indicates, he sees a contrast between different areas of the province in terms of the progress of social change. On the whole, he considers the western parts to be less developed. Darling was the author of two related books on Punjab society: *The Punjab peasant in prosperity and debt* (London: Oxford University Press, 1925); and *Wisdom and waste in the Punjab village* (London: Oxford University Press, 1934). His autobiography, *Apprentice to power: India 1904-1906* (London: Hogarth Press, 1961), is a delightful account of his life as a young man in the Punjab before the first world war, especially in Dera Ghazi Khan in the south-west of the province.

408 **A Punjabi village in Pakistan.**
Zekiye Eglar.   New York: Columbia University Press, 1960. 240p.
3 maps. bibliog.

An ethnographic account of a village in Gujrat district in northern Punjab based on an extended stay in the early 1950s. All aspects of village life are covered, but special attention is paid to the family and to the position of women. The author, as both a woman and a Muslim, had privileged access to the domestic sphere. The main analytical focus of the book is on the institution of *vartan bhanji*, the exchange of gifts and favours particularly at the time of marriages, which serves to integrate village society.

409 **Zentrale Gewalt in Nager (Karakorum): politische Organisationsformen, ideologische Begründungen des Königtums und Veränderungen in der Moderne.** (Central power in Nager [Karakorum]: forms of political organization and ideological foundations of kingship and transformations in the modern period.)
Jürgen Frembgen. Wiesbaden, West Germany: Franz Steiner Verlag, 1985. 241p. 5 maps. bibliog. (Beiträge zur Südasienforschung Südasien-Institut Universität Heidelberg, no. 103).

This is a work of political anthropology which discusses state forms in the Karakoram region in the northern mountains and in particular the kingdom that existed in Nager for several centuries until its absorption into Pakistan in 1972. Frembgen discusses the segmentary and unitary elements within the state.

410 **Social structure of Pakistan's Brahui-Baluchi population.**
Yuri Gankovsky. *Journal of South Asian and Middle Eastern Studies*, vol. 5, no. 4 (Summer 1982), p. 57-73.

A general account of the Baluchi and Brahui peoples. The article is a useful synthesis of material from a wide range of census and other sources.

411 **Guardians of the Khaibar: the social organization and history of the Afridis of Pakistan.**
David M. Hart. Lahore: Vanguard Books, 1985. 208p. 6 maps. bibliog.

This is a study by an anthropologist whose approach is very much that of the traditional ethnographer, although in the circumstances in which he had to work in the late 1970s he had to rely heavily on interview and historical material rather than on direct observation. The Afridi are the Pukhtun tribe which lives in the area of the Khyber pass. Hart discusses their kinship organization and history, and compares Pukhtun tribal structure to that of the Berber in North Africa.

412 **Relocation of a Punjab Pakistan community.**
John J. Honigmann. *Middle East Journal*, vol. 8, no. 4 (Autumn 1954), p. 429-44.

This is a detailed anthropological study of a village established on newly irrigated land in the Thal region of West Punjab. Most of the inhabitants were from Ludhiana district in East Punjab and had come as refugees in 1947. Honigmann takes an optimistic view of the village's development.

413 **Panjab castes.**
Denzil Ibbetson. Delhi: B. R. Publishing Corporation, 1974. 338p.

First published as a separate volume in 1916, this was originally part of the 1881 Census Report where it was entitled 'The races, castes and tribes of the Panjáb'. A classic of colonial ethnography, it displays the official urge to classify the people who made up the population of the Indian empire and to define the characteristics which supposedly distinguished one group from another. After an initial chapter discussing general features of caste in the Punjab (which at this point included much of what is now the North-West Frontier Province), Ibbetson discusses in detail a very large number of social groups, making comments on their traditions, practices and way of life.

414 **Generosity and jealousy: the Swat Pukhtun of northern Pakistan.**
Charles Lindholm. New York: Columbia University Press, 1982.
321p. bibliog.
An anthropological case-study of a Pukhtun village in the Swat valley of northern Pakistan. Lindholm uses a range of techniques derived from anthropology and psychology but acknowledges in his introduction the singular depth of insight derived from his close friendship and cooperation with one particular individual in the village. Lindholm's central concern is to uncover the basic structure of Pukhtun society and culture and in particular the tension between the value attached in it to hospitality and the fierce competiton which is otherwise characteristic. He finds at least part of the answer to lie in the value attached to friendship.

415 **Astor: eine Ethnographie.** (Astor: an ethnography.)
Adam Nayyar. Wiesbaden, West Germany: Franz Steiner Verlag,
1986. 120p. map. bibliog. (Beiträge zur Südasienforschung Südasien-
Institut Universität Heidelberg, vol. 88)
Astor is a valley settlement on the northern side of Nanga Parbat in northern Pakistan. Nayyar's account of the people that live there concentrates on their traditional world-view and religious practices, especially the role of the *shaman*. He also discusses the recent impact of Islam on the region. Appendices give the text and German translations of representative *shaman* and lineage songs.

416 **Livestock symbolism and pastoral ideology among the Kafirs of the
Hindu Kush.**
Peter Parkes. *Man* (n.s.) vol. 22, no. 4 (Dec. 1987), p. 637-60.
A specialist exercise in cultural anthropology which looks at the ritual and the moral values of Kalasha (or Kafir) pastoralists of Chitral. This tiny non-Muslim group makes livestock husbandry an exclusively male activity and links this division of labour to a dichotomy of the natural environment into male and female domains.

417 **Baluch fishermen in Pakistan.**
Stephen Pastner. *Asian Affairs*, vol. 9 (o.s. vol. 65), no. 2 (June
1978), p. 161-7.
This is a descriptive article for a more general audience by a professional anthropologist who spent time among the fishermen of the Baluchistan coast in 1976-77. He describes an adaptable group who are broadly content with their life despite increasing pressure from the outside world.

418 **The competitive saints of the Baluch.**
Stephen L. Pastner. *Asian Affairs*, vol. 11 (o.s. vol. 67), no. 1
(Feb. 1980), p. 37-42.
Pastner here provides a brief but evocative sketch of the role of Baluchi sufis in the life of the nomads of Baluchistan.

419 **Agriculture, kinship and politics in southern Baluchistan.**
Stephen Pastner, Carroll McC. Pastner. *Man*, (n.s.), vol. 7 (1972),
p. 128-36.
This article explores the complex relations between land-use practices, especially irrigation, kinship and marriage, and politics in the Makran region of southern Baluchistan. The authors draw special attention to the fluidity of kinship ties and local political arrangements and see a link with a pattern of land use in which the stress is on individual rather than group decision-making.

420 **The social organization of the Marri Baluch.**
Robert N. Pehrson, compiled and analysed by Fredrik Barth. New York: Wenner-Gren Foundation for Anthropological Research, 1966. 127p. map. bibliog. (Viking Fund Publication in Anthropology, no. 43).
The author died during the course of his fieldwork in 1954-55, and his rough draft was revised subsequently by the distinguished anthropologist Fredrik Barth. The Marri are a nomadic tribe who live mainly in north-east Baluchistan. Pehrson stayed in their camps and collected data on such topics as kinship, relations between the sexes, and tribal structure. As an ethnographic work it is primarily of use for anthropologists, but the material would be accessible to the non-specialist.

421 **Rites and ceremonies of Hindus and Muslims.**
Compiled by H. A. Rose. New Delhi: Amar Prakashan, 1983. 228p.
This typical piece of colonial ethnography was first published in 1908 and was put together by the compiler from material in earlier census reports for the Punjab. Topics covered include pregnancy, birth, betrothal, marriage and death observances, with separate sections in each case for Hindus and Muslims. A final chapter covers the subject of fictive kinship.

422 **Ethnologie und Geschichte: Festschrift für Karl Jettmar.** (Ethnology and history: *Festschrift* for Karl Jettmar.)
Edited by Peter Snoy. Wiesbaden, West Germany: Franz Steiner Verlag, 1983. 654p. 2 maps. bibliog. (Beiträge zur Südasienforschung Südasien-Institut Universität Heidelberg, vol. 86).
This *Festschrift* in honour of the leading foreign scholar of the northern regions of Pakistan, includes contributions from 56 scholars from across the world. Most are written in German but there are some in English and a couple in French. For the most part they relate to the archaeology, ethnology and history of the Hindu Kush region in Pakistan and Afghanistan.

423 **The Jat of Pakistan.**
Sigrid Westphal-Hellbusch, Heinz Westphal. Berlin: Duncker & Humblot, 1964. 110p. bibliog.
The Jats who are the subject of this piece of ethnographic research have little if anything to do with the numerous Jat population of the Punjab but are a nomadic tribe of the Indus delta. The authors describe the results of fieldwork carried out in 1955-56, and examine topics such as tribal organization and economic activities, as well as discussing links between the group and similar tribes in Iraq.

Social Structure. Regional

The tigers of Baluchistan.
See item no. 14.

Mountain people.
See item no. 35.

Words for my brother: travels between the Hindu Kush and the Himalayas.
See item no. 75.

Mizh: a monograph on government's relations with the Mahsud tribe.
See item no. 195.

The last Wali of Swat: an autobiography as told to Fredrik Barth.
See item no. 273.

The profile of popular Islam in the Pakistani Punjab.
See item no. 356.

Die Religionen des Hindukusch. (The religions of the Hindukush.)
See item no. 367.

Class and power in a Punjabi village.
See item no. 385.

Pakistan society: Islam, ethnicity and leadership in South Asia.
See item no. 386.

Kinship in West Punjab villages.
See item no. 387.

The politics of dependency: a village in West Punjab.
See item no. 388.

Caste, patti and faction in the life of a Punjab village.
See item no. 394.

***Zat* and *qoum* in Punjabi society: a contribution to the problem of caste.**
See item no. 401.

The endless day: some case material on Asian rural women.
See item no. 434.

Social Change and Social Issues

424 Settlement and social change in Asia.
Wolfram Eberhard. Hong Kong: Hong Kong University Press, 1967.
492p. maps. bibliog. (Collected Papers of Wolfram Eberhard, vol. 1).
Most of the papers in this volume deal with China but three are to do with Pakistan.
The first, 'Colony villages in the Punjab', reviews the manner in which first the colonial
and later the Pakistan government designed the canal colonies in the Punjab. The
second is a very useful bibliography, 'Studies on Pakistan's social and economic
conditions: a bibliographic note', which lists a number of unpublished theses in Punjab
universities completed since 1930 dealing with these issues, mainly at village level. The
third, 'Modern tendencies of Islam in Pakistan', adds little to the subject.

425 Tourismus in Hunza: Beziehungen zwischen Gästern und Gastgebern.
(Tourism in Hunza: relations between guests and hosts.)
Jürgen Frembgen. *Sociologus* (n.s.), vol. 33, no. 2 (1983), p. 174-85.
Hunza in the northern mountains of Pakistan is seen by many as a 'Shangri-la' and it
has attracted many tourists in recent years. In the spirit of recent anthropological
questioning of the impact of tourism on hitherto remote groups, the author looks at the
negative consequences in Hunza on the integrity of local cultural patterns.

**426 Poverty, voluntary organizations and social change: a study of an urban
slum in Pakistan.**
Sabeeha Hafeez. Karachi: Royal Book Company, 1985. 248p. bibliog.
This is an action-oriented, although rather jargonized study of the Lyari area of
Karachi and of the local and outside voluntary groups which are active there. Hafeez
describes them collectively as 'change actors' and examines in detail the type of work
they undertake.

427 **Drug addiction and rehabilitation of addicts in Pakistan.**
Edited by Anwar-ul-Haq, Umar Farooq.   Lahore: Pakistan
Sociological Association, 1979. 218p.

This volume contains 25 papers presented to a conference held in Faisalabad in
November 1977 on a problem that has since become more acute, especially as a result
of changes in the drug traffic following the Afghanistan crisis. The participants were
mainly sociologists and medical specialists; the subjects of the papers ranged from
analyses of the origins of drug addiction in society to practical methods for controlling
the growing of the opium poppy.

428 **Rural development in Pakistan.**
Akhter Hameed Khan, introduction by Akbar S. Ahmed.   Lahore:
Vanguard Books, 1985. 307p.

Akhter Hameed Khan has been a major figure in Pakistani thinking on issues of rural
development, if often more of a gadfly than a mainstream policy-maker, and this
volume includes a selection of his papers and essays. The emphasis throughout his
career, from his time at the Comilla Academy of Rural Development on, has been on
decentralizing administration and increasing popular involvement in development. One
of the papers provides a brief autobiography. The introduction by Akbar S. Ahmed is
mainly biographical and includes a note on the inside story of the Daudzai project.

429 **Rural development in Pakistan.**
Shoaib Sultan Khan.   Delhi: Vikas, 1980. 161p.

The author of this study was at one time director of the Pakistan Academy of Rural
Development in Peshawar and reflects in this book on the meaning of rural
development in a country like Pakistan and appropriate strategies to achieve it. Much
of the volume is devoted to a consideration of one particular effort to stimulate
development in the Daudzai area of North-West Frontier Province in the early 1970s
through encouraging cooperation between officials and the local population (see
previous entry). The writer was particularly influenced by the earlier work of Akhter
Hameed Khan.

430 **Cultural barriers to Pakistan's quest for unity.**
Stephen Pastner.   *Journal of Developing Societies*, vol. 3, no. 1 (April
1987), p. 25-45.

An anthropologist's view of the tension within Pakistan between universalist Islam and
particularist ethnic traditions. Pastner argues that the short-term measures taken by the
government to reduce social and economic tensions, for example the encouragement of
labour export to the Middle East, may in the end exacerbate some of the country's
problems.

431 **Pakistan's rural development.**
Mushtaqur Rahman.   Hong Kong: Asian Research Service, 1983.
175p. 14 maps. bibliog.

An evaluation by a geographer of the Integrated Rural Development Programme
introduced by Z. A. Bhutto in 1972. Following a general discussion of rural
development there are case-studies drawn from all regions of Pakistan. The author
gives a pessimistic assessment of the programme which he sees as being imposed from
above and proposes an alternative approach based on greater popular participation.

Squatter settlements in Pakistan: the impact of upgrading.
See item no. 684.

Between basti dwellers and bureaucrats: lessons in squatter settlement upgrading in Karachi.
See item no. 689.

Women and society

432 **Women in the Muslim world.**
Edited by Lois Beck, Nikki Keddie. Cambridge, Massachusetts; London: Harvard University Press, 1978. 698p. bibliog.

Despite the title, most of this volume is concerned with the Middle East, and there is only one essay on Pakistan, an anthropological study by Carroll McC. Pastner on 'The status of women and property on a Baluchistan oasis in Pakistan'. In the first section, 'General perspectives on legal and socio-economic change', there are some references to Pakistani material.

433 **Nizam-i-Islam: processes and conflicts in Pakistan's programme of Islamisation, with special reference to the position of women.**
Lucy Carroll. *Journal of Comparative and Commonwealth Politics*, vol. 20, no. 1 (March 1982), p. 57-95.

The author is concerned with the difficulties created by efforts to Islamize Pakistan's legal system and uses a detailed case-study of the family law position of women to illustrate her points.

434 **The endless day: some case material on Asian rural women.**
Edited by T. Scarlett Epstein, Rosemary A. Watts. Oxford, England; New York; Toronto; Sydney; Paris; Frankfurt: Pergamon Press, 1981. 179p. bibliog. (Pergamon International Library, Women in Development Series, vol. 3).

Two chapters in this volume, both with an anthropological orientation, are concerned with Pakistan. The first, by Akbar S. Ahmed and Zeenat Ahmed, entitled '"Mor" and "Tor": binary and opposing models of Pukhtun womanhood', discusses the role of women in upholding the basic Pukhtun values embodied in the notion of *pukhtunwali*. The second, by Naveed-i-Rahat, 'The role of women in reciprocal relationships in a Punjab village', sees a similar role for women in a village near Islamabad, although she also emphasizes the ability of women to manipulate those values to their own ends.

435 **Women in Muslim family law.**
John L. Esposito. Syracuse, New York: Syracuse University Press, 1982. 155p. bibliog.

Esposito discusses the issues involved in the position of women under Muslim family law, and the dilemmas facing those who wish to change it. He uses Pakistan and Egypt as his principal case-studies.

436 **The metropolitan women in Pakistan: studies.**
Sabeeha Hafeez. Karachi: Royal Book Company, 1981. 406p.
This is a collection of six related studies on the conditions of life of women in Karachi. The author is a sociologist who conducted sample surveys to collect much of the data used. Groups studied include career-oriented middle-class women, factory workers, housewives and slum-dwellers.

437 **Women's seclusion and men's honor: sex roles in north India, Bangladesh, and Pakistan.**
David G. Mandelbaum. Tucson, Arizona: University of Arizona Press, 1988. 153p. bibliog.
Mandelbaum was a distinguished American anthropologist, and this was the last book he wrote before his death in 1987. In it he takes an anthropological perspective on the position of women in South Asia and on the significance of seclusion or *purdah*. He argues that in South Asia, as elsewhere, gender relations are linked to other cultural themes, especially to men's honour and prestige. An earlier highly influential work on the same subject, although it deals only with Muslim women in and around Delhi, is by Cora Vreede-de Stuers, *Parda: a study of Muslim women's life in northern India* (Assen, The Netherlands: Van Gorcum, 1968).

438 **Women between cultures: the lives of Kinnaird College alumnae in British India.**
Michelle Maskiell. Syracuse, New York: Syracuse University, Maxwell School of Citizenship and Public Affairs, 1984. 202p. 2 maps. bibliog. (Foreign and Comparative Studies/South Asian series, no. 9).
Originally a thesis, this work looks first at the question of education for women in colonial Punjab and the establishment of Kinnaird College in Lahore in 1913 as a missionary institution, and then at the graduates of the college and the way their lives were altered. Maskiell concludes that despite the opportunities that a college education offered, the basic structure of family-centred life remained the norm for most.

439 **The extended family: women and political participation in India and Pakistan.**
Edited by Gail Minault. Delhi: Chanakya, 1981. 312p.
The theme of this collection of essays is political participation rather than the extended family in the sociological sense. Two papers deal with Muslim women during the pre-independence period, and one with women's groups and the 1961 Muslim Family Laws Ordinance in Pakistan.

440 **Women of Pakistan: two steps forward, one step back?**
Edited by Khawar Mumtaz, Farida Shaheed. London; Atlantic Highlands, New Jersey: Zed Press, 1987. 196p. bibliog.
A pioneering work by two women academics and activists on the history of women's movements in Pakistan, particularly the Women's Action Forum. After an account of

the general position of women, the editors, who are in fact primarily responsible for the whole book, describe the activities of the forum in opposing the Zia régime's policies towards women.

441 **Purdah: separate worlds and symbolic shelter.**
Hanna Papanek. *Comparative Studies in Society and History*, vol. 15, no. 3 (June 1973), p. 289-325.
The author uses published material on India and Pakistan, and her own substantial experience of life in Pakistan to discuss the pattern of purdah in South Asia among Muslim and Hindu communities, and the way it meshes with systems of status, dependency, and the maintenance of moral standards.

442 **Rural women and the family: a study of a Punjabi village in Pakistan.**
Abdur Rauf. *Journal of Comparative Family Studies*, vol. 18, no. 3 (Autumn 1987), p. 403-15.
Based on a study of a village in Faisalabad district, the article delineates the subordinate position of women within the family, especially in matters of property. It identifies a gap between expressed attitudes and actual practice.

443 **Women of South Asia: a guide to resources.**
Carol Sakala. Millwood, New York: Kraus International Publications, 1980. 517p.
Besides a good range of bibliographical entries, including articles and theses as well as books, this guide includes a chapter by Emily Hodges, 'Libraries, archives and other resources in Pakistan for the study of women', p. 437-47.

444 **Pakistani women: a socioeconomic and demographic profile.**
Edited by Nasra M. Shah, foreword by Syed Nawab Haider Naqvi. Islamabad: Pakistan Institute of Development Economics; Honolulu, Hawaii: East-West Population Institute, East-West Center, 1986. 412p. map. bibliog.
This substantial contribution brings together data from a wide range of census and other survey sources to produce as comprehensive a picture as possible of the position of women in Pakistan. Besides collating the data, itself a major task, the contributors apply appropriate analytical techniques to achieve as accurate and dynamic a picture as possible. The first part of the book deals with the demographic position, while in the second part topics such as health, education, employment and family planning issues are discussed. A useful appendix reviews all the relevant census and other data sources.

Women's status and fertility change in Pakistan.
See item no. 303.

A Punjabi village in Pakistan.
See item no. 408.

Social Change and Social Issues. Women and society

Islamic reassertion in Pakistan: the application of Islamic laws in a modern state.
See item no. 522.

Politics

General

445 Pakistan general elections: 1970
Iftikhar Ahmad. Lahore: South Asian Institute, Punjab University, 1976. 159p. bibliog.

After a general review of previous elections in Pakistan, this work provides separate chapters on the contestants, the issues, the campaign and the results of Pakistan's first ever general election. The final two chapters look at the results in terms of socio-economic factors and at trends in political leadership as revealed by the elections. Within the confines of a narrowly based election study, there is much useful material and analysis.

446 Government and politics in Pakistan.
Mushtaq Ahmad. Karachi: Space Publishers, 1970. 3rd ed. 392p. bibliog.

A well-established and reliable, if old-fashioned textbook on the subject. Ahmad treats each phase of Pakistan's political history in turn, from the parliamentary period before 1958 to the military rule of General Yahya Khan. For each phase he reviews critically the institutional developments and the economic and social policies pursued. There is however little discussion of the social background.

447 Contemporary Pakistan: politics, economy and society.
Edited by Manzooruddin Ahmed. Durham, North Carolina: Carolina Academic Press, 1980. 269p.

The papers collected in this volume were originally presented at a conference in New York in 1978, with contributions arranged thematically into sections on politics, economy, and society. Many of them are concerned specifically, and often from a distinctly critical position, to review the Bhutto period and the 1977 elections. The immediacy of response is both a strength and a weakness. Other papers, particularly in the last section, take a longer-term perspective.

448 **Pakistan: human rights violations and the decline of the rule of law.**
London: Amnesty International, 1982. 57p.

Amnesty International's report covers constitutional developments in the period after the coup of 1977 and the incidence of arbitrary arrests, imprisonments without trial, torture and death in police custody, and other aspects of what it regards as unacceptable abuses of human rights.

449 **Asian Survey.**
Berkeley, California: University of California, Institute of International Studies, 1961- . monthly.

This widely read journal carries articles in the first instance from academic analysts but also from other specialists in the domestic and international affairs of Asia. There are frequent contributions on Pakistan and on the South Asian region. Each February there is an article reviewing the previous year's developments in the country.

450 **The Jamaat-i-Islami of Pakistan: political thought and political action.**
Kalim Bahadur. Delhi: Chetana, 1977. 228p. bibliog.

A critical study of the Jamaat-i-Islami, the fundamentalist political organization founded by Maulana Maududi. The book deals successively with the antecedents of the Jamaat and its early activities before independence; the role of the Jamaat in Pakistan's politics up to 1971, especially its efforts to establish an Islamic constitution, and its organizational structure and ideology.

451 **The state, religion and ethnic politics: Afghanistan, Iran and Pakistan.**
Edited by Ali Banuazizi, Myron Weiner. Syracuse, New York: Syracuse University Press, 1986. 390p. 6 maps.

This useful collection of essays contains contributions on Pakistan from four leading US scholars, Leonard Binder, Stephen Cohen, Selig Harrison, and John Esposito. The themes of the work's title are addressed in the context of Pakistan's past and present situation.

452 **Zia's Pakistan: politics and stability in a frontline state.**
Edited by Craig Baxter. Boulder, Colorado; London: Westview Press, 1985. 122p. (Westview Special Studies on South and Southeast Asia).

The American academics who produced this set of papers reflect on what appeared at the time to be a turning point in Zia's rule when he introduced in 1985 a measure of civilian participation. The central theme of the collection is the issue of the degree of legitimacy enjoyed by the Zia régime among different groups, and the factors that might affect that legitimacy, for example the Afghan situation and economic issues.

453 **Pakistan: the gathering storm.**
Benazir Bhutto. Delhi: Vikas, 1983. 116p.

This reproduces a political manifesto issued by Benazir Bhutto when President Zia was at the height of his power and the Pakistan People's Party was officially proscribed. In vigorous language she condemns the Zia régime for its dictatorial ways and puts forward the demand for a return to democracy on the basis of the 1973 constitution. She also sets out a programme for economic and foreign policy.

454 **"If I am assassinated ...".**
Zulfikar Ali Bhutto, foreword by Pran Chopra. Delhi: Vikas, 1979. 240p.
Written secretly while he was on trial and eventually smuggled out of prison, this is Bhutto's defence of himself against the accusations that had been made against his government by General Zia. Besides responding vigorously to the charges of election rigging, etc., he goes on the offensive and accuses his opponents of being in league with foreign powers (by which is clearly meant the USA) alarmed at his popularity and at his nuclear policies.

455 **Pakistan: a political study.**
Keith Callard. London: George Allen & Unwin, 1957. 355p. bibliog.
An early but useful study of Pakistan's political system in which Callard sees Pakistan as a country in search of a political identity of its own and questions the necessary applicability of the norms of Western democracy. Starting from independence he discusses party politics, constitution-making and the federal structure, and the role of Islam. Appendices summarize the 1956 constitution and list central government ministers and provincial governors and chief ministers.

456 **Pakistan: transition from military to civilian rule.**
Golam W. Choudhury. Buckhurst Hill, England: Scorpion, 1988. 256p. bibliog.
Completed in July 1988, although there is a brief epilogue which refers to the death of President Zia the following month, this is a sympathetic account of what the author calls Zia's 'great experiment of blending Islam and democracy' in Pakistan. Some of the book is descriptive of events in the last few years, especially in the constitutional field, but there is also a substantial amount of background information and discussion. Two long chapters discuss the Islamization process.

457 **Pakistan: the roots of dictatorship. The political economy of a praetorian state.**
Edited by Hassan Gardezi, Jamil Rashid. London: Zed Press, 1983. 394p. map. bibliog.
A collection of essays by radical Pakistani academics, most of whom were working abroad in 1983. The focus is the persistence of military rule and its origins in the country's social and economic structure. There are sections on the external dimension, particularly what the contributors see as Pakistan's dependent position vis-à-vis the United States, and on Islam and the manipulation of ideology. The book was published in Pakistan in abbreviated form as *Pakistan: the unstable state*.

458 **Imperialism and revolution in South Asia.**
Edited by Kathleen Gough, Hari P. Sharma.   New York; London:
Monthly Review Press, 1973. 470p.

This collection of essays by radical scholars includes several on Pakistan. The one that has had the greatest influence on subsequent scholarship is the important piece by Hamza Alavi on 'The state in postcolonial societies: Pakistan and Bangladesh'. Originally published in *New Left Review*, no. 74 (July-Aug. 1972), this challenges the appropriateness of traditional Marxist views on the position of the state in Asian and African countries and argues that because of the particular configuration of class forces in many such states, including Pakistan, the state and the military-bureaucratic oligarchy that controls it has a degree of relative autonomy from the main propertied classes. There are also useful articles by Hassan N. Gardezi, Feroz Ahmed, and Saghir Ahmad.

459 **State and ideology in the Middle East and Pakistan.**
Fred Halliday, Hamza Alavi.   London: Macmillan, 1988. 267p.

The only chapter on Pakistan is in fact by Hamza Alavi: 'Pakistan and Islam: ethnicity and ideology', p. 64-111. Alavi argues from a sociological perspective that the Pakistan movement was about Muslim material interests rather than Islam. The argument is presented mainly in historical terms, but there is some discussion of the post-independence period and of the Zia years.

460 **Politics in Pakistan: the struggle for legitimacy.**
Louis D. Hayes.   Boulder, Colorado: Westview; Epping, England:
Bowker, 1984. 203p. bibliog.

The author argues in the course of this general study of Pakistani politics that successive régimes have failed to achieve legitimacy for themselves both because of the difficulties of locating a stable source of political authority within the Islamic tradition and because of failures of political leadership since independence. It would be suitable for a student readership.

461 **Politics in the post-military state: some reflections on the Pakistani experience.**
Gerald A. Heeger.   *World Politics*, vol. 29, no. 2 (Jan. 1977),
p. 242-62.

This article, written before the Zia coup, addresses theoretical questions about the ability of civilian régimes which come after periods of military rule to establish firmly rooted democratic institutions. Pointing to the often arbitrary and 'patrimonial' strategies pursued by Bhutto, Heeger was pessimistic about the prospects.

462 **Land to the tiller: the political economy of agrarian reform in South Asia.**
Ronald J. Herring.   New Haven, Connecticut, London: Yale
University Press, 1983. 314p. 4 maps. bibliog.

A comprehensive study of the subject within the framework of which there is a chapter devoted to Pakistan with the title 'Land ceilings in Pakistan: an agrarian bourgeois revolution?'. Herring sees the reforms of the 1970s as part of a process whereby the traditional landlord class was brought within the fold of 'progressive, enlightened gentry', without alienating its support from the régime. The author has covered much of the same ground, with particular emphasis on the political dimension, in 'Zulfikar Ali Bhutto and the "eradication of feudalism" in Pakistan', *Comparative Studies in Society and History*, vol. 21, no. 4 (Oct. 1979), p. 519-57.

463 Pakistan in crisis: an interview with Eqbal Ahmad.
Nubar Housepian. *Race and Class*, vol. 22, no. 2 (Autumn 1980), p. 129-46.

Eqbal Ahmad is a well-known radical scholar who in this interview describes at some length his immediate reactions to and analysis of the Zia régime. He sees the situation in terms of simultaneous crises of legitimation, state power, integration, economy and external relations. He draws particular attention to divergence under Zia between the interests of the army and the bureaucracy.

464 Elite politics in an ideological state.
Asaf Hussain. Folkestone, England: Dawson, 1979. 212p. bibliog.

This is a fairly general study of Pakistan's politics from a sociological perspective. Hussain first discusses the special quality of Pakistan as an 'ideological state', and the inappropriateness of using Western models of government to assess and judge its political progress. He then devotes most of the book to a detailed analysis of the existing political system, which he sees as dominated by a number of élite groups which he lists as the landowning élites, the bureaucratic élites, the religious élites, the industrial élites, the professional élites and the military élites, before concluding that Pakistan will not progress in a truly Islamic direction so long as the power of the élite remains unchallenged.

465 Pakistan: Zia and after.
Anthony Hyman, Muhammed Ghayur, Naresh Kaushik. London: Asia Publishing House, 1988. 137p.

This book was completed within a month of President Zia's death in August 1988 as a review of his years in power. It makes up in immediacy and vigorous comment what it may lack in depth and reflectiveness.

466 Generals in politics: Pakistan 1958–1982.
Mohammad Asghar Khan. London; Canberra: Croom Helm, 1983. 230p.

The author himself is a retired Air Marshal and leader of a political party, the Tehrik-i-Istiqlal. He claims to be vehemently opposed to any form of military rule, although he played an ambiguous role in the events that led up to the coup of 1977. His book is for the most part, however, an account and justification of his own involvement in politics from 1968 on. It includes his clashes with Bhutto as well as with Zia.

467 Interest groups and development: business and politics in Pakistan.
Stanley A. Kochanek. Delhi: Oxford University Press, 1983. 393p. bibliog.

A detailed study of the place of business interest groups within the Pakistan political system from a political science perspective. Kochanek concludes that there has been very slow development of modern interest groups in Pakistan, as opposed to the use of more personal channels of influence, and that this is related to more general characteristics of the Pakistan political system. There is also a great deal of useful information on business in general.

468 **Contemporary problems of Pakistan.**
Edited by J. Henry Korson. Leiden, The Netherlands: E. J. Brill, 1974. 151p.

Although there is no indication of the fact, this volume is a reprint of a special issue of the *Journal of African and Asian Studies*, vol. 8, nos 3-4 (July and October 1973). Altogether seven articles are included, all of them studying one or another aspect of Pakistan under Bhutto. Some are of an ephemeral nature and their authors have written more recently on the same themes (for example in Manzooruddin Ahmed, *Contemporary Pakistan: politics, economy and society*, [q.v.]); others, for example those by Baxter on the political role of the large landowning families in the Punjab and by Rahman on the treatment of Islam in the 1973 constitution, are of more lasting significance.

469 **Power and privilege: influence and decision-making in Pakistan.**
Robert LaPorte, Jr. Berkeley, California; Los Angeles: University of California Press, 1975. 225p. bibliog.

This is a study of the political élite in Pakistan and its participation in decision-making during the period since 1947. LaPorte is concerned on the one hand to argue that the élite is not as monolithic as it has sometimes been portrayed, especially with the emergence of an articulate middle class, and on the other to suggest that Pakistan politics were still in the early 1970s 'elite-controlled and elite-directed'. The study is based to some extent on analysis of political developments but also incorporates assessments gathered systematically from American diplomats and others who had served in Pakistan.

470 **Pakistan People's Party and Pakistan's democracy.**
Maleeha Lodhi. *Journal of South Asian and Middle Eastern Studies*, vol. 6, no. 3 (Spring 1983), p. 20-31.

The author discusses the reasons for the failure of the Pakistan People's Party to mount an effective challenge to the régime of President Zia. These are attributed to organizational and leadership weaknesses going back to the formation of the party.

471 **The politics of development: the case of Pakistan, 1947–1958.**
Talukder Maniruzzaman. Dacca: Green Book House, 1971. 191p. bibliog.

Originally a thesis, this is a study of the period from independence up to the 1958 coup which argues that despite the obvious political instability of these years a degree of 'political development', as defined in terms of prevalent theories in the 1960s, did take place. Maniruzzaman is particularly concerned with the development of interest groups.

472 **Ethnic preference and public policy in developing states.**
Edited by Neil Nevitte, Charles H. Kennedy. Boulder, Colorado:
Lynne Rienner, 1986. 203p.

This book includes a chapter by Kennedy, published in a shorter version in *Asian Survey*, vol. 24, no. 6, on the 'Politics of redistributional preference in Pakistan' (p. 63-93). In it he discusses the regional tensions within Pakistan that have become more pronounced over the years, despite the unifying factor of Islam. As in other countries which face similar problems, a system of quotas has been introduced for recruitment to the public services and Kennedy discusses the operation of the system.

473 **The political economy of Pakistan 1947–85.**
Omar Noman. London; New York: KPI, 1988. 218p. bibliog.

This is a political history of Pakistan which seeks to relate forms of government to developments in the economy and consequent change, or lack of change, in the class structure of the country. The book is in three parts dealing, respectively, with the pre-1971 period, the Bhutto phase, and the Zia years up to the lifting of Martial Law.

474 **An analysis of contemporary Pakistani politics: Bhutto versus the military.**
Sameel Ahmed Qureshi. *Asian Survey*, vol. 19, no. 9 (Sept. 1979), p. 910-21.

Sameel Ahmed Qureshi is in fact a pseudonym for a Pakistani political observer who writes here of the circumstances of Zulfikar Ali Bhutto's fall and in particular his trial and execution. The author argues strongly for Bhutto's innocence.

475 **Public opinion and political development in Pakistan, 1947–1958.**
Inamur Rahman. Karachi: Oxford University Press, 1982. 282p. bibliog.

Originally a PhD thesis, this book uses the categories of American political science. It makes perhaps excessive claims for the role of the press during the period studied but nevertheless includes some useful material on public opinion in the pre-Ayub Khan period. The work is based on a survey of four leading newspapers of the time – *Dawn*, *Pakistan Times*, *Pakistan Observer*, and *Nawa-i-Waqt* (Urdu).

476 **The military and politics in Pakistan, 1947–86.**
Hasan-Askari Rizvi, foreword by Fazal Muqeem Khan. Lahore:
Progressive, 1986. 3rd ed. 339p. bibliog.

Rizvi traces the history of the relationship between the army and the political system of Pakistan from the situation in pre-independence India through the various phases of civilian government and military rule up to the Zia period. He attributes the frequency of military interventions to the weakness of Pakistan's political institutions, but argues that military rule is not a solution. The third edition is a substantially revised and extended version of the earlier editions published in 1974 and 1976 respectively. Appendices include statements by successive military rulers on why they are taking power.

477 **The political system of Pakistan.**
Khalid B. Sayeed.   Boston: Houghton Mifflin, 1967. 321p. 3 maps.
bibliog.

Sayeed begins with the pre-1947 origins of Pakistan's politics before moving on to a thematic analysis of the government system, the place of Islam, the problem of regionalism, political parties, development in the rural sector, and international relations. The framework of the study is a developmental approach derived from the political science of the time.

478 **Politics in Pakistan: the nature and direction of political change.**
Khalid bin Sayeed.   New York: Praeger, 1980. 194p. map.

An interesting general survey of Pakistan's political development which, unlike Sayeed's earlier work (see previous entry), emphasizes the colonial origins of the Pakistani state and the importance of the class basis of successive régimes. Sayeed sees the Bhutto régime as Bonapartist in the Marxist sense in its efforts to act as arbiter between class interests, and stresses the importance of the petty bourgeoisie in its overthrow.

479 **Political development in Pakistan.**
Karl von Vorys.   Princeton, New Jersey: Princeton University Press, 1965. 341p.

The author starts his analysis from the assumptions that economic and social change can come about only if there is an adequate political leadership capable of giving direction and that such direction needs to be carefully planned. He regards General Ayub Khan, who was in power at the time he wrote, as having the necessary leadership qualities. The first part of the book sets out the background to Pakistan's political system; in the second von Vorys discusses in more detail the programmes adopted by Ayub. He concludes with an analysis of the presidential election of 1965. Appendices include extracts from the 1962 constitution and President Ayub's inaugural address after his electoral victory.

480 **Pakistan under martial law, 1977–1985.**
Mohammad Waseem.   Lahore: Vanguard Books, 1987. 246p.

This is a revised collection of the author's contributions to the *Muslim*, one of Pakistan's leading English-language newspapers, between 1983 and 1985. The approach in fact is as much academic as journalistic and taken together the articles form a connected analysis of Pakistan's politics during the Martial Law period and more generally. There are also some useful sketches of a number of leading Pakistani politicians.

481 **Politics and the state in Pakistan.**
Mohammad Waseem.   Lahore: Progressive, 1989. 555p.

This is a substantial and important work on the state in Pakistan. The author integrates his historical and theoretical material to provide an analysis of Pakistan politics in terms of the role of the state as an initiator of economic development on the one hand and as the focus of the struggle between classes and regions on the other.

482 **The March 1977 elections in Pakistan: where everyone lost.**
M. G. Weinbaum. *Asian Survey*, vol. 17, no. 7 (July 1977), p. 599-618.

A detailed account by an academic who was in Pakistan at the time of the disputed elections. Weinbaum covers the immediate run up, the elections themselves, and the early stages of the agitation by the Pakistan National Alliance (PNA) which led eventually to the military coup. A more general review of the political situation at the time by Lawrence Ziring can be found in the same issue: 'Pakistan: the campaign before the storm', p. 581-98.

483 **The politics of Pakistan: a constitutional quest.**
Richard S. Wheeler. Ithaca, New York; London: Cornell University Press, 1970. 346p. 3 maps. bibliog. (South Asian Political Systems).

An introductory account of Pakistan's politics which is centred on constitutional questions and the search for consensus. The historical background and the social and economic setting are covered, before detailed treatments of the periods 1947-58 and 1958-69.

484 **White paper on the performance of the Bhutto regime.**
Islamabad: Government of Pakistan, 1979. 4 vols.

Following the coup of July 1977 and the subsequent postponing of the elections, the government of General Zia published a number of white papers designed to show the Bhutto years in a negative light. The one referred to here deals with allegations concerning Bhutto's personal conduct, the treatment of the fundamental institutions of the state, the use of state power against his opponents, and the economic policies pursued during the 1972-77 period. Facsimiles of relevant documents are included. While the tone is harsh and the documents have a clear political motivation, they are important sources for the study of the period. Two earlier white papers published in 1978 dealt respectively with the misuse of the media during the Bhutto period and the allegations of rigging during the 1977 elections. Bhutto's response to the earlier white papers is to be found in his *"If I am assassinated ..."* (q.v.).

485 **The states of South Asia: problems of national integration.**
Edited by A. Jeyaratnam Wilson, Denis Dalton. London: C. Hurst, 1982. 343p.

A *Festschrift* for a distinguished scholar of South Asian politics, Professor W. H. Morris-Jones, who himself worked primarily on India, this volume includes articles on the pre-1947 origins of Pakistani political issues by Khalid bin Sayeed, and on the condition of Pakistan at the beginning of the 1980s by Ataur Rahman, as well as references in some of the other contributions.

486 **Indian Muslim refugees in the politics of Pakistan.**
Theodore P. Wright, Jr. *Journal of Commonwealth and Comparative Politics*, vol. 12, no. 2 (July 1974), p. 189-205.

This is a general review of the *muhajirs* or refugees who came from India in 1947 and their political fortunes. Wright deals especially with the situation during the Ayub Khan years and with the refugees' position in Sindh, where their dominance of Karachi and other urban areas led to considerable rivalry with the local Sindhi population.

487 **Pakistan in its fourth decade: current political, social, and economic situation and prospects for the 1980s.**
Edited by Wolfgang-Peter Zingel in collaboration with Stephanie Zingel-Avé Lallemant. Hamburg: Deutsches Orient Institut, 1983. 374p. bibliog. (Mitteilungen des Deutschen Orient-Instituts, no. 23).

A collection of papers based on a conference held in Hamburg in 1980 to discuss the contemporary situation in Pakistan. Separate sections are devoted to constitution and law, ideology and regionalism, the economy, and foreign policy. The majority of the contributors are German or based in Germany, but others are from Pakistan, Britain and North America. The book was reprinted in Pakistan in two volumes in 1985 with the title *Pakistan in the 80s* (Lahore: Vanguard Books).

488 **Pakistan: the enigma of political development.**
Lawrence Ziring. Boulder, Colorado: Westview Press; Folkestone, England: Dawson, 1980. 294p. 2 maps. bibliog.

A general overview of Pakistan's political development which covers all the main themes, including the dominance of the army and bureaucracy, ethnic tensions, and problems of constitution-making. The enigma of the title refers to Pakistan's failure to achieve a stable and legitimate political structure.

Pakistan: a nation in making.
See item no. 3.

Breaking the curfew: a political journey through Pakistan.
See item no. 56.

Passage to Peshawar: Pakistan between the Hindu Kush and the Arabian sea.
See item no. 73.

Can Pakistan survive? The death of a state.
See item no. 249.

Pakistan: military rule or people's power.
See item no. 250.

Pakistan under Bhutto 1971–1977.
See item no. 253.

Pakistan: failure in national integration.
See item no. 257.

Persistent praetorianism: Pakistan's third military regime.
See item no. 259.

The Ayub Khan era: politics in Pakistan, 1958–1969.
See item no. 262.

Pakistan: the long view.
See item no. 263.

Friends not masters: a political autobiography.
See item no. 275.

The battle of ideas in Pakistan.
See item no. 506.

Der Indisch–Pakistanische Konflikt und seine wirtschaftlichen und sozialen Kosten für Pakistan in den Jahren 1958–1968. (The Indo–Pakistani conflict and its economic and social costs for Pakistan in the years 1958–1968.) *See* item no. 587.

Asian drama: an inquiry into the poverty of nations.
See item no. 608.

Pakistan: country report.
See item no. 611.

Land reforms in Pakistan: a historical perspective.
See item no. 666.

Rural development in Bangladesh and Pakistan.
See item no. 670.

Exports, politics, and economic development: Pakistan 1970–1982.
See item no. 671.

Regional

489 **Focus on Baluchistan and Pushtoon question.**
Edited by Feroz Ahmed.   Lahore: People's Publishing House, 1975.
116p.
The articles included in this collection were originally published in *Pakistan Forum* (a radical journal published in Canada) in 1973. The purpose of the collection was to open up the regional question in the aftermath of the secession of Bangladesh and to advocate a solution based on the rights of all national groups in the country. The individual articles provide somewhat general and rather brief accounts of the historical and social situation in the two provinces of Baluchistan and North-West Frontier Province (NWFP).

490 **Pakistan's western borderlands: the transformation of a political order.**
Edited by Ainslie T. Embree.   New Delhi: Vikas, 1977. 158p. 2 maps.
bibliog.
A collection of papers originally presented to a seminar in New York on developments in NWFP and Baluchistan. The linking theme is the analysis of the stresses encountered as areas peripheral to the British Indian empire are integrated into the new unit of Pakistan. The authors are historians and anthropologists as well as political scientists, but it is the political theme that is dominant.

491 Ethnic conflict in South Asia.
Edited by Asghar Ali Engineer. Delhi: Ajanta, 1987. 223p.

The rising tide of ethnic violence in South Asia is the focus of this collection of papers presented originally to a conference in Nepal organized by a Sri Lankan institute. There are seven contributions on Pakistan. Most of them deal with the violence in Karachi and in Sindh more generally between Muhajirs, Pukhtuns, and Sindhis.

492 In Afghanistan's shadow: Baluch nationalism and Soviet temptations.
Selig S. Harrison. New York; Washington, DC: Carnegie Foundation for International Peace, 1981. 228p. 7 maps.

Selig Harrison, a scholar and a journalist, writes here of the strategic location of the Baluch areas, which lie across the Iran–Pakistan border, and discusses the desire in the region for political autonomy or independence. Although the purpose of the book is to stimulate public debate in the United States on policy towards the region – and Harrison argues for a restricted role designed to limit risk – it also makes a significant contribution to a general understanding of Baluchistan.

493 Centre–province relations in Pakistan under President Zia: the government's and the opposition approaches.
C. G. P. Rakisits. *Pacific Affairs*, vol. 61, no. 1 (Spring 1988), p. 78-97.

The author argues that President Zia's policy of Islamization was accompanied by a degree of centralization which was seen by the smaller provinces as the 'Punjabization' of Pakistan society; this in turn provoked a degree of consensus among the political parties on the need for an alternative approach to centre–province relations. The author gives particular attention to developments in Sindh.

494 The Baluchis and the Pathans.
Robert G. Wirsing. London: Minority Rights Group, 1981. 23p. map. bibliog.

A brief and succinct account of the past history and present position of these two major ethno-linguistic groups in Pakistan (and also in Iran and Afghanistan). It is designed to inform the reader of the political and economic pressures to which they are currently subjected as a result of domestic and international developments. Similar ground is covered by the same author's 'South Asia: the Baluch frontier tribes of Pakistan', in Robert G. Wirsing (ed.), *Protection of ethnic minorities: comparative perspectives* (New York; Oxford; Toronto; Sydney; Paris; Frankfurt: Pergamon Press, 1981), p. 277-312.

The narrow smile: a journey back to the north-west frontier.
See item no. 68.

Indian Muslim refugees in the politics of Pakistan.
See item no. 486.

Islam and politics

495 Islam and Pakistan.
Freeland Abbott. Ithaca, New York: Cornell University Press, 1968.
242p. bibliog.

This is a relatively early treatment of the subject which besides relies entirely on English-language sources and on translations. It nevertheless remains valuable for its historical sweep and the warmth of its understanding of the dilemmas inherent in interpreting new social realities through established religious beliefs.

496 Parliament, parties, polls and Islam: issues in the current debate on religion and politics in Pakistan.
Mumtaz Ahmad. *American Journal of Islamic Social Sciences*, vol. 2, no. 1 (July 1985), p. 15-28.

A review of the debates in Pakistan over the structure and institutions of a properly Islamic political system. The author is primarily concerned with the debates during the Zia régime and the largely unsuccessful efforts of the government to establish a consensus among the intellectual and political élite on how to proceed.

497 Maulana Maududi and the Islamic state.
Sayed Riaz Ahmad. Lahore: People's Publishing House, 1976. 192p. bibliog.

Originally a doctoral thesis, this is a general study of Maududi's thinking on political matters. Apart from expounding his principal views, as found especially in *Islamic law and constitution* (q.v.), Ahmad examines the development of his ideas against the background of changing political circumstances in Pakistan and compares them with those of other advocates of an Islamic state.

498 The concept of an Islamic state: an analysis of the ideological controversy in Pakistan.
Ishtiaq Ahmed. London: Frances Pinter, 1987. 235p. bibliog.

Ahmed reviews a number of positions taken by Pakistani writers since 1947 on the question of how Quranic laws and injunctions could be made the foundation of a political order. Although some of his subjects have been studied more than once by earlier writers, Ahmed's work is valuable for its systematic approach and for its interesting discussion of the relationship between divine will and human reason.

499 The politics of Islamic reassertion.
Edited by Mohammed Ayoob. London: Croom Helm, 1981. 298p.

William Richter contributes the chapter on Pakistan to this collection of country studies published in the wake of the Iranian revolution. Most of the chapter is devoted to the measures introduced by the Zia régime and to their political impact.

500 Pakistan's ideology and ideologues.
Ikram Azam. Lahore: Progressive, 1982. 177p. bibliog.

Ikram Azam is a prolific writer who is committed to the idea that Pakistan is held together by its Islamic ideology. The present work traces the emergence of the ideology of Pakistan in the work of Jinnah, Iqbal, and other leading figures. The book itself can best be seen as an ideological statement.

501 **Religion and politics in Pakistan.**
Leonard Binder. Berkeley, California, Los Angeles: University of California Press, 1961. 440p.

The focus of this important work is the framing of the constitution of 1956 and the attempts by the *ulama* and religiously oriented politicians to make it what they considered a genuinely Islamic one. Binder discusses in detail the attitudes of the various groups and the successive compromises that were reached, culminating in 1954 with the effective defeat of the *ulama's* position in favour of a modernist approach. Two appendices reproduce the views of the Board of Talimat-i-Islamia, the representative of the *ulama*.

502 **L'Islam et l'état dans le monde d'aujourd'hui.** (Islam and the state in the contemporary world.)
Edited by Olivier Carré. Paris: Presses Universitaires de France, 1982.

This collection of essays contains a chapter by Marc Gaborieau on 'Rôles politiques de l'Islam au Pakistan' (p. 189-203). He reviews the role of Islam in Pakistan since its creation and looks at the tension between modernists, traditionalists and fundamentalists. He covers the debates on the form of the constitution and trends after 1977.

503 **Modern Islamic political thought: the response of the Shī'ī and Sunnī Muslims to the twentieth century.**
Hamid Enayat. London: Macmillan, 1982. 225p.

This valuable work by an Iranian scholar concentrates on Egyptian and Iranian writers but devotes substantial space to Maududi and makes some reference to other South Asian writers such as Iqbal and Azad. The comparative framework is useful.

504 **Islamization: religion and politics in Pakistan.**
John L. Esposito. *The Muslim World.* vol. 72, nos 3-4 (July-Oct. 1982), p. 197-223.

A review of changes introduced by the Zia régime up to 1982 in the fields of law, economics, education and the position of women, together with a brief examination of the underlying ideological debate. The article is based on published sources and on interviews conducted by the author with President Zia and other leading figures in the régime.

505 **The politics of sufism: redefining the saints of Islam.**
Katherine Ewing. *Journal of Asian Studies*, vol. 42, no. 2 (Feb. 1983), p. 251-68.

In this interesting article based on fieldwork carried out in the mid-1970s, the author discusses the policy of successive governments since 1958 towards the hereditary saints or *pirs* who play such an important role in religious life in Pakistan. Both Ayub Khan and Bhutto sought to bring the shrines under more direct government control to limit their political power but at the same time to allow the government to benefit from the

Islamic symbols associated with them. President Zia continued the same policy, although his political strategy emphasized the role of the *ulama* rather than the *pirs*. In the process of exercising greater control, the government has also sought to redefine the role of the *pir* in terms of an educator rather than a spiritual intermediary.

506   **The battle of ideas in Pakistan.**
Sibte Hasan.   Karachi: Pakistan Publishing House, 1986. 280p.

A group of related articles by a well-known Pakistani critic and writer on the theme of secularism, in which the author's concern is to link secularism as an ideology to progressive social change. Hasan traces the development of secularism historically as well as making comparisons with the situation in other Muslim countries such as Egypt and Turkey. He concludes with two chapters on the battle of ideas in modern Urdu literature and on Iqbal, his prototypical humanist.

507   **Islamization: an analysis of religious, political and social change in Pakistan.**
Riaz Hassan.   *Middle Eastern Studies*, vol. 21, no. 3 (July 1985), p. 263-84.

A review of the Islamization process during the Zia period which takes seriously the views and motives of the proponents of Islamization in Pakistan while at the same time placing them in social context. The article concludes that ironically even if it were successful Islamization might succeed in creating new social schisms in place of those it had overcome. Appendices include the preamble to the 1973 constitution and the text of a statement by a group of *ulama* in 1951 on the basic principles of an Islamic state.

508   **Islamisation of Pakistan.**
Afzal Iqbal.   Lahore: Vanguard Books, 1986. 198p. bibliog.

This is a review by a prominent writer and former diplomat of the issues involved in the question of Islamization in Pakistan. The author outlines what he considers to be the main thrust of the movement for Pakistan and examines the debates over how Pakistan's character as a Muslim society should be incorporated into constitutional provisions. He examines the Zia period in detail up to 1985. The Islamic provisions of Pakistan's successive constitutions are included as appendices.

509   **Islam, politics and the state: the Pakistan experience.**
Edited by Asghar Khan.   London: Zed Press, 1985. 281p.

A collection of essays critical of the way Islam has been used and interpreted by the rulers of Pakistan, especially in the period since 1977. The editor is a prominent political figure, and the authors of the individual essays are all well-established academics, mostly with a radical orientation. The subjects range from general overviews of the historical and contemporary relationship of Islam and politics, through studies of individual figures such as Maududi, to analyses of official cultural and scientific policy. There are also essays dealing with the crisis of the Pakistan state, problems of national integration, and Pakistan's geopolitical imperatives.

510 **Pakistan's Shia movement: an interview with Arif Hussaini.**
Maleeha Lodhi. *Third World Quarterly*, vol. 10, no. 2 (April 1988),
p. 806-17.

Arif Hussaini, who was murdered in August 1988, was the principal leader of
Pakistan's Shia minority and had transformed the Tehrik-i-Nifaz-i-Fiqah-i-Jafria into a
significant political force. In this interview he discusses the role of the Tehrik, the
position of the Shia community in Pakistan, and his views on the Iranian revolution
and world affairs generally. There is a general treatment of the Shia position by Saleem
Qureshi, 'The politics of the Shia minority in Pakistan', in Dhirendra Vajpeyi and
Yogendra K. Malik (eds), *Religious and ethnic minorities in South Asia* (Delhi:
Manohar, 1989), p. 109-38.

511 **The Islamic law and constitution.**
Sayyid Abul Aᶜlā Maududi. Lahore: Islamic Publications, 1983. 8th
ed. 412p.

This book is in fact a compilation of the writings and speeches of Maududi, the founder
of Pakistan's fundamentalist Jamaat-i Islami, on politics and constitutionalism within
the framework of Islam. First published in 1955 and in a greatly enlarged edition in
1960, it has become the basic text for understanding Maududi's thought in this area.
He argues throughout that the establishment in Pakistan of a truly Islamic state, based
strictly on the Quran and the Sunna, is both necessary and feasible. He indicates that
such a state would give authority under God to an elected amir and a consultative
assembly or majlis-i-shura.

512 **Faith and power: the politics of Islam.**
Edward Mortimer. London: Faber & Faber, 1982. 432p. 5 maps.

Mortimer, a distinguished British journalist, here seeks to understand, through a series
of case-studies, the interrelationship of Islamic belief and the politics of the societies to
which its adherents belong. The chapter devoted to Pakistan reviews the demand for
Pakistan and the various ways in which Islam has played a part in politics since
independence.

513 **From Jinnah to Zia.**
Muhammad Munir. Lahore: Vanguard Books, 1980. 2nd ed. 183p.

The author, a former Chief Justice of Pakistan and a prominent intellectual figure, uses
this book (originally published in 1979) to develop an argument against the notion that
Pakistan should be some form of theocracy and in favour of the view that it should be a
democracy. He argues that the intention of Jinnah to create a secular state was
progressively undermined by his successors. There is considerable implicit criticism of
the Zia régime. The book was written as a contribution to political debate in Pakistan
and is not always easy to follow without some prior knowledge of events, but it is not
an ephemeral work.

514 **Among the believers: an Islamic journey.**
V. S. Naipaul. London: André Deutsch, 1981. 399p.

A journal by the distinguished writer of his visit to a number of Muslim countries. A
third is devoted to Pakistan, which he visited in 1979. Through an intensely personal
account of his encounters with individuals, Naipaul raises a series of issues concerning

Islam itself and those countries which are seeking to unite Islam and politics. His own observations bring little comfort to the fundamentalist.

515 Islam in the political process.
Edited by James Piscatori. Cambridge, England: Cambridge University Press, 1983. 240p.

This collaborative volume compares the roles that Islam plays in the politics of a number of countries, some in the Middle East, others elsewhere. A chapter by David Taylor, 'The politics of Islam and Islamization in Pakistan' (p. 181-98) examines the situation before and after independence.

516 Islam and development: the Zia regime in Pakistan.
Saleem Qureshi. *World Development*, vol 8, nos 7-8 (July-Aug. 1980), p. 563-75.

The article covers what has become familiar ground in its treatment of the types of measures introduced by the Zia régime, but Qureshi looks in more detail than most other writers at those areas affecting economic development and at the assumptions underlying the measures that were taken.

517 Report of the court of inquiry constituted under Punjab Act II of 1954 to enquire into the Punjab disturbances of 1953.
Lahore: Superintendent, Government Printing, Punjab, 1954. 386p.

Generally referred to as the Munir report after its chairman Mr Justice Munir, this report is in the first instance a detailed account of the anti-Ahmadi disturbances in Lahore in 1953 which were the first occasion after independence that the government faced a large-scale challenge on the streets which was brought to an end only by the imposition of martial law. It is also however a wide-ranging discussion and critique of the idea of an Islamic state in Pakistan.

518 Islam in the modern world.
Erwin I. J. Rosenthal. London: Cambridge University Press, 1965. 416p. bibliog.

The author, an authority on medieval Islamic thought, conducted a comparative study in the early 1960s on the way Islam has adapted to the modern world. The result is a sensitive account of constitutional debates about the place of Islam on the one hand and of debates within Islam on the other. A major part of the book relates to Pakistan, especially to the discussions there in the 1950s.

519 South Asian politics and religion.
Edited by Donald Eugene Smith. Princeton, New Jersey: Princeton University Press, 1966. 563p.

This old but still important collection of articles has a separate section on 'Pakistan: the politics of Islamic identity' which contains six contributions. Of particular significance are Charles Adams's piece on Maududi, and Fazlur Rahman's on Muslim family laws.

520 **Islam in modern history.**
Wilfred Cantwell Smith.   Princeton, New Jersey: Princeton University Press, 1957. 317p.

Smith reflects in his *magnum opus* on the course of Islamic history and the dynamic force within it of religious aspiration. A substantial chapter is devoted to Pakistan and the dilemmas inherent in the quest for an Islamic way of life.

521 **Pakistan: Islam, politics, and national solidarity.**
Anwar Hussain Syed.   New York: Praeger, 1982. 203p.

A valuable study of the uses that have been made of Islam in Pakistan politics to create a sense of national solidarity. Syed argues that such solidarity is unlikely to flow from a simple emphasis on religious identity and suggests that a democratic political system is a prerequisite for its full development.

522 **Islamic reassertion in Pakistan: the application of Islamic laws in a modern state.**
Edited by Anita M. Weiss.   Syracuse, New York: Syracuse University Press, 1986. 146p. bibliog.

A collection of eight essays on the dimensions and significance of the Islamization programme from 1979 on. Apart from two general reviews of the broader context, there are three studies of the economic aspects, and individual treatments of the effects on women and the political implications of the programme. A particularly interesting piece by Richard Kurin (published earlier in *Asian Survey*, vol. 25, no. 8 (Aug. 1985), p. 852-62) looks at the impact (or lack of impact) on the Islam practised in the countryside.

Muslims and political representation in colonial India: the making of Pakistan.
See item no. 230.

Islam and modernity: transformation of an intellectual tradition.
See item no. 374.

The Jamaat-i-Islami of Pakistan: political thought and political action.
See item no. 450.

Pakistan: transition from military to civilian rule.
See item no. 456.

From the Anglo-Mohammedan law to the Shariah: the Pakistan experiment.
See item no. 528.

Constitutional and Legal System

523 The constitution of the Islamic republic of Pakistan 1956.
Karachi: Government of Pakistan, Ministry of Law, 1956. 224p.

Although its formulation was a protracted and painful process and in the end it was never fully implemented, the 1956 constitution maintained much of the structure of the colonial government, and also of the parliamentary system. Islam was recognized but treated as separate from the state. The constitution also incorporates the decision made in 1955 to merge all the previous provinces in West Pakistan into a single province.

524 The constitution of the republic of Pakistan 1962.
Karachi: Government of Pakistan, Manager of Publications, 1962. 134p.

Promulgated in March 1962 to replace the 1956 constitution, this gave Pakistan a presidential form of government. Designed very much to meet the wishes of Ayub Khan, it provided for the election of 'basic democracies' at the local level, the members of which formed an electoral college for the election of the president and of other bodies. The preliminary work in preparing the constitution was done by a constitutional commission, whose report was also published in 1962 (*Report of the Constitutional Commission, Pakistan, 1961.* Karachi: Manager of Publications, 1962).

525 The constitution of the Islamic Republic of Pakistan, 1973, as amended up to March 1988.
Makhdoom Ali Khan. Karachi: Pakistan Publishing House, 1986 (*sic*, in fact 1988). 347p.

Technically the 1973 constitution, introduced during the Bhutto régime, remained the only constitutional framework for Pakistan throughout the Zia years and thereafter, although its provisions were of course overridden by Martial Law from 1977 to 1985. The constitution was, however, radically amended by the 8th Amendment, passed in late 1985, as well as by earlier measures. The present work is a standard text of the constitution as it stood after the 8th Amendment, with footnotes which indicate every change that was made after 1973. It also includes the text of a number of important documents from the Zia period, including the Political Parties Act of 1962, as amended in 1985, and the 1986 rules for the registration of political parties. There is, however, no index to the book nor commentary on the individual clauses. The introduction discusses general legal issues and assumes a knowledge of the relevant political history.

526 Aspects of the Frontier Crimes Regulation in Pakistan.
Willard Berry. Durham, North Carolina: Duke University Program in Comparative Studies on Southern Asia, 1966. 122p. bibliog. (Monographs and Occasional Papers Series, no. 3).

The focus of this monograph is the way the British and the Pakistan governments have handled the question of the legal norms to be followed in the tribal areas of the Frontier. The Frontier Crimes Regulation of 1901 and the Criminal Law Amendment of 1963 both assumed that there is space in Pakistan (or British India) for two sets of legal norms, although the 1963 measure gives greater weight to formal rules. After the Ayub Khan coup of 1958 both the president and the then chief justice justified this legal pluralism as the basis for an indigenous legal system, although it was in turn criticized as simply a cover for executive arbitrariness. The author of this monograph, based on a careful reading of the relevant legal cases and secondary anthropological literature, provides an account from a legal sociological perspective, of the implications of these legal measures for social change and national development.

527 Constitutional development in Pakistan.
G. W. Choudhury. London: Longman, 1969. 2nd ed. 277p. bibliog.

The standard account of constitutional development in Pakistan up to and including the passing of the 1962 constitution which introduced a presidential system and a form of indirect democracy. The author describes in some detail the 1962 constitution, in whose framing he had a role as honorary advisor to the Constitution Commission. He discusses the earlier, largely fruitless efforts to find a constitutional framework which would satisfy all interests. The present work, which is a substantially revised and extended version of the first edition, published in 1959, also largely supersedes the author's *Democracy in Pakistan*, published in 1963 which, despite its title, was primarily concerned with constitutional development. On the purely legal side, Ivor Jennings, *Constitutional Problems in Pakistan* (London: Cambridge University Press, 1957) reproduces the texts of the major judgments in the Federal Court which arose out of the crisis created in 1954 by the dismissal by the governor-general of the first Constituent Assembly and discussed in chapter 7 of Choudhury's book. An older work on the subject is Alan Gledhill's *Pakistan: the development of its laws and constitution* (London: Stevens, 1957 [The British Commonwealth: The Development of its Laws and Constitutions, vol. 8]).

528 From the Anglo-Mohammedan law to the Shariah: the Pakistan experiment.
Afaq Haydar. *Journal of South Asian and Middle Eastern Studies*, vol. 10, no. 4 (Summer 1987), p. 33-50.

After an outline of the *sharia*, the author discusses briefly the measures taken in Pakistan to install it in place of the existing legal system, and the difficulties encountered in the process.

529 **Family law in Pakistan.**
David S. Pearl. *Journal of Family Law*, vol. 9, no. 2 (1969),
p. 165-89.
A review for lawyers who are not specialists on Pakistan on the background to the
Muslim Family Laws Ordinance of 1961. Pearl reports that at the time he wrote the
ordinance had not made much impact.

530 **A textbook on Muslim personal law.**
David Pearl. London; Sydney; Wolfeboro, New Hampshire: Croom
Helm, 1987. 2nd ed. 284p. bibliog.
First published in 1979, this is intended primarily for the specialist but is accessible to
others interested in family law among Muslims. Pearl places special emphasis on
Muslims of the Indian subcontinent and refers frequently to law cases from India and
Pakistan.

531 **Local self government in Pakistan.**
Syed Abdul Quddus. Lahore: Vanguard Books, 1981. 402p. bibliog.
This work is focused on the restoration by the Zia régime in 1979 of local government
institutions, albeit on a non-party basis. Three-quarters of the book is in fact devoted
to reproducing the texts of the relevant government ordinances. There is a somewhat
wordy introduction which looks at local self-government from a number of angles.

532 **A code of Muslim personal law.**
Tanzil-ur-Rahman. Karachi: Hamdard National Foundation, 1978,
1980. 2 vols. bibliog.
This is a comprehensive work, mainly for the specialist, which approaches the subject
through establishing a codification designed to reduce the differences between the
various schools of law within Islam. Each section is followed by a commentary, often at
considerable length, on the issues raised and the sources followed.

533 **An introduction to Islamic law.**
Joseph Schacht. Oxford, England: Clarendon Press, 1964. 304p.
bibliog.
Joseph Schacht was an Islamicist as much as a lawyer, and this important work
examines law as a historical phenomenon. The first part of the book discusses the
evolution of Islamic law; the second looks at such primary themes as property, family,
and criminal law.

534 **Partnership and profit-sharing in Islamic law.**
Muhammad Nejatullah Siddiqi. Leicester, England: Islamic
Foundation, 1985. 111p. bibliog. (Islamic Economic Series, no. 9).
Originally written in Urdu, this is a general introduction to the principles that underlie
Islamic approaches to commercial law. *Shirkah* and *mudarabah* are described as the
two principal forms of business partnership that do not contravene the Islamic ban on
interest (*riba*).

535 **Constitutional legitimacy: a study of the doctrine of necessity.**
   Leslie Wolf-Phillips.   London: Third World Foundation, 1979. 79p.
   (Third World Foundation Monographs, no. 6).

This useful study looks in a comparative perspective at the legal arguments put forward to support the imposition of martial law at various times in Pakistan's history and to ensure a measure of constitutional continuity. The author discusses four instances, viz. the governor-general cases of 1955, *Dosso* (1958), *Asma Jilani* (1972) and *Begum Bhutto* (1977). Each case produced a different response from the judges. An abridged version was published as an article in *Third World Quarterly*, vol. 1, no. 4 (Oct. 1979), p. 97-133.

Nizam-i-Islam: processes and conflicts in Pakistan's programme of Islamisation, with special reference to the position of women.
See item no. 433.

Women in Muslim family law.
See item no. 435.

Religion and politics in Pakistan.
See item no. 501.

South Asian politics and religion.
See item no. 519.

Government and Administration

536 **Administrative problems in Pakistan.**
Edited by Guthrie S. Birkhead.   Syracuse, New York: Syracuse
University Press, 1966. 223p. 2 maps.

The seven essays collected in this volume were all written by American scholars
connected with Syracuse University and the Administrative Staff College in Lahore.
The common concern is with the importance of public administration to the success of
plans for economic development. The individual chapters cover basic democracies,
agriculture, business organizations, and individual government agencies, and proposals
for administrative reform.

537 **Asian bureaucratic systems emergent from the British imperial
tradition.**
Edited by Ralph Braibanti.   Durham, North Carolina: Duke
University, Commonwealth Studies Center, [n.d.]. 733p. (Duke
University Commonwealth-Studies Center Publication no. 28).

The purpose of this volume was to engage in a comparative study of bureaucratic
systems in Asian countries in the context of efforts at the time the work was written to
bring such systems into line with developmental requirements. Braibanti himself
contributed a long chapter on 'The higher bureaucracy of Pakistan' (p. 209-353) and
there is relevant material in the chapters by B. Cohn on the recruitment and training of
British officials during the early colonial period and by H. Tinker on the structure of
the British imperial heritage. Braibanti contributed a chapter on 'Public bureaucracy
and judiciary in Pakistan' to another comparative volume, *Bureaucracy and political
development*, edited by Joseph LaPalombara (Princeton, New Jersey: Princeton
University Press, 1963).

538 **Research on the bureaucracy of Pakistan: a critique of sources,
conditions, and issues, with appended documents.**
Ralph Braibanti.   Durham, North Carolina: Duke University Press,
1966. 569p. (Duke University Commonwealth-Studies Center
Publication no. 26).

In the 1960s the bureaucratic system of Pakistan became of considerable interest to
foreign, especially American scholars who were concerned with the overall economic
progress of the country. The present volume makes a case for the importance to
researchers of the considerable volume of reports and documents on the bureaucracy
issued mainly after (but in some cases before) 1947. It then discusses in substantial and
very helpful detail these sources, and provides necessary background information on
the organization of government. The work covers not only central government but
local institutions and public corporations. There is a separate chapter devoted to legal
research. Fifteen documents appendices are included. These are for the most part
extracts from speeches designed to illustrate general attitudes towards bureaucratic
change.

539 **Babus, Brahmans and bureaucrats: a critique of the administrative
system in Pakistan.**
Nazim (pseud. for Hassan Habib).   Lahore: People's Publishing
House, 1973. 144p.

A collection of articles and papers writen in 1970-71 which argue for a radical overhaul
of a system which the author believes is a legacy of the colonial past. He is particularly
concerned to eliminate the 'Babu–Brahman–Bureaucrat complex' and replace it with
modern, professional and specialized management. At the time the book was
published, Hassan Habib was principal of the Pakistan Administrative Staff College.

540 **District administration in West Pakistan: its problems and challenges.**
Edited by Inayatullah.   Peshawar: Pakistan Academy for Rural
Development, 1964. 336p.

This volume contains the papers given at a conference in 1964 which drew together
academics and professional administrators to discuss the problems in adapting
Pakistan's district level administration to the requirements of the post-independence
situation as represented by the introduction of the basic democracies scheme by Ayub
Khan.

541 **Bureaucracy in Pakistan.**
Charles H. Kennedy.   Karachi: Oxford University Press, 1987. 246p.
bibliog.

A detailed study of the bureaucracy in Pakistan which discusses its central political role
since independence in the context both of its own institutional history since before
independence and of the general political history of the country. Kennedy is
particularly good on the changes brought about during the Bhutto period and after.

542 **Administrative training and development: a comparative study of East Africa, Zambia, Pakistan, and India.**
Edited by Bernard Schaffer.   New York; Washington, DC; London: Praeger, 1974. 445p. (Praeger Special Studies in International Economics and Development).

The work as a whole focuses on the role of training and training institutions in meeting developing countries' needs. There is a contribution by Ken Cabatoff on the National Institute of Public Administration (NIPA) in Lahore. Basing himself on fieldwork at the end of the 1960s, he discusses the tensions between staff and students over the purpose of the institution and the type of training that it imparted, and over their respective roles.

The men who ruled India.
See item no. 117.

Punjab settlement manual.
See item no. 183.

Armed Forces

543 **The Indo–Pak clash in the Rann of Kutch.**
Saeed Ahmad.   Rawalpindi, Pakistan: Army Education Press, [1973].
149p. 6 maps.
A detailed account, primarily from the military point of view, of the clashes in the first
half of 1965 between Indian and Pakistani forces in the Rann of Kutch area which lies
across the extreme southern section of the Indo–Pakistan border. Although not a full-
scale war, these clashes were an important prelude to the September 1965 war. The
volume includes the text of the ceasefire agreement of 30 June 1965.

544 **The Pakistan army.**
Stephen P. Cohen.   Berkeley, California; Los Angeles; London:
University of California Press, 1984. 177p. bibliog.
This is a comprehensive and reliable account by the leading US specialist on the
military in South Asia. After discussing the general organization and recruitment of the
army, including its domination by men from particular regions, especially the northern
Punjab, Cohen turns to the officer corps, its general attitudes, political involvement,
ideological orientation and strategic outlook.

545 **Battle for Pakistan: the air war of 1965.**
John Fricker.   Shepperton, England: Ian Allan, 1979. 192p. map.
A strictly military account by a British journalist and writer on affairs of the air war in
September 1965. The author had full cooperation from the Pakistan Air Force and is
therefore in a position to give a detailed narrative of the actions that were fought. He
also discusses the reasons for the air superiority that was achieved by the Pakistan side.
The book is well illustrated by photographs.

144

546 **History of the Pakistan Air Force, 1947–1982.**
Syed Shabbir Hussain, M. Tariq Qureshi, foreword by M. Anwar
Shamim. [?Karachi]: [?Pakistan Air Force], 1982. 332p.

An official history illustrated with many photographs which covers the Pakistan Air
Force from its inception at the time of independence to the 1980s. Like most such
histories it is full of precise detail of the formation of squadrons and of specific
operations during Pakistan's wars with India and the men who took part in them.
There are also more general sections on organization and training.

547 **Pakistan's nuclear development.**
Ashok Kapur. London; New York; Sydney: Croom Helm, 1987.
258p.

A careful and scholarly study of Pakistan's nuclear programme since the 1950s by an
Indian specialist in international relations based in Canada. Kapur argues that it is only
since the early 1970s that the programme has been primarily military in orientation. He
advocates a private dialogue between India and Pakistan to improve mutual
understanding in this critical area. Another relevant work is *Nuclear power in
developing countries: an analysis of decisionmaking*, edited by James Everett Katz and
Onkar S. Marwah (Lexington, Massachusetts; Toronto: Lexington Books, 1982),
which contains a review of Pakistan by Shirin Tahir-Kheli, although there is no direct
consideration of the military aspects.

548 **The first round: Indo–Pakistan War 1965.**
M. Asghar Khan, foreword by Altaf Gauhar. London: Islamic
Information Services, 1979. 146p.

The author was commander-in-chief of the Pakistan Air Force until July 1965, two
months before the war broke out, and was familiar with the diplomatic as well as
military background. During the war itself he was active in obtaining military supplies
from friendly countries such as China and Turkey. The book, written we are told in
1966-67, combines personal reminiscence with observations on the actions and
decisions of the principal actors on the Pakistan side. He is critical of United States
policy towards the combatants and of Ayub Khan for agreeing to a ceasefire rather
than continuing the military action at a moment when he thinks a breakthrough might
have been made. He remarks in the introduction that the war 'appears now to have
been fought for no purpose'.

549 **The martial races of India.**
George MacMunn. London: Sampson Low, Marston & Co, (c.1933).
368p. 2 maps.

The concept of the martial race is now seen as closely associated with the ideology of
imperialism, but it was widely accepted in the period before independence and its
traces still linger. In this classic statement MacMunn, an army general, outlines the
history of armies in India from classical to modern times. His chapters on the British
period lay much stress on the 'martial races' of the Punjab.

550 **A matter of honour: an account of the Indian army, its officers and men.**
Philip Mason. London: Jonathan Cape, 1974. 580p. maps. bibliog.

Philip Mason, a distinguished writer and member of the Indian Civil Service, writes here of the Indian army from its 17th- and 18th-century origins to its partition, along with the rest of the Indian empire, at the time of independence. He emphasizes the contribution made by the Indian army to British causes elsewhere in the world, notably during the two world wars. This is both a scholarly work, as in the discussion of the 'martial races' approach to recruitment, but also a well-written popular account.

551 **Bugles and a tiger: a personal adventure.**
John Masters.   London: Michael Joseph, 1956. 335p.

A personal memoir of his life as a young soldier on the North-West Frontier by the well-known novelist. He took part for a while in the military operations in Waziristan from 1936 to 1939, and reflects on the outlook and attitudes of the participants on both sides.

552 **Nation building and the Pakistan army, 1947–1969.**
Raymond A. Moore, Jr., foreword by Altaf Qadir.   Lahore: Aziz, 1979. 384p.

Unlike most studies of the military, this work concentrates explicitly on what the author calls the nation-building activities of the Pakistan army in the period up to 1969. The first chapters cover the role of the army in its purely military capacity as a defender of the country's internal and external security, but most of the book is concerned with such issues as its involvement in disaster relief and the activities of the Fauji (army) Foundation in promoting industrial development.

553 **Our defence cause: an analysis of Pakistan's past and future military role.**
M. Attiqur Rahman.   London; Sydney; Toronto: White Lion, 1976. 263p. bibliog.

This book is a reflective discussion by a retired general of the weaknesses in Pakistan's defence planning in the light of the defeat in the 1971 war with India. His suggestions for change, which draw on comparative examples from the Napoleonic wars on, extend from relatively minor points of detail to proposals for greater openness in military affairs.

554 **Going nuclear.**
Leonard Spector.   Cambridge, Massachussetts: Ballinger, 1987. 370p. maps. (A Carnegie Endowment Book).

Spector is one of the leading US specialists on nuclear proliferation. This volume, one of a series sponsored by the Carnegie Endowment for International Peace, reviews the evidence for nuclear weapons programmes in a number of countries, including Pakistan and India. A list of each country's known nuclear installations is given. Spector brings his account up to late 1986, and concludes that Pakistan is actively seeking a nuclear weapons capability. He is the author of two earlier volumes in the series: *Nuclear proliferation today* (New York: Vintage Books, 1984), and *The new nuclear nations* (ibid., 1985).

Witness to surrender.
See item no. 260.

The story of soldiering and politics in India and Pakistan.
See item no. 281.

The military and politics in Pakistan, 1947–86.
See item no. 476.

Foreign Relations

General

555 **China Pakistan relations 1947–1980: documents.**
Edited by K. Arif. Lahore: Vanguard Books, 1984. 300p.
The 209 documents included in this volume are almost all public statements and communiqués. Although the formulae used are, as would be expected, often stereotyped, taken together the documents illustrate the increasingly close relationship between Pakistan and China since 1947. There is a useful set of appendices which bring together otherwise scattered statistical information on economic relations and on arms supplies from China to Pakistan.

556 **Pakistan's Soviet policy: one step forward, two steps back.**
Muhammad R. Azmi. *Asian Profile*, vol. 15, no. 2 (April 1987), p. 167-78.
Azmi reviews the relationship before and after the 1979 Soviet intervention in Afghanistan and argues that Pakistan should take steps to improve its relations with the USSR, in part to reduce the perceived threat from India.

557 **The myth of independence.**
Zulfikar Ali Bhutto. London: Oxford University Press, 1969. 188p.
The late prime minister's most extended statement of his position on international relations, and an important document for understanding his world view. It was written shortly after he had resigned as Ayub Khan's foreign minister and just before his foundation of the Pakistan People's Party. Through a survey of Pakistan's foreign relations since 1947, in which the conflict with India is seen as the central feature, he argues against the link with the United States which had been so important to Pakistan in the late 1950s and early 1960s. He describes the USA as unreliable and the alliance itself as an infringement of Pakistan's sovereignty. The book also makes a case for close relations with China, in the fostering of which Bhutto had a large part.

558 **The Indian ocean: region of conflict or 'peace zone'?**
Dieter Braun, translated by Carol Geldart, Kathleen Llanwarne.
London: C. Hurst; Canberra: Croom Helm, 1983. 228p. 6 maps.
bibliog.
First published in German in 1982 (*Der Indische Ozean: Konfliktregion oder 'Zone des Friedens'?*, Baden-Baden, West Germany: Nomos Verlagsgesellschaft [Internationale Politik und Sicherheit, vol. 9]), this is a study by a German specialist in security issues of the whole Indian Ocean region in terms both of global and regional factors. There is a valuable chapter which reviews the history of the zone of peace idea, first put forward by Sri Lanka and then taken up by India.

559 **Pakistan's foreign policy: an historical analysis.**
S. M. Burke. London: Oxford University Press, 1973. 432p. bibliog.
A standard history of Pakistan's foreign policy by a former Pakistani diplomat. Burke organizes his material into three periods: 1947-53, the non-aligned years; 1954-62, the aligned years; and 1963-70, a period of reappraisal. A brief postscript covers the period up to July 1972 and the Simla agreement. The focus of the book is very much on Indo–Pakistan relations, and on the bearing of those on relations with the rest of the world, but it is not exclusively devoted to them.

560 **Perspectives on Pakistan's foreign policy.**
Edited by Surendra Chopra. Amritsar, India: Guru Nanak Dev University Press, 1983. 476p.
The 26 articles included in this work, all but two by Indian scholars, arose out of a seminar in 1982. Some are general in scope, others provide detailed case-studies. There are some rather stereotyped comments, but as a whole the volume is useful both for its detail and as an Indian perspective.

561 **India, Pakistan, Bangladesh, and the major powers: politics of a divided subcontinent.**
G. W. Choudhury. New York: Free Press; London: Collier Macmillan, 1975. 276p. bibliog.
The author organizes his study by describing and analysing in turn the relations since 1947 between the countries of the subcontinent and the USSR, the USA and China, especially in the context of the Bangladesh crisis and its aftermath. He argues that on the whole the great powers, the USSR especially, have complicated rather than eased the way to peace in the region.

562 **Islam in foreign policy.**
Edited by Adeed Dawisha. Cambridge, England: Cambridge University Press, 1983. 191p.
This is a companion volume to that edited by J. Piscatori, *Islam in the political process* (q.v.). In the present collection there is a piece on Pakistan, 'In search of an identity: Islam and Pakistan's foreign policy', by Shirin Tahir-Kheli, in which she discusses the growing importance in the 1970s of the Islamic dimension but notes that such a policy may carry costs in terms of involvement in the Middle East's regional conflicts.

563 **Pakistan in a changing world: essays in honour of K. Sarwar Hasan.**
Edited by Masuma Hasan.   Karachi: Pakistan Institute of
International Affairs, 1978. 258p. 3 maps.

Seven Pakistani and four foreign scholars contributed to this volume in honour of the
founder-secretary of the Pakistan Institute of International Affairs. Subjects are mostly
in the field of Pakistan's foreign relations, and cover many aspects ranging from the
1965 war with India to Pakistan's relations with Australia. This is a useful collection.

564 **Pakistan and the Iran–Iraq war.**
Suroosh Irfani.   *Journal of South Asian and Middle Eastern Studies*,
vol. 9, no. 2 (Winter 1985), p. 55-66.

Throughout the war from 1980 to 1988 Pakistan was able to maintain a neutral stance
and to keep links with both sides. This article discusses its policy in historical,
economic and strategic perspective. An earlier article written before the fall of the
Shah in 1979 is Shirin Tahir-Kheli's 'Iran and Pakistan: cooperation in an area of
conflict', *Asian Survey*, vol. 17, no. 5 (May 1977), p. 474-90.

565 **Security in Southern Asia 1: the security of Southwest Asia.**
Zalmay Khalilzad.   Aldershot, England: Gower, 1984. 191p.

South-west Asia is defined here as Pakistan, Afghanistan and Iran and is seen as a
region of instability and crisis. The purpose of the book, a product of a research
programme at the International Institute of Strategic Studies in London on regional
security issues, is to provide an integrated account of threats to the region's security
arising from domestic instability, regional rivalries, especially the Kashmir issue, and
superpower involvement in the area.

566 **Soviet–American relations with Pakistan, Iran and Afghanistan.**
Edited by Hafeez Malik.   London: Macmillan Press, 1987. 431p.

This volume is made up of the papers presented to a conference in 1984 convened to
consider US policy in South-west Asia in the light of developments in Iran and
Afghanistan. Most of the contributors are American academics and security specialists,
but there are chapters from Agha Shahi, former foreign minister of Pakistan, and
from a group of Soviet scholars. Pakistan's bilateral relations with its neighbours and
the great powers are reviewed, and there are chapters also on the security implications
of internal problems.

567 **Defense planning in less-industrialized states: the Middle East and South
Asia.**
Edited by Stephanie G. Neuman.   Lexington, Massachusetts;
Toronto: Lexington Books, 1984. 315p. maps.

This volume arose out of concern in the USA to understand more closely the processes
whereby planning of defence policies takes place in the volatile areas of the Middle
East and South Asia. The chapter on Pakistan is contributed by Shirin Tahir-Kheli,
with a commentary by Stephen Cohen. Tahir-Kheli characterizes Pakistan's defence
planning as essentially reactive and lacking long-term perspective.

568 **Pakistan Horizon.**
Karachi: Pakistan Institute of International Affairs, 1948- . quarterly.
This is the main journal in Pakistan devoted to Pakistan's international relations. As well as research articles on a range of specific and more general topics, each issue includes two chronologies, 'Pakistan and the world', and 'Chronicle of international affairs', and copies of selected documents relevant to Pakistan.

569 **Anglo–Pakistan relations, 1947–1976.**
M. Aslam Qureshi.   Lahore: Research Society of Pakistan, 1976.
395p. bibliog. (Publications of the Research Society, no. 38 [*sic*, in fact 33]).
Originally a doctoral thesis, this work describes in detail relations between the two countries as they emerged from the trauma of partition in 1947. The author focuses on particular events and developments such as the Kashmir question, Pakistan's membership of Western military alliances, and its fraught relations with Afghanistan. A final chapter covers the Bangladesh crisis and Z. A. Bhutto's subsequent decision to take Pakistan out of the Commonwealth (reversed by his daughter in 1989). Anthony Hyman's article, 'Pakistan and the Commonwealth: an expanding organization?', *Round Table*, no. 307 (July 1988), p. 293-302, offers a historical perspective.

570 **The frontiers of Pakistan: a study of frontier problems in Pakistan's foreign policy.**
Mujtaba Razvi.   Karachi; Dhaka: National Publishing House, 1971.
339p. 8 maps. bibliog.
A comprehensive analysis from a Pakistani perspective of the country's frontiers, based largely on historical and geographical material. The author sees Pakistan as especially concerned to finalize its 'territorial personality', the limits of which had been somewhat hazy at the time of independence owing to the British imperial policy of relying on buffer zones. Whereas a settlement with Iran was easy to achieve, it was not so with India and Afghanistan, where conflict extended beyond the narrow question of border demarcation. The work includes the text of a number of important documents, including the Radcliffe Award of 1947, the Indus Waters Treaty, and the Tashkent Declaration.

571 **United States – Pakistan relations.**
Edited by Leo E. Rose, Noor A. Husain.   Berkeley, California: University of California, Institute of East Asian Studies, 1985. 270p. (Research Papers and Policy Studies, no. 13).
The eighteen papers collected in this volume were originally presented to a conference held in 1984 and organized jointly by the University of California and the Institute of Strategic Studies in Islamabad. Themes covered included economic and security relations between Pakistan and the United States, and discussions of the impact on the US–Pakistan relationship of wider international issues, for example the Arab–Israeli conflict, where the two countries have rather different perceptions and interests. The papers are for the most part oriented towards the relationship between the two countries at the time the conference was held but are quite broad-ranging in scope.

572 **The regional imperative: the administration of U.S. foreign policy
towards South Asian states under presidents Johnson and Nixon.**
Lloyd I. Rudolph, Susanne Hoeber Rudolph (et al.).   New Delhi:
Concept Publishing, 1980. 465p.

The studies collected together in this volume were originally prepared by US
academics as part of an official project to review US foreign policy, and focus on issues
that were current in the mid-1970s. Two papers deal specifically with Pakistan. Philip
Oldenburg examines the way the US government responded to the 1971 crisis, while
Gerald A. Heeger discusses the way in which US policy towards Pakistan was
formulated in the immediate aftermath of the creation of Bangladesh. An important
article on US policy in 1971 by a senior US official at the time of the Bangladesh crisis,
Christopher Van Hollen, is reproduced as an appendix, and there are substantial
references to Pakistan in other contributions.

573 **China and Pakistan: diplomacy of an entente cordiale.**
Anwar Hussain Syed.   Amherst, Massachusetts: University of
Massachusetts Press; Karachi: Oxford University Press, 1974. 259p.
map.

Syed traces and comments upon Pakistan–China relations since the early 1950s. He
discusses China's role at the time of the Indo–Pakistan war of 1965 and its difficult
position during the 1971 civil war. He sees the relationship from the Pakistani side as
part of a pattern of 'small nation' behaviour. Another study which touches briefly on
the relationship is by Wayne A. Wilcox, *India, Pakistan and the rise of China* (New
York: Walker & Co, 1964).

574 **The Saudi–Pakistani military relationship: implications for U.S. policy.**
Shirin Tahir-Kheli, William O. Staudenmaier.   *Orbis*, vol. 26, no. 1
(Spring 1982), p. 155-71.

The authors discuss the domestic and international factors which gave impetus to the
relationship in the 1970s and review the implications for US strategy in the Middle
East. In general they consider it to have been a helpful development.

575 **The United States and Pakistan: the evolution of an influence
relationship.**
Shirin Tahir-Kheli.   New York: Praeger, 1982. 167p. bibliog. (Studies
of Influence in International Relations).

Pakistan and the United States have a longstanding military and diplomatic connection
dating back to the mid-1950s, but the relationship has often been fraught and uneasy.
Tahir-Kheli's interesting study discusses the two sides' divergent perceptions of the
threats each faced and concludes that in practice the two were able to influence each
other on only a limited number of occasions. She discusses the evolution of the
relationship from its beginning up to the Afghan crisis and devotes a chapter to the
nuclear issue, where the United States has signally failed to influence Pakistan.

576 **The enduring entente: Sino–Pakistani relations 1960–1980.**
Yaacov Vertzberger, foreword by T. P. Thornton.   New York:
Praeger, 1983. 112p. map. (Washington Papers, vol. 10, no. 95).

A useful study of relations between Pakistan and China. Vertzberger describes the historical development of the relationship and locates it in the strategic and diplomatic requirements of the two countries.

577 **Pakistan enters the Middle East.**
M. G. Weinbaum, Gautam Sen. *Orbis*, vol. 22, no. 3 (Fall 1978), p. 595-612.

This gives an overview of Pakistan's relations with its Middle East neighbours since independence, and especially after 1971 when Bhutto consciously sought to build up links. The authors see the Middle East as a major component of Pakistan's future foreign policy.

578 **Pakistan's search for a foreign policy after the invasion of Afghanistan.**
W. Howard Wriggins. *Pacific Affairs*, vol. 57, no. 2 (Summer 1984), p. 284-303.

A review of the alternative strategies open to Pakistan after the Soviet invasion of Afghanistan at the end of 1979. Wriggins looks at the implications of relying heavily on the USA, the eventual strategy followed, and also at possibilities of improving links with India, before turning to Pakistan's stance towards the USSR. He concludes that Pakistani policy-makers pursued an adroit and multifaceted policy in difficult circumstances.

Making the new Commonwealth.
See item no. 243.

Pakistan in its fourth decade: current political, social, and economic situation and prospects for the 1980s.
See item no. 487.

Islam, politics and the state: the Pakistan experience.
See item no. 509.

South Asian insecurity and the great powers.
See item no. 584.

The security of South Asia: American and Asian perspectives.
See item no. 586.

South Asia: too late to remove the bomb.
See item no. 589.

India

579 **Pakistan's nuclear dilemma: energy and security dimensions.**
Akhtar Ali. Karachi: Economist Research Unit, 1984. 218p. bibliog.

A careful review of the positions of India and Pakistan over nuclear power and nuclear weapons. The author argues, contrary to powerful voices in Pakistan in the 1970s and

1980s, that the country has benefited little from keeping its nuclear option open, and that it would be better for it to sign the Nuclear Non-Proliferation Treaty without linking this to India's doing so. There is a 60-page appendix reviewing Pakistan's energy needs and sources of supply.

580 **Bangla Desh documents.**
New Delhi: Government of India, Ministry of External Affairs, [1971]. 719p.

This volume was produced in 1971 after the Pakistan army's intervention in East Bengal, as part of the Indian diplomatic efforts to try to bring international pressure to bear on the Pakistan government to end the civil war and allow the large number of refugees in India to return home. It includes large numbers of short extracts from Pakistani and Indian sources, mainly official documents and statements, covering the 1970-71 period. There are also extracts to illustrate international press reaction.

581 **India, Pakistan, and the great powers.**
William J. Barnds. London: Pall Mall Press, 1972. 388p. 3 maps. bibliog.

The author worked for many years as an analyst for the US government, and during that time developed an interest in the relationships between South Asia and the rest of the world. This book reviews the complex patterns of US and USSR involvement in the region, the consequences of the Indo–China war of 1962 and the Indo–Pakistan war of 1965, and the choices facing the USA in its policy towards the region. Barnds concludes with an argument for less military involvement through arms supplies and more support for long-term economic development in the region.

582 **The Indo–Pakistani conflict.**
Russell Brines. London: Pall Mall Press, 1968. 481p. 4 maps. bibliog.

This is an account by a journalist of the Indo–Pakistan war of 1965. Brines's purpose is to identify the broader historical forces which drove the two sides into a major military conflict, and he therefore devotes much of his book to the background of hostility between the two countries. He blames the Soviet Union and China for exploiting the situation and using India and Pakistan as proxies for their own conflicts.

583 **Mainsprings of Indian and Pakistani foreign policies.**
S. M. Burke. Minneapolis, Minnesota: University of Minnesota Press, 1974. 308p. bibliog.

This is in some ways a companion piece to Burke's more detailed account of Pakistan's foreign policy, *Pakistan's foreign policy: an historical analysis* (q.v.). In the first part he discusses the broad historical and cultural framework. In the second, he again describes the development of foreign policy after independence, but in comparative terms.

584 **South Asian insecurity and the great powers.**
Edited by Barry Buzan, Gowher Rizvi. London: Macmillan, 1986. 257p.

The theoretical framework for this work is Buzan's concept of a security complex as an appropriate unit of analysis in the field of international relations. South Asia is one such security complex and the book looks at various factors that impinge on it. These include domestic problems in India and Pakistan, specifically regional rivalries, especially the Indo–Pakistan tension on which there is a chapter by Rizvi, and supra-regional conflicts, including superpower competition. The editors conclude that Pakistan is likely to play a pivotal role, for good or ill, in future developments in the region.

585 **Pakistan's relations with India: 1947–1966.**
G. W. Choudhury. London: Pall Mall Press, 1968. 341p. bibliog.
A careful and meticulous history of the subject by a political scientist who was also a minister in the government of Yahya Khan. Although written from a Pakistani perspective, it seeks to provide an essentially factual account. Separate chapters are devoted to the Kashmir dispute and trade and water disputes, as well as to the more general development of each country's foreign policy. The book ends with the 1965 war.

586 **The security of South Asia: American and Asian perspectives.**
Edited by Stephen Philip Cohen. Chicago; Urbana, Illinois: University of Illinois Press, 1987. 290p. maps.
Cohen brought together a number of leading academics, journalists and public figures from South Asia and the United States to produce this work, which does indeed provide perspectives on the main security issues in the South Asian region. Wherever possible, contributors to the volume look at situations from other people's points of view. There are also four chapters which seek to provide 'visions of the future', and appendices on the military balance of power and on the consequences for the region if there were to be a nuclear conflict.

587 **Der Indisch–Pakistanische Konflikt und seine wirtschaftlichen und sozialen Kosten für Pakistan in den Jahren 1958–1968.** (The Indo–Pakistani conflict and its economic and social costs for Pakistan in the years 1958–1968.)
Hans Frey. Wiesbaden, West Germany: Franz Steiner Verlag, 1978. 234p. bibliog. (Beiträge zur Südasienforschung Südasien-Institut Universität Heidelberg, vol. 38).
This is a more general work than its title might suggest. Frey traces the development of regional and communal differences in the pre- and post-independence periods and their consequences for domestic as well as Indo–Pakistan relations. He also assesses the direct impact of Indo–Pakistan conflicts on the two countries in terms of increased defence spending and other costs.

588 **Kashmir: a study in India–Pakistan relations.**
Sisir Gupta. London: Asia Publishing House, 1966. 511p. bibliog.
This is the most authoritative statement from an Indian writer on Kashmir, and a work whose careful analysis of all aspects of the situation makes it invaluable for any serious student of the subject. Gupta traces the course of the conflict from the period just before independence, through the tangled events of the 1947-49 period and the initial involvement of the United Nations, to the stalemate in the 1950s. A final chapter reviews possible ways forward. The work was completed before the 1965 war, but Gupta reviews its implications in a brief preface.

589   **South Asia: too late to remove the bomb.**
Richard N. Haass.   *Orbis*, vol. 32, no. 1 (Winter 1988), p. 107-18.
After reviewing recent developments, especially in the nuclear field, Haass concludes that Indo–Pakistan relations remain very unstable. He argues that the USA has no option but to be involved in the region but that the margin for error is very small.

590   **The process of priority formulation: US foreign policy in the Indo–Pakistani war of 1971.**
Dan Haendel.   Boulder, Colorado: Westview Press, 1977. 428p. bibliog.
Originally a dissertation and making little effort to hide its origins, this work discusses the relevance of a range of theoretical models to the events of 1971. Haendel is particularly concerned to see how far US decisions, for example to maintain formal neutrality, can be explained in terms of a theory of rational choice.

591   **Nuclear proliferation: Islam, the bomb and South Asia.**
Rodney W. Jones, foreword by Amos A. Jordan, Jr.   Beverly Hills, California; London: Sage Publications, 1981. 88p. bibliog. (Washington Papers, vol. 9, no. 82).
A US policy-oriented analysis of Pakistan's and India's nuclear programmes which assesses the chances of restricting the proliferation of nuclear weapons in the South Asian region. Written at the beginning of the 1980s, it covers only the first few years of the two countries' nuclear programmes but is useful both for its succinct and balanced account of developments and for its analysis of the issues at stake in discussions of nuclear proliferation in the region.

592   **Danger in Kashmir.**
Josef Korbel.   Princeton, New Jersey: Princeton University Press, 1954. 351p. 2 maps. bibliog.
An early but still valuable account of the Kashmir dispute by a member of the UN commission which tried in the early stages to bring about an agreed solution. Korbel describes the background and origins of the dispute and then goes into detail on the work of the UN and its representatives. Appendices include relevant UN documents.

593   **The Indus rivers: a study of the effects of partition.**
Aloys Arthur Michel.   New Haven, Connecticut; London: Yale University Press, 1967. 595p. 9 maps. bibliog.
The Indus Waters Treaty of 1960, concluded with the help of the World Bank, brought to an end years of uncertainty and recrimination between India and Pakistan over the use for irrigation of the Indus and its tributaries, which pay no heed to the boundaries established in 1947. Michel's study traces the development of irrigation in the region before 1947, the political consequences of partition in 1947, the framing of the treaty and its subsequent implementation in the two countries. Most of his fieldwork was carried out in Pakistan rather than India. A detailed account of the negotiations that produced the treaty is *Indus waters treaty: an exercise in international mediation*, by Niranjan D. Gulhati (Bombay: Allied Publishers, 1973). Gulhati was head of the Indian negotiators during the critical stages. Both his and Michel's works include the text of the treaty.

The Indo–Pak clash in the Rann of Kutch.
See item no. 543.

Pakistan's nuclear development.
See item no. 547.

The first round: Indo–Pakistan War 1965.
See item no. 548.

Going nuclear.
See item no. 554.

Pakistan's foreign policy: an historical analysis.
See item no. 559.

The frontiers of Pakistan: a study of frontier problems in Pakistan's foreign policy.
See item no. 570.

Economy

594 The impact of international migration on economic development in Pakistan.
Jonathan Addleton. *Asian Survey*, vol. 24, no. 5 (May 1984), p. 574-96.
The focus of this article is migration to the Gulf in the 1970s. Addleton looks at the size and composition of the flows of workers, at government policy, at the impact on the economy, especially through the way the workers' remittances were invested, and finally at the consequences of declining rates of migration and remittances.

595 The management of Pakistan's economy, 1947-82.
Viqar Ahmed, Rashid Amjad. Karachi: Oxford University Press, 1984. 315p. (UGC Monograph Series in Economics).
This work was written primarily for economics students in Pakistan but would be valuable for anyone wanting basic data and information on trends in the Pakistan economy since independence. It contains sections on the macro framework, economic decision-making in a historical perspective, agriculture, industrial and commercial policies, and the financing of economic development.

596 Trade, finance and development in Pakistan.
J. Russell Andrus, Azizali F. Mohammed. Karachi: Oxford University Press, 1966. 289p. bibliog.
A largely descriptive work which deals first with the importance of trade to Pakistan's development and then with a number of aspects of the banking system and public finance. A final chapter covers development planning. The same authors published *The Economy of Pakistan* in 1958 (London: Oxford University Press).

597 Annual Report.
Karachi: State Bank of Pakistan. annual.
Published a few months after the end of each financial year, the *Annual Report* is in two

parts. The first reviews the general state of the economy and the current situation with respect to the money supply, banking, public finance, etc. The second is a statistical appendix which provides detailed figures on selected economic indicators, national accounts, agriculture, manufacturing and mining, money and banking, the capital market, prices, the balance of payments, foreign trade and government finance. Although there is some overlap with the *Economic Survey* (q.v.) the authors of the State Bank document are more detached in tone and cover financial issues in considerably more detail. The *Bulletin* of the State Bank, published monthly, contains items of economic news and information, but most of its space is given over to statistical tables which more or less duplicate and update those in the *Annual Report*.

598 **Pakistan's development priorities: choices for the future.**
Edited by Shahid Javed Burki, Robert LaPorte, Jr.   Karachi: Oxford University Press, 1984. 390p.

A collection of articles by leading economists on the state of the Pakistan economy at the beginning of the Sixth Plan period. The book is organized into sections dealing with the historical background to the economy, sectoral priorities in agriculture, industry and resource mobilization, human resource development and delivery systems. A concluding chapter identifies priorities for the attention of the country's economic planners. The sections dealing with sectoral priorities and human resources are perhaps the most valuable, but the book as a whole is an important, if in some respects over-optimistic, review of the state of the economy in the 1980s. A shorter version of S. Lieberman's article on population was published in *Population and Development Review*, vol. 8, no. 1 (March 1982), p. 85-120, under the title 'Demographic perspectives on Pakistan's development'.

599 **Pakistan: energy planning in a strategic vortex.**
Charles K. Ebinger.   Bloomington, Indiana: Indiana University Press, 1981. 155p. map. bibliog.

This is a policy-oriented study by a US expert on the energy situation facing Pakistan after the oil price rises of the 1970s. He concludes that Pakistan faces a serious energy crisis and that its nature and the solutions to it are as much political as economic. The international implications are also drawn out.

600 **Economic Survey.**
Islamabad: Government of Pakistan, Ministry of Finance, Economic Adviser's Wing. annual.

Produced each year on the eve of the budget, i.e. in June, the *Economic Survey* reviews the general state of the economy in the previous financial year (in Pakistan, July-June). A lengthy statistical appendix provides time-series data on all important economic indicators, including estimates for the year under review. Much of the material is very detailed and the commentary naturally reflects current government concerns. Used with care the *Economic Survey* is the best starting point for serious economic analysis. From 1986 onwards, a *Statistical Supplement* has been issued in October to complete the figures for the previous financial year.

Economy

601 **Development policy II – the Pakistan experience.**
Edited by Walter P. Falcon, Gustav F. Papanek. Cambridge,
Massachusetts: Harvard University Press, 1971. 267p.

A series of essays on specific aspects of Pakistan's economic development by members
of Harvard's Development Advisory Service. Topics covered include agriculture,
exports, and entrepreneurship. Although the individual authors have mostly written
elsewhere on their subjects, the collection is a useful one and illustrates the prevalent
policy orientation at the time. An earlier volume, *Development policy – theory and
practice*, edited by Gustav F. Papanek (Cambridge, Massachusetts: Harvard University
Press, 1968), contains three papers relating to Pakistan.

602 **Growth and inequality in Pakistan.**
Edited by Keith Griffin, Azizur Rahman Khan. London: Macmillan,
St Martin's Press, 1972. 282p. bibliog.

This is a collection of articles published for the most part in the *Pakistan Development
Review* in the second half of the 1960s, in which the authors question some of the
assumptions that had been made in development economics generally and specifically
in the case of Pakistan. Criticism is directed against a number of other economists,
Gustav Papanek for example, who worked in Pakistan during the 1960s. Their main
concern is with the implications for equality of the type of growth-oriented policies
pursued during the 1960s. Some of the contributions deal directly with questions of
income distribution, others look at the implications for such questions of agricultural
and industrial policy.

603 **A compendium of Pakistan's economy.**
Irfan-ul-Haque. Karachi: Royal Book Company, 1987. 461p. bibliog.

This is a collection of 61 previously published papers and articles on various aspects of
the economy. Regrettably, no indication is given as to the date or place of original
publication, but for the most part they were written during the 1980s for economic and
financial magazines in Pakistan. Many relate to the general state of the economy but
there are others on monetary policy and other macro-economic issues and on industry,
agriculture, and trade. The papers are very often based on government statistics and
provide an easy way into them, although the articles also assume considerable
background knowledge of the economy.

604 **Domestic resource mobilization in Pakistan: selected issues.**
Nizar Jetha, Shamshad Akhtar, Govinda Rao. Washington, DC:
World Bank, 1984. 133p. (World Bank Staff Working Papers, no. 632).

The question of raising the domestic savings rate by mobilizing additional resources
either through taxation or through private savings has been a major policy issue in
Pakistan for a number of years. This World Bank study reviews the situation in respect
of direct and indirect taxation, personal saving and company saving, and makes a
number of recommendations with a view to raising the overall levels. Appendices
outline in a clear and simple way the taxation structure at the time the report was
written.

160

605 **The economic growth of Pakistan.**
Sergei Kamanev [*sic*, Kamenev].   Lahore: Vanguard Books, 1985.
169p. bibliog.
This is a general review of Pakistan's economy by a Soviet scholar. Kamenev takes as his raw material the national accounts produced since 1947 and found in various official statistical publications. He then uses these data to discuss the structure of the economy, for example industrial and agricultural production and public finance, and how it has changed over time. The study ends in 1971.

606 **The political economy of Pakistan.**
Shahid Kardar.   Lahore: Progressive Publishers, 1987. 318p.
This is a collection of 29 newspaper and magazine articles published in the 1984-86 period mainly in *Dawn*, *Viewpoint*, and the *Herald*. Many aspects of economic policy are covered by the writer, a journalist and economist who is highly critical of the current social and economic system in Pakistan.

607 **Money and banking in Pakistan.**
S. A. Meenai.   Karachi: Oxford University Press, 1984. 3rd ed. 308p.
bibliog.
This standard work by a senior official of the State Bank of Pakistan aims at and achieves a comprehensive review of the subject. First issued in 1967, the book describes the various categories of banks and credit institutions in the country, and then discusses the way monetary policy is handled. A final chapter in the third edition looks at Islamization and the moves to switch to non-interest-based forms of lending.

608 **Asian drama: an inquiry into the poverty of nations.**
Gunnar Myrdal.   New York: Twentieth Century Fund, 1968. 3 vols.
2 maps. (A Twentieth Century Fund Study).
This justly famous work takes South Asia as its principal example in its discussion of the many political, social and economic factors which affect the ability of Asian countries to achieve equitable and stable forms of development. There is a separate chapter on Pakistan's political problems, and the country is mentioned frequently in other sections of the work.

609 **Pakistan's economy through the seventies.**
Syed Nawab Haider Naqvi, Khwaja Sarmad.   Islamabad: Pakistan
Institute of Development Economics, 1984. 180p. bibliog.
The authors provide a thorough review, based on an extensive statistical appendix, of what happened to the Pakistan economy between 1969/70 and 1979/80 in terms of agricultural and industrial production, domestic resource availability, foreign trade, and aid and development. They identify a series of long-term problems which were not resolved despite the relatively good annual growth rates in GDP. A related study which looks at the whole period since independence is by Khwaja Sarmad, *A review of Pakistan's development experience (1949–50 to 1979–80)* (Islamabad: Pakistan Institute of Development Economics, 1984 [Research Reports Series, no. 140]).

Economy

610 Pakistan and Gulf Economist.
Karachi: Economist Publications, 1960- . weekly.

Published from 1960 to 1982 as the *Pakistan Economist*, this is a general economic and political magazine which carries articles on a wide range of topics related to Pakistan, the Gulf, and world affairs generally. There is a short statistical section at the end of each issue.

611 Pakistan: Country Report.
London: Economist Intelligence Unit, 1955- . quarterly.

Previously entitled *Quarterly Economic Review*, this examines current trends in the economy under such thematic headings as agriculture, industry, energy, foreign trade, and aid and development. There is also a section on political developments. The reports aim to interpret as well as to describe. An annually updated *Country Profile* places current economic and political developments in longer-term perspective.

612 Pakistan Development Review.
Islamabad: Pakistan Institute of Development Economics, 1960- . quarterly.

This is the main journal for professional discussion of development issues in Pakistan. Some papers are highly technical but many are accessible to the non-professional. Some articles published in the journal are subsequently incorporated into books or are collected into edited works. Other important articles are not, however, and research on any aspect of Pakistan's economic development should begin with the *Review*. As well as economics in the narrow sense, it also includes frequent contributions on demographic and other issues.

613 Pakistan Economic and Social Review.
Lahore: University of the Punjab, Department of Economics, 1952- . biannual.

This longstanding journal is concerned primarily with issues of economic development and with related social questions.

614 Lectures on development strategy, growth, equity and the political process in southern Asia.
Gustav F. Papanek. Islamabad: Pakistan Institute of Development Economics, 1986. 147p. bibliog. (Lectures in Development Economics, no. 5).

This volume includes the text of three lectures by Papanek in Islamabad in which he compares the results of the different economic strategies pursued in Pakistan, India, Bangladesh, Sri Lanka and Indonesia in terms of growth and equity, and the relationship between the two. He is keenly aware of the political dimension. The discussion that his lectures provoked, much of which focused on the Pakistan experience, is reproduced *in extenso*, as are the comments at each lecture of Syed Nawab Haider Naqvi.

615 **Pakistan's development: social goals and private incentives.**
Gustav F. Papanek.   Cambridge, Massachusetts: Harvard University
Press, 1967; Karachi: Oxford University Press, 1968. 354p. bibliog.

Papanek was one of the earliest and most important of the foreign advisers who
worked in Pakistan during the 1950s and 1960s, and this is his most important study of
the country's economy. In it he outlines and applauds what he regards as the sensible
and pragmatic approach taken by the Ayub Khan government towards the private
sector. The final chapter is titled 'The social utility of greed'. There is a substantial
statistical appendix.

616 **Economic development in South Asia: proceedings of a conference held**
by the International Economic Association at Kandy, Ceylon.
Edited by E. A. G. Robinson, Michael Kidron.   London: Macmillan,
St Martin's Press, 1970. 585p.

The papers collected here arose from a concern to compare the economic experiences
of India and Pakistan in their quests for development. A conference was subsequently
held in the late 1960s at which for the most part paired papers by Indian and Pakistani
economists on such topics as agricultural development, the role of the public sector,
choice of techniques, trade and foreign aid were presented and discussed. The volume
includes brief summaries of the discussions that took place on the papers.

617 **The economy of Pakistan: a select bibliography.**
Akhtar H. Siddiqui.   Karachi: Institute of Development Economics,
1963. 162p.

Siddiqui brings together 4,248 items on the economy of Pakistan, many of them from
highly specialized periodicals. The entries are arranged under subject headings, but
there are no annotations. A supplement was published in 1967 covering the period
1963–65. Siddiqui is the compiler of many other bibliographies, for example
Agriculture in Pakistan: a selected bibliography (Rawalpindi: United States Agency for
International Development, 1969) and *A guide to Pakistan government publications,*
1958–70 (Karachi: National Book Centre, 1973).

618 **Growth and development in Pakistan 1955–1969.**
Joseph J. Stern, Walter P. Falcon.   Cambridge, Massachusetts: Center
for International Studies, Harvard University, 1970. 88p. (Occasional
Papers in International Affairs, no. 23).

A useful and compact review of Pakistan's economic development from the inception
of planning in 1955 to the end of the Ayub Khan period. The agricultural, industrial
and social sectors are examined in turn.

619 **The economic consequences of divided India: a study of the economy of**
India and Pakistan.
C. N. Vakil.   Bombay: Vora, 1950. 555p. bibliog.

This work, to which a number of scholars besides Vakil also contributed, provides a
benchmark for studies of the later development of the Pakistan economy, as well as
providing detailed material on the immediate impact of the partition and economic
relations between India and Pakistan. Chapters cover the refugee problem, agriculture,
industry, mining, transport, trade and finance.

Economy

620 **World Development Report.**
World Bank.   New York: Oxford University Press, 1978- . annual.
This is an annual publication which provides an easy and reliable way to view a country's economy in comparison with others. The first part of each report reviews trends in the world economy, particularly as they affect Third World countries. The second, 'World development indicators', is a set of 30 or so statistical tables covering topics ranging from the structure of production and balance of payments to demographic trends and social indicators.

Pakistan: its resources and development.
See item no. 30.

The Cambridge Economic History of India.
See item no. 108.

Class structure and economic development: India and Pakistan since the Moghuls.
See item no. 115.

Economic history of Pakistan.
See item no. 258.

The export of manpower from Pakistan to the Middle East, 1975–1985.
See item no. 322.

Pakistan in its fourth decade: current political, social, and economic situation and prospects for the 1980s.
See item no. 487.

Islam and development: the Zia regime in Pakistan.
See item no. 516.

Islamic reassertion in Pakistan: the application of Islamic laws in a modern state.
See item no. 522.

Pakistan's nuclear dilemma: energy and security dimensions.
See item no. 579.

Planning

621 The first five year plan, 1955–60.
Karachi: Government of Pakistan, National Planning Board, 1958.
652p. map.

An earlier version of the plan had been published in May 1956 but was then withdrawn because of opposition from landed interests annoyed by some of the recommendations. The final version was approved in April 1957, nearly halfway through the plan period (which ran from April 1955 to March 1960). The document reviews the general state of the economy in both the private and the public sectors and then makes its recommendations, setting targets, identifying projects and proposing policy measures as necessary. The overall aim was a growth in gross national product (GNP) during the plan period of approximately 15 per cent. Considerable emphasis was placed on agriculture and irrigation.

622 The second five year plan (1960–65).
Karachi: Government of Pakistan, Planning Commission, 1960. 414p.

Prepared by the government of Ayub Khan and reflecting his pragmatic orientation, this is a somewhat shorter document than that prepared for the first plan, although the basic approach to development remained much the same. The second five-year plan achieved many of its objectives. *A final evaluation of the second five-year plan (1960–65)*, was published by the Planning Commission in 1966.

623 The third five year plan (1965–70).
Karachi: Government of Pakistan, Planning Commission, 1968. 605p.
map.

An initial draft of the third plan was published in August 1964 to elicit comments. It then had to be revised in the light of financial and other difficulties flowing from the September 1965 war with India. The revisions are indicated in a separately paginated 36-page appendix, 'Revised phasing, sectoral priorities and allocations of the third five year plan (1965–70)'.

Planning

624 **The fourth five year plan (1970–75).**
Islamabad: Government of Pakistan, Planning Commission, 1970.
574p.

Produced in the period immediately after the agitation against President Ayub and as the crisis over East Pakistan was beginning to develop, the fourth plan reflects these developments, although it follows the standard pattern of describing each specific sector of the economy and setting targets to be achieved in the immediate future. *Reports of the advisory panels for the fourth five-year plan* (Islamabad: Government of Pakistan, Planning Commission, 1970, 2 vols), published at the same time, gives a clearer picture of the differences among economists over the direction the plan should take. The first volume in fact consists of separate reports submitted by the East and West Pakistani members of the general panel.

625 **The fifth five year plan (1978–83).**
Karachi: Government of Pakistan, Planning Commission, 1978. 266p.

The fourth plan was aborted because of the 1971 civil war and the subsequent change of régime in West Pakistan. After the overthrow of Bhutto, who had used a series of annual plans for economic policy purposes, the Zia régime produced a fifth five-year plan in 1978 which emphasized higher levels of resource mobilization and improved efficiency. As usual, the plan document consists of sections on broad strategy and sectoral programmes and a statistical review.

626 **The sixth five year plan 1983–88.**
Islamabad: Government of Pakistan, Planning Commission, [n.d. (1986)]. 647p.

The document sets out the general planning strategy for the sixth plan (July 1983-June 1988), which was designed to produce GDP growth of 6.5 per cent through greater private sector investment and higher savings levels generally. Each sector of the economy including human resources is given a chapter in which past performance is reviewed and in which targets are set and projects identified for the sixth plan. A statistical appendix sums up past performance and the sixth plan targets.

627 **7th five year plan 1988–93 and perspective plan 1988–2003 (draft).**
Islamabad: Government of Pakistan, Planning Commission, 1988.
714p.

Published a few weeks before the official start of the seventh plan in July 1988 and prepared during the Zia period, this draft follows the pattern of previous plan documents in reviewing the past and setting future targets, although there is no separate statistical section. The seventh plan as set out here continues the emphasis of the sixth on the private sector. The document also includes a perspective plan which sets out the basic economic framework for longer-term development up to 2003.

628 **Studies in development planning.**
Edited by Hollis B. Chenery. Cambridge, Massachusetts: Harvard University Press, 1971. 422p. bibliog. (Harvard Economic Studies, vol. 136).

This collection of rather technical studies in the methodology of economic planning includes two papers on Pakistan: by A. MacEwan on problems of intersectoral and interregional resource allocation in the context of divisions between East and West Pakistan, and by Carl Gotsch on the application of linear programming to problems of agricultural policy.

629 **Development strategy for the sixth plan 1983–88: an IPS task force report.**
Islamabad: Institute of Policy Studies, 1983. 137p.
This is an attempt by a group of economists to produce an alternative strategy for Pakistan's economic development which is more in keeping with an Islamic position. The authors emphasize the importance of achieving development based on indigenous resources and in line with the Islamic principles of justice and welfare. More specifically, they argue for greater investment in agriculture and greater attention to regional development.

630 **Federal and sovereign: a policy framework for the economic development of Pakistan.**
Lahore: Independent Planning Commission, 1985. 179p.
Intended as a blueprint for an alternative path of economic development, this report was produced by a group of left-wing economists, journalists and others to stimulate public debate over the policy issues at stake. The style is deliberately popular. The commission members argue that a radical restructuring and decentralization of power within the country is the only way forward if just and equitable economic development is to take place.

631 **The strategy of economic planning: a case study of Pakistan.**
Mahbub ul Haq.   Karachi: Oxford University Press, 1966. 2nd ed. 266p.
First published in 1963, this has been an influential book in the history of Pakistan planning. The author, who eventually became minister of finance in the 1980s, had been associated earlier with the Planning Commission and here argues for a much bolder approach to planning if Pakistan is to make rapid progress towards self-reliant economic growth.

632 **A short-term model for Pakistan economy: an econometric analysis.**
Nurul Islam.   Lahore; Karachi; Dacca: Oxford University Press, 1965. 148p.
The purpose of an econometric model is to aid decision-makers in their work by indicating the effect of changes in one part of the economy on other parts. In this technical monograph, Islam constructs such a model for the Pakistan economy and organizes existing data to provide a statistical estimation of it.

633 **Planning and development in Pakistan: review and alternatives 1947–1982.**
M. L. Qureshi.   Lahore: Vanguard Books, 1984. 428p.
The author of this critical analysis of Pakistan's development strategy worked both as an academic economist and as a policy-maker, and was at one time chief economist in the Pakistan Planning Commission. In the first part of the book, Qureshi reviews the extent to which past strategies have succeeded in meeting basic needs and achieving

equitable distribution of income. The second part puts forward suggestions for an alternative approach based on decentralization of planning and better use of existing resources.

634 **Western economists and eastern societies.**
George Rosen. Baltimore, Maryland; London: Johns Hopkins University Press, 1985. 270p. (Johns Hopkins Studies in Development).
This interesting book by someone who himself belongs to the group he describes is about the work of the many Western, especially American economists who worked as advisers in South Asia in the 1950s and 1960s under the auspices of the Ford Foundation. In the case of Pakistan this means particularly the Harvard Advisory Group, which exercised a major influence on economic policy during the Ayub Khan period and was involved in the establishment of the Pakistan Institute of Development Economics. Rosen describes the ways in which the initial naive assumptions and 'myths' of some of the advisers had to be modified, but his overall assessment of their impact is positive.

635 **River basin planning: theory and practice.**
Edited by Suranjit K. Saha, Christopher J. Barrow. Chichester, England; New York; Brisbane; Toronto: Wiley, 1981. 357p. maps. bibliog.
The purpose of this volume, which originated in a 1980 colloquium, is to stimulate interest in the practical study of river basin planning. M. J. Shepperdson contributed a paper, 'The development of irrigation in the Indus river basin, Pakistan', p. 191-213, which looks at the demographic, environmental, and socio-economic consequences of the development of irrigation in Pakistan.

636 **Planning in Pakistan: organization and implementation.**
Albert Waterston, assisted by C. J. Martin, Fritz A. Steuber.
Baltimore, Maryland: Johns Hopkins Press, 1963. 150p. map. bibliog.
An early but still useful work which describes in detail the way Pakistan's first three five-year plans were formulated and implemented. Waterston and his colleagues are concerned with such issues as the relationship between the plans and the budgetary policy of the government, which was often at odds with planning objectives.

Pakistan's development priorities: choices for the future.
See item no. 598.

Bestimmungsgründe und Alternativen divergierender regionaler Wachstums-verläufe in Entwicklungsländern: eine theoretische und empirische Analyse unter besonderer Berücksichtigung der Regionalentwicklung in Ost- und Westpakistan, 1947–1970. (Determinants of and alternatives to diverging regional growth paths in developing countries: a theoretical and empirical analysis with special reference to regional development in East and West Pakistan.)
See item no. 649.

Planning for education in Pakistan: a personal case study.
See item no. 693.

Standards of Living

637 **Lebensverhältnisse ländlicher Familien in Westpakistan: eine Typisierung ländlicher Haushalte als Grundlage für entwicklungspolitische Maßnahmen, dargestellt am Beispiel von sechs Dörfern im Distrikt Peshawar, Westpakistan.** (Conditions of life of rural families in West Pakistan: a typology of rural households as a foundation for political development measures, based on the example of six villages in Peshawar district, West Pakistan.) Herbert Albrecht. Saarbrücken, West Germany: Verlag der SSIP-Schriften – D. Breitenbach, 1971. 328p. bibliog. (Sozialökonomische Schriften zur Agrarentwicklung, no. 3).

A socio-economic study of six villages which discusses social stratification, patterns of landholding, consumption levels and other aspects of rural life. Albrecht is concerned to relate changes in type and status of household to stages in family life-cycles.

638 **Rural–urban migration and the urban poor in Pakistan.** V. Belokrenitsky. *Journal of South Asian and Middle Eastern Studies*, vol. 8, no. 1 (Fall 1984), p. 35-46.

The author discusses the economic conditions of the migrants to the towns who have been displaced from the land by the mechanization of agriculture, most of whom have had to search for jobs in the low-productivity 'informal' sector and in service occupations. He examines the social framework of migrants' lives, and concludes that traditional structures continue to play an important part.

639 **Asie du Sud: traditions et changements.** (South Asia: traditions and transformations.)
Edited by Marc Gaborieau, Alice Thorner.   Paris: Éditions du Centre National de la Recherche Scientifique, 1979. 676p. (Colloques Internationaux du Centre National de la Recherche Scientifique).

The most important paper on Pakistan in this conference volume is by M. J. Shepperdson, p. 531-41, 'Health policies and planning in Pakistan'. Shepperdson reviews the overall position on the health front and examines government programmes to improve it, with special attention to the 1965-76 period. He argues that malaria eradication has in the past absorbed a disproportionate share of resources.

640 **Long-term trends in income distribution in Pakistan.**
Stephen Guisinger, Norman L. Hicks.   *World Development*, vol. 6, nos 11-12 (Nov.-Dec. 1978), p. 1271-80.

A review of the evidence on income distribution from 1951 to 1975 using data from a variety of sources. The authors conclude, contrary to both popular perception and orthodox economic theory, that income inequality did not worsen in the 1964-72 period of relatively rapid economic growth, largely because of rises in agricultural incomes. Their tentative conclusion for the 1972-75 period is that while the real wages of some sectors of the organized industrial workforce may have risen, stagnation elsewhere meant that overall income inequality increased.

641 **The structure of disparity in developing agriculture: a case study of the Pakistan Punjab.**
Shigemochi Hirashima.   Tokyo: Institute of Developing Economies, 1978. 138p. bibliog. (I.D.E. Occasional Papers Series, no. 16).

The existence of sharp disparities of income between landowners and landless which do not disappear as a result of the type of agricultural development experienced in countries such as Pakistan is treated in this case-study as a historically based phenomenon. Hirashima goes back to the introduction of irrigation during the late 19th century to show how institutional and technological factors interact to sustain existing disparities.

642 **Working with statistics of quality of life: Pakistan, 1960 to 1983.**
Haroon Jamal, Salman Malik.   *The Developing Economies*, vol. 25, no. 3 (Sept. 1987), p. 270-80.

A pioneering effort to construct a physical quality of life index for Pakistan for the period stated, using data from official sources. A physical quality of life index seeks to measure a country's progress in social rather than narrowly economic terms, for example in the fields of health and education. The authors conclude that over the 23 years studied Pakistan has made no major breakthroughs.

643 **Poverty in rural Asia.**
Edited by Azizur Rahman Khan, Eddie Lee.   Bangkok: International Labour Organization Asian Employment Programme, 1984. 276p.

This volume produced under the auspices of the ILO looks at the extent and nature of poverty in rural Asia. M. Irfan and Rashid Amjad contribute a chapter on poverty in rural Pakistan (p. 19-47). In it they review the findings of empirical research in the 1960s and 1970s. They find that the evidence remains insufficient for firm conclusions but that the major economic changes that took place in agriculture during this time did not necessarily lead to much amelioration of poverty.

644 **Welfare implications of sugar pricing in Pakistan.**
Mahmood Hasan Khan. *Food Policy*, vol. 11, no. 3 (Aug. 1986), p. 253-8.
Khan reviews the consequences of the high levels of protection given to sugar producers in Pakistan since the mid-1970s. These have led to a rapid increase in output but not to increases in productivity. Using partial equilibrium analysis, he argues that private profit has been at the expense of the consumer.

645 **The quality of life in Pakistan: studies in social sector economics.**
Edited by Ijaz Nabi. Lahore: Vanguard Books, 1986. 401p. bibliog.
A series of important studies, some of them reprinted from specialist journals, on the less tangible aspects of economic development which nevertheless have a major bearing on the well-being of the individual. The initial section contains articles on the overall position of Pakistan in comparison with other countries, and on the regional position internally. Thereafter there are sections on health, education, and housing. Where necessary, the studies are technical, but most are easy for the non-specialist to follow. Except for the introduction, the articles do not go beyond 1982 in their coverage.

646 **Underdevelopment, poverty and inequality in Pakistan.**
S. M. Naseem. Lahore: Vanguard Books, 1981. 323p. bibliog.
The author, a distinguished economist, examines Pakistan's economic performance since independence so as to survey in an integrated fashion 'the consequences of the economic strategies and policies adopted during the period, for economic development, income redistribution and poverty alleviation'. Naseem is particularly concerned with the agrarian situation.

647 **Rural poverty in South Asia.**
Edited by T. N. Srinivasan, Pranab K. Bardhan. New York: Columbia University Press, 1988. 565p.
Most of this substantial volume is concerned with India but one article by Shahid Javed Burki, 'Poverty in Pakistan: myth or reality?', p. 69-88, considers Pakistan. Burki's argument is that Pakistan no longer suffers quite the same acute poverty that it did up to the 1970s and as is to be found elsewhere in South Asia, partly because of labour migration to the Middle East and partly because of the economic development that has taken place both in industry and in agriculture. He points, however, to the difficulties in interpreting the available data.

648 **The political economy of healthcare in Pakistan.**
S. Akbar Zaidi. Lahore: Vanguard Books, 1988. 342p.
This is a series of separate studies on the general subject of the provision of healthcare facilities in Pakistan. As the title indicates, the author links the problems he identifies, such as the urban bias in the provision of medical services in Pakistan, to structural

characteristics of Pakistan society. Nearly half the work is taken up by a survey-based study entitled 'Medical students: their socio-economic background and urban choice', carried out jointly with Salman Malik in 1984. For this, 358 students in Sindh medical colleges were interviewed. The paper includes the tabulated results and the full text of a number of the interviews.

Growth and inequality in Pakistan.
See item no. 602.

Regional disparities

649 **Bestimmungsgründe und Alternativen divergierender regionaler Wachstumsverläufe in Entwicklungsländern: eine theoretische und empirische Analyse unter besonderer Berücksichtigung der Regionalentwicklung in Ost- und Westpakistan, 1947–1970.**
(Determinants of and alternatives to diverging regional growth paths in developing countries: a theoretical and empirical analysis with special reference to regional development in East and West Pakistan.) Heinz-Dietmar Ahrens.   Wiesbaden, West Germany: Franz Steiner Verlag, 1978. 392p. bibliog. (Beiträge zur Südasienforschung Südasien-Institut Universität Heidelberg, vol. 42).
This is a mathematically based study of economic development strategies designed to maximize overall growth and regional distribution at the same time. Ahrens sets up a simulation exercise to test what the effects of different strategies might have been in the case of East and West Pakistan. There is practical discussion of such issues as transfer of foreign exchange from one wing to the other and the allocation of foreign aid.

650 **Die Problematik regionaler Entwicklungsunterschiede in Entwicklungsländern: eine theoretische und empirische Analyse dargestellt am beispiel Pakistans unter Verwendung der Hauptkomponentenmethode.**
(The problem of regional differences in development in developing countries: a theoretical and empirical analysis based on the example of Pakistan through the use of the principal components method.) Wolfgang-Peter Zingel.   Wiesbaden, West Germany: Franz Steiner Verlag, 1979. 554p. maps. bibliog. (Beiträge zur Südasienforschung Südasien-Institut Universität Heidelberg, vol. 51).
Using rigorous statistical methods, Zingel explores the degree and nature of regional disparities in economic development in Pakistan up to the beginning of the 1970s. He establishes a basis on which to classify all the districts of the country. He then examines the possible explanations for these differences in terms of past government policy.

Pakistan: failure in national integration.
See item no. 257.

Private industrial investment in Pakistan 1960–1980.
See item no. 652.

Industry

651 **Entrepreneurship in the Third World: risk and uncertainty in industry
in Pakistan.**
Zafar Altaf.   London; New York; Sydney: Croom Helm, 1988. 224p.
bibliog.

This book discusses different types of entrepreneurial behaviour in Pakistan in the light
of the specific political environment there. The author blames the propensity of
successive governments to intervene in the economy for producing an unstable
situation for entrepreneurial activity. The value of the work is rather reduced by poor
organization and layout. An earlier work by Altaf on the same subject is *Pakistani
entrepreneurs* (London: Croom Helm, 1983).

652 **Private industrial investment in Pakistan 1960–1980.**
Rashid Amjad.   Cambridge, England: Cambridge University Press,
1982. 257p. bibliog. (Cambridge South Asian Studies, no. 26).

This important work studies levels of investment in industry in the 1960s and seeks to
explain the high rates in the early years of the decade and the markedly lower ones
after 1965. The author finds the key factor to be foreign aid inflows, high levels of
which combined with an overvalued exchange rate permitted highly profitable
investment to be made in the earlier period. After 1965 a foreign exchange constraint
and the imposition of controls on investment limited new projects. The author draws
attention to the concentration of control over industrial assets in this period and to the
increase in interregional inequality, as well as to the higher levels of foreign
indebtedness that resulted from the policies followed.

653 **The structure of protection in developing countries.**
Bela Balassa and associates.   Baltimore, Maryland; London: Johns
Hopkins Press, 1971. 375p.

This is a study for the World Bank and the Inter-American Development Bank on
protection of industries, a major topic in development economics. Seven countries

174

were studied following a common methodology. The study of Pakistan is by Stephen R. Lewis, Jr. and Stephen E. Guisinger. They describe the complex system used at the time to protect Pakistan's nascent industries, especially the system of multiple exchange rates.

654 **Foreign aid and industrial development in Pakistan.**
Irving Brecher, S. A. Abbas.   London: Cambridge University Press, 1972. 271p. bibliog. (Perspectives on Development, no. 1).
A specialized study of the interaction between flows of foreign aid to Pakistan up to the late 1960s and economic development, particularly in the industrial sector. A series of case-studies are presented in both the public and private sectors. The authors conclude that aid during the period studied was a major factor in Pakistan's growth but that to be effective aid must always be tied to appropriate institutional change in the recipient country, not least so as to avoid increasing income disparities.

655 **Pakistan: industrialization and trade policies.**
Stephen R. Lewis, Jr.   London; New York; Karachi: Oxford University Press for OECD, Paris, 1970. 214p. bibliog.
A technical study of the impact of government policy towards manufacturing exports on the rate and composition of industrial growth. The work is valuable for its description of the various policy instruments and its statistical appendix, as well as for its discussion of the rapid industrial growth that occurred in the 1960s, and of the effect of policy on regional disparities between East and West Pakistan.

656 **Pakistan's big businessmen: Muslim separatism, entrepreneurship, and partial modernization.**
Hanna Papanek.   *Economic Development and Cultural Change*, vol. 21, no. 1 (Oct. 1972), p. 1-32.
This is an important study of the role played by migrants from India, especially Bombay and Gujarat, in the development of an indigenous capitalist class. Papanek sets the business activities of the largest families in historical and sociological context.

657 **Industrial concentration and economic power in Pakistan.**
Lawrence J. White.   Princeton, New Jersey: Princeton University Press, 1974. 212p. bibliog.
This study, using tools derived from the study of industrial organization in developed countries, looks at the degree of concentration of industrial control in Pakistan in the late 1960s, a period when the position of the so-called '22 families' who owned much of the organized sector of industry as well as banks was under public scrutiny. White seeks to understand how such concentrations occur and their likely economic and non-economic effects. He concludes with a review of the initial measures taken by the incoming Bhutto government at the beginning of 1972.

Interest groups and development: business and politics in Pakistan.
See item no. 467.

Agriculture

658 **Pakistan: the political economy of rural development.**
Edited by Karamat Ali. Lahore: Vanguard Books, 1982. 381p.
This is a useful collection of twelve articles on various aspects of Pakistan's agricultural sector, with the general theme of the two-way interaction between technological change and political power. Topics covered include land reform, agricultural taxation and the introduction of tractors into agriculture. All but the first and last articles are reprinted from various specialist journals, some of which would not easily be available except in a large library.

659 **Irrigation development planning: aspects of Pakistan experience.**
I. D. Carruthers. Ashford, England: Wye College, Department of Economics, 1968. 67p. bibliog. maps. (Agrarian Development Studies, no. 2).
A study of the economic factors affecting the design of irrigation projects, based on practical experience of work in the lower Indus region. The author discusses the best methods of project appraisal and concludes with a discussion of the vital but very sensitive issues of pricing policy and agricultural taxation.

660 **An appraisal of wheat market policy in Pakistan.**
Peter A. Cornelisse, Syed Nawab Haider Naqvi. *World Development*, vol. 17, no. 3 (March 1989), p. 409-19.
This is a brief article based on a large-scale research project into current policies towards wheat marketing and the role of government agencies. The article argues for a more market-oriented approach in view of the improvement in the levels of wheat production since the 1960s.

661 **Irrigation and drainage in the world: a global review.**
K. K. Framji, I. K. Mahajan. New Delhi: International Commission
on Irrigation and Drainage, 1969. 2nd ed. 2 vols.

First published in 1955, this work provides a comprehensive review of the subject in all
the world's major countries. Pakistan is dealt with in the second volume, p. 791-847.
The chapter reviews the climatic and geological background and then lists the main
irrigation works that have been constructed. It also deals with the drainage schemes
that have been put in hand from 1959 onwards to deal with the serious problems of
waterlogging and salinity that have developed in the wake of irrigation projects. It also
covers the legal and administrative aspects of the subject.

662 **Prices, taxes and subsidies in Pakistan agriculture, 1960–1976.**
Carl Gotsch, Gilbert Brown. Washington, DC: World Bank, 1980.
108p. map. (World Bank Staff Working Paper, no. 387).

This is a technical paper intended for economists and others involved in agricultural
policy-making. The particular focus is on the relationship between prices paid to the
farmer (fixed or heavily influenced by government) and agricultural investment. The
authors conclude that although for political reasons prices paid for some crops have
been kept artificially low, in general price levels were sufficient to allow for steady
growth in the period studied.

663 **Impact of agricultural research and extension on crop productivity in
Pakistan: a production function approach.**
Mahmood Hasan Khan, Ather Hussain Akbari. *World Development*,
vol. 14, no. 6 (June 1986), p. 757-62.

A brief review of the subject using advanced statistical techniques. The authors
conclude that in the past Pakistan has invested low amounts in these areas and that the
marginal return on further investment would be very high.

664 **Irrigation management in Pakistan: four papers.**
Douglas J. Merrey, James M. Wolf. Digana, Sri Lanka: International
Irrigation Management Institute, 1986. 66p. maps. bibliog. (IIMI
Research Paper, no. 4).

The papers included in this volume review the irrigation situation in Pakistan and
attempt to provide some answers to the question of why an area which, with irrigation,
could be highly fertile has not fulfilled its potential. The three papers by Merrey look
at local-level sociological and ecological processes which affect the way the irrigation
system operates. That by Wolf is concerned with how the operation and maintenance
of the system is funded.

665 **The agrarian economy of Pakistan: issues and policies.**
Ijaz Nabi, Naved Hamid, Shahid Zahid. Karachi: Oxford University
Press, 1986. 337p. bibliog. (UGC Monograph Series in Economics).

Intended for professional economists and advanced students, this work provides a
sophisticated review of alternative theoretical approaches to the study of agricultural
development, and then examines in detail the relationship between farm size and
productivity, tenancy, linear programming approaches to farmers' decision-making,
and rural–urban migration. The three authors make the best of the available data.

666 **Land reforms in Pakistan: a historical perspective.**
Edited by Syed Nawab Haider Naqvi, Mahmood Hasan Khan, M.
Ghaffar Chaudhry. Islamabad: Pakistan Institute of Development
Economics, 1987. 216p.

This is in fact a collection of key documents illustrating the history of proposals to
change the structure of landholding in Pakistan up to 1959. Included in the volume, in
whole or in large part, are the reports of the Government Hari Enquiry Committee,
1947-48 (together with a minute of dissent by M. Masud); the Agrarian Committee
appointed by the Pakistan Muslim League, 1949; the Land Reforms Commission,
1959; and chapter seventeen of the first five-year plan. There is an introductory chapter
by the editors which sets the documents in context and concludes that little has actually
happened to change the rural status quo.

667 **The green revolution in Pakistan: implications of technological change.**
Leslie Nulty, foreword by Arthur Gaitskell. New York; Washington;
London: Praeger, 1972. 150p. map. bibliog. (Praeger Special Studies in
International Economics and Development).

This useful although now rather dated study looks at the substantial increases in
agricultural output, mainly wheat, that were beginning to be achieved in the late 1960s,
within the wider context of the Pakistan economy. She argues that some farmers in
Pakistan were well placed to take advantage of the increased availability of water and
fertilizer but that without corresponding changes in the distribution of land the benefits
of agricultural development were likely to remain concentrated in the hands of a few.
She also argues against the need to maintain artificially high prices for agricultural
products as a means of stimulating production.

668 **Political regimes, public policy and economic development: agricultural
performance and rural change in two Punjabs.**
Holly Sims. New Delhi; Newbury Park, California; London: Sage,
1988. 206p.

The Punjab before 1947 was a single geographical unit, and the fate of the two halves
after a purely political division therefore becomes an interesting issue for comparative
economic and political study. The demonstrably superior agricultural performance of
Indian Punjab is attributed in this carefully researched study, which included intensive
interviews with farmers on both sides of the border, to the impact of greater political
participation in the Indian political system and to a more effective administrative
system. An earlier study of the same subject, which looked primarily at output
comparisons, was by Chandra Prabha, 'Districtwise rates of growth in agricultural
output in East and West Punjab during the pre-partition and post-partition periods',
Indian Economic and Social History Review, vol. 6, no. 4 (Dec. 1969), p. 347-50.

669 **Rural development in Pakistan.**
Edited by Richard Stanford. Durham, North Carolina: Carolina
Academic Press, 1980. 164p. bibliog.

This is a set of short papers which emerged out of a visit to Pakistan in 1973 by a group
of American academics. The writers are mainly Pakistani academics and government
officials who met and talked with the group in order to explain to it the problems of
rural development in Pakistan and the way the government had tried to tackle them.
The tone of most of the papers is simple and straightforward and the volume as a

whole would be useful as background for undergraduate students of economic development as well as for a wider audience.

670 **Rural development in Bangladesh and Pakistan.**
Edited by Robert D. Stevens, Hamza Alavi, Peter J. Bertocci.
Honolulu, Hawaii: University Press of Hawaii, 1976. 399p. bibliog.
Just over half of the papers in this collection, most of which were originally presented to a conference in 1971, deal with Pakistan. While the general theme is rural development and the interrelationship of economic and social change, the range of topics covered and the disciplinary approaches adopted are quite broad. Stevens identifies the five main themes as agricultural stagnation and growth, the regional effects of agricultural growth, changing political and social relationships, impending crises, and implications for the role of government and political institutions.

The wealth and welfare of the Punjab.
See item no. 180.

Pakistan's rural development.
See item no. 431.

Land to the tiller: the political economy of agrarian reform in South Asia.
See item no. 462.

The economy of Pakistan: a select bibliography.
See item no. 617.

Welfare implications of sugar pricing in Pakistan.
See item no. 644.

The economics of camel transport in Pakistan.
See item no. 677.

West Pakistan: rural education and development.
See item no. 695.

Trade

671 **Exports, politics, and economic development: Pakistan 1970–1982.**
John Adams, Sabiha Iqbal.   Boulder, Colorado: Westview Press,
1983. 257p. bibliog.

The emphasis of this work is very firmly on the political aspects of Pakistan's trade
performance during the Bhutto period and the first five years of President Zia's
régime. The authors argue that policy has to be seen as arising from the interplay of
political interests. They also show how export performance in turn feeds back into the
distribution of income and influence among the groups involved.

672 **Foreign Trade Statistics.**
Islamabad: Government of Pakistan, Federal Bureau of Statistics,
1955- . quarterly.

Initially published on an annual basis, these statistics provide detailed information on
Pakistan's imports and exports of all commodities. The information is summarized in
other statistical publications of the Government of Pakistan, for example the *Statistical
Yearbook*, and these figures would be needed only by those interested in one particular
product or with some other very specialized interest.

673 **Pakistan's trade with Eastern bloc countries.**
Michael Kidron.   New York; Washington; London: Praeger, 1972.
131p.

The author presents a general argument on the economic relationship between Eastern
bloc countries and countries of the South or Third World, and uses Pakistan as a case-
study. Whereas the general argument is based on a theoretical analysis of world power
relations, the case-study is 'austerely empirical'. The book discusses the sharp rise in
Pakistan's trade with Eastern bloc countries in the 1960s, which in 1969-70 reached
11.6 per cent of the total, but concludes that, as in fact turned out to be the case,
prospects for further growth were limited. There is a detailed statistical section.

674 **Pattern of foreign trade of Pakistan.**
Karachi: Chamber of Commerce and Industry, 1984. 2nd ed. 278p.
Based on official sources, this publication summarizes Pakistan's trade with each one of its trading partners. For each country there is a summary statement of the balance of trade from 1969/70 to 1982/83 and a list of the items traded from 1979/80 on. Summary tables are also included. An earlier edition was published in 1977.

Trade, finance and development in Pakistan.
See item no. 596.

The structure of protection in developing countries.
See item no. 653.

Pakistan: industrialization and trade policies.
See item no. 655.

Transport

675 Relics of the Raj.
C. J. Gammell.   London: G.R.Q. Publications, 1985. 96p. maps.

South Asia is well known as the part of the world where steam engines still play a major role in railway transport, and it has duly attracted attention from railway enthusiasts. The present volume is made up mainly of black and white photographs of engines taken in the early 1980s. The Pakistan railway system gets its proportionate share of attention. In addition to the photographs, there is a map of the system and a list of the classes of steam engines in use.

676 Boats and boatmen of Pakistan.
Basil Greenhill.   Newton Abbot, England: David & Charles, 1971. 191p. 2 maps.

Written before the break-up of Pakistan, this work naturally devotes most of its space to the amphibious conditions of East Bengal, but there are two chapters on West Pakistan. One is on the traditional fishing boats of the coast near Karachi, the other on the boats used on the fast-flowing rivers of the northern areas. The fieldwork on which the book is based was mostly carried out in the 1950s. The author is a specialist in traditional methods of boat-building and his work is a significant contribution. The book wears its learning lightly, however, and would be of fairly wide interest.

677 The economics of camel transport in Pakistan.
Alan Heston, H. Hasnain, S. Z. Hussain, R. N. Khan.   *Economic Development and Cultural Change*, vol. 34, no. 1 (Oct. 1985), p. 121-41.

This interesting article reports the results of a survey in 1982 carried out by the Pakistan Agricultural Research Council in order to assess the current position of camels in the Pakistan economy at a time when many of their traditional functions are being performed mechanically. The conclusion is that for some types of activity camel power remains economically competitive, for example short-haul freight in towns and cities, but that the cost of fodder is a key variable.

678 **Hundred years of Pakistan Railways: Pakistan Western Railways**
1861–1961, Pakistan Eastern Railways 1862–1962.
M. B. K. Malik.   Karachi: Government of Pakistan, Ministry of
Railways and Communications, 1962. 226p. 15 maps. bibliog.

Produced under official auspices, this work covers a remarkably wide range of topics, including the expansion of the railway system, details of employee welfare, and the technical details of rolling stock so beloved by enthusiasts. The book is illustrated by many black and white photographs.

Statistics

679 Environment Statistics of Pakistan.
Islamabad: Government of Pakistan, Federal Bureau of Statistics,
Statistical Division, 1984- . annual.

This publication brings together existing statistical data on natural resources, energy, land, human settlement and pollution to provide an overall view of Pakistan's environment, although the preface acknowledges gaps in the coverage.

680 Pakistan Statistical Yearbook.
Karachi: Government of Pakistan, Statistics Division, Federal Bureau
of Statistics, 1952- . annual.

The most authoritative statistical source for Pakistan, this volume provides over 600 pages of statistics covering all aspects of Pakistan life, but with a strong emphasis on the economic. Currently, there are twenty sections including: climate; population; labour; agriculture; manufacturing; energy and mining; transport; money and banking; insurance and joint stock companies; balance of payments; public finance; cooperative societies; health; education; society and culture; national accounts; prices; foreign trade; foreign aid; and development planning. As far as possible, the tables cover the past ten years. The *Yearbook* was first published in 1952 but began to appear on an annual basis only somewhat later. From time to time special retrospective editions are published, for example *Twenty-five years of Pakistan in statistics, 1947–72*.

681 Statistical Pocket Book of Pakistan.
Karachi: Statistics Division, Federal Bureau of Statistics, [c.1962-].
annual.

Closely related to the previous entry, this covers effectively the same fields as the *Yearbook*, except foreign aid, but presents the figures in a much more concise and abbreviated form. In size it lives up to its title.

184

682 **Statistical Yearbook/Annuaire statistique.**
New York: United Nations, [c.1950-]. annual.
The United Nations statistical yearbook contains summary statistics on population, economy, communications, education and other topics. Although derived for the most part from Pakistani sources, and thus overlapping with the *Pakistan Statistical Yearbook* (q.v.), the data in the UN source have been processed and presented in such a way that Pakistan can be compared to other countries. A number of specialized UN agencies produce statistical information from which information on Pakistan can be derived. Among these are UNESCO (*Statistical Yearbook*); ILO (*Yearbook of Labour Statistics*); IMF (*International Financial Statistics* [monthly]). Pakistan is not, however, a member of WHO.

Annual report.
See item no. 597.

Economic survey.
See item no. 600.

World development report.
See item no. 620.

Urban Development

683 **Karachi.**
Mohamed Amin, Duncan Willetts, Brian Tetley. Karachi: Pak American Commercial, 1986. 136p.
This is a glossy introduction to the city, primarily aimed at a tourist market. There are numerous photographs.

684 **Squatter settlements in Pakistan: the impact of upgrading.**
Maarten L. Kool, Dik Verboom, Jan J. van der Linden. Lahore: Vanguard Books, 1988. 182p. bibliog.
The focus of this study, one of the results of a long-term Dutch research project in Karachi, is a long-established squatter settlement in Karachi which in 1977 was selected for regularization and upgrading. Surveys in 1977, 1979, 1981, 1983 and 1987 allowed the researchers to trace in great detail the way this affected the residents. Their conclusions are that the upgrading has been only a partial success.

685 **Lahore: Entwicklung und räumliche Ordnung seines zentralen Geschäftsbereich.** (Lahore: development and spatial organization of its central business area.)
Josef Mayer. Erlangen, West Germany: Fränkischen Geographischen Gesellschaft, 1979. 196p. 10 maps. bibliog. (Erlangen Geographische Arbeiten, Sonderband no. 9).
A detailed analysis, originally submitted as a doctoral dissertation, on the urban geography of Lahore, or rather of its central business area. Each individual locality in the bazaar and its economic activities is described. The focus of the work is the distinctive spatial organization of the area, with each trade or activity being concentrated in one small area, despite the absence of any formal 'planning'.

686　The new capitals of India, Pakistan and Bangladesh.
　　　Sten Nilsson.　Lund, Sweden: Studentlitteratur, 1973. 230p. maps.
There is a brief mention of Lahore and a more extended coverage of Karachi,
Pakistan's capital immediately after independence, but the main Pakistan section of
this book is a substantial essay on Islamabad. As well as looking at the historical and
political context in which Islamabad was planned and constructed, the author discusses
the outlook of the city's principal designer, the Greek architect and planner C. A.
Doxiadis. He then examines the different ways in which the architects of the individual
buildings conceived their task and comments on their relative success. There are
numerous, not always very well produced, plans and illustrations.

687　Lahore: urban development in the third world.
　　　Mohammad A. Qadeer.　Lahore: Vanguard Books, 1983. 282p. 13
　　　maps. bibliog.
This is a study of the process of urban change in a large Third World city. Qadeer,
himself a native of Lahore and with a wide comparative knowledge, sees the city as a
totality and explores the impact on it, and on the quality of life of its citizens, of the
rapid changes of the post-independence period. He is sceptical of some of the
'solutions' that have been put forward to resolve the 'urban crisis', but suggests that
with appropriate policy shifts a decent life for Lahore's citizens can be achieved.

688　Urban biographies.
　　　Grenfell Rudduck. Karachi: Government of Pakistan, Planning
　　　Commission, 1965. 127p. 3 maps. (Study no. P.P.&H 19).
Rudduck, an architect and town planner, worked as an adviser to the Planning
Commission in the field of urban development in the late 1950s. In this work he
presents three brief but still useful historical studies of Karachi, Lahore and Dhaka
written primarily from a town planning perspective.

689　Between basti dwellers and bureaucrats: lessons in squatter settlement
　　　upgrading in Karachi.
　　　J. W. Schoorl, J. J. van der Linden, K. S. Yap.　Oxford, England:
　　　Pergamon Press, 1983. 305p. maps. bibliog.
The volume contains a series of articles emerging out of a twelve-year involvement by
the Amsterdam Free University in slum improvement work in Karachi. After a section
dealing with sociological perspectives, the authors examine a number of government
housing projects and come to pessimistic conclusions about the possibility of their
effecting real improvements.

690　'Exploring the neglected': a study of fruit and vegetable hawkers in
　　　Karachi.
　　　Shahid Zahid, with the assistance of Robert E. Klitgaard, Sajjad
　　　Akhtar.　Karachi: Applied Economics Research Centre, University of
　　　Karachi, 1977. mimeo. 111p. (Research Report, no. 8).
This is a useful study of one part of the 'informal sector' in Karachi. The numerous
fruit and vegetable hawkers in the city were studied intensively in 1975-76. There is
information in the report based on direct and lively observation of the actual workings
of the distribution system from wholesale market to street level, as well as data on the

background of the hawkers in terms of area of origin, date of migration to Karachi, etc., as well as their attitudes and outlook.

Poverty, voluntary organizations and social change: a study of an urban slum in Pakistan.
See item no. 426.

Education

691 **Primary education and national development: a case study of the conditions for expanding primary education in West Pakistan with an introductory discussion of educational planning in relation to different aspects of national development and education.**
Rodney Åsberg.   Stockholm: Almqvist & Wicksell, 1973. 388p. maps. bibliog. (Göteborg Studies in Educational Sciences, no. 10).
This study, based on fieldwork carried out in 1969-70, begins from an academic perspective but is throughout concerned with the need for the creation of universal literacy and primary education in Pakistan, with the obstacles to the achievement of this goal and with the possible non-formal routes to it.

692 **Education in South Asia: a bibliography.**
Philip G. Altbach, Denzil Saldanha, Jeanne Weiler.   New York; London: Garland Publishing, 1987. 360p. (Garland Reference Library of Social Science, vol. 390).
The 1,419 entries are arranged into chapters on a thematic basis and cover sociological as well as organizational and pedagogical aspects of the subject. There are relatively few entries on Pakistan, but this reflects the state of the literature.

693 **Planning for education in Pakistan: a personal case study.**
Adam Curle.   London; Sydney; Wellington: Tavistock, 1966. 208p. map. bibliog.
The author was associated with the Planning Commission in Pakistan in the late 1950s and again more briefly in the 1960s during the preparation of the third five-year plan, working first on social issues and then on education. Here he discusses both the question of planning for educational development in the Pakistan context and his own role as one of the tribe of foreign experts who were so important in the earlier stages of economic and social planning there. The tone throughout is personal but there is

plenty of discussion of the major issues involved in expanding the range of educational provision in the conditions prevailing in Pakistan.

694 Data analysis for development.
Robert E. Klitgaard. Karachi: Oxford University Press, 1985. 142p. (UGC Monograph Series in Economics).

This work is designed as a tool to teach elementary statistics to Pakistani students of economics and allied subjects. The value of the book here lies in its use of case-studies derived from data collected by members of the Applied Economics Research Centre at the University of Karachi which would not otherwise be available. Most are derived from concrete problems in Karachi city or in Sindh. Five of the eight examples relate to aspects of education, for example the economics of teacher training, and the factors affecting pupil performance in different types of schools.

695 West Pakistan: rural education and development.
Abdur Rauf. Honolulu, Hawaii: East-West Center Press, 1970. 173p. bibliog.

Rauf reviews the progress made in West Pakistan after independence in various areas of rural development. As well as education in the formal sense, programmes for agricultural development are examined in some detail.

696 Education in search of fundamentals.
Parwaiz Shami. Karachi: National Book Foundation, 1976. 368p.

A collection of thirteen articles which cover a wide range of topics, for example 'Professional competence of teachers', 'The home and the school', and 'The educative process and leisure'. The style is literary rather than empirical; the author is concerned to identify the broad trends in Pakistan society and their educational implications.

Science and Technology

697 **Science in Pakistan (1947–1977).**
M. I. D. Chughtai.   Lahore: Pakistan Association for the
Advancement of Science, 1978. 22p. (Occasional Publication).
A brief survey by the president of the Pakistan Association for the Advancement of
Science of the progress made in scientific research after independence. Chughtai lists
the various institutions in the country and outlines the policies towards science adopted
by successive governments.

698 **Science and the human condition in India and Pakistan.**
Edited by Ward Morehouse.   New York: Rockefeller University
Press, 1968. 230p.
Based on a conference held in 1966, this volume reflects the view that the spread of
scientific knowledge is the most important precondition of social progress. The
participants were senior scholars and scientists from India, Pakistan and the United
States and the scope of the papers ranges from specific areas of applied science to
discussions of general issues to do with scientific education and the role of government.
Some of the papers are specifically concerned with Pakistan, while others make
comparisons between India and Pakistan.

699 **Herb drugs and herbalists in Pakistan.**
Khan Usmanghani, Gisho Honda, Wataru Miki.   Tokyo: Institute for
the Study of Languages and Cultures of Asia and Africa, 1986. 281p.
bibliog. (Studia Culturae Islamicae, 28).
Although it is far from obvious from the introduction, this book, the result of
comparative work by a Japanese team on traditional systems of medicine in the Middle
East, consists primarily of a translation (alongside the original Urdu text) of a
handbook for the traditional physician or *hakim* in South Asia, prepared by Hakim
Muhammad Said of the Hamdard Foundation, the largest producer of traditional or
unani medicines in Pakistan. The recipes and uses for all the medicines are included,

Science and Technology

and there are photographs of each herb used in their preparation. The book also includes a 25-page translation of a family history by Hakim Muhammad Said which would be useful to anyone interested in traditional Muslim society and perhaps to medical anthropologists.

Islam, politics and the state: the Pakistan experience.
See item no. 509.

Pakistan's nuclear dilemma: energy and security dimensions.
See item no. 579.

Literature

Urdu

700   **Ghazals of Ghalib.**
Edited by Aijaz Ahmad.   New York: Columbia University Press,
1971. 174p.

This is an interesting experiment in translation. The editor, an Urdu scholar, has
selected a number of extracts from Ghalib's *ghazals* and provided a literal translation
together with notes on the vocabulary used and its deeper resonances. These have then
been given to English-language poets to produce their own versions. Some of these
remain quite close to the original, others are much freer renderings. For some *ghazals*
several versions are included.

701   **The shore and the wave.**
Aziz Ahmad, translated by Ralph Russell.   London: George Allen &
Unwin, 1971. 167p. (UNESCO Asian Fiction Series).

The author, well known as a scholar of Islam in South Asia, published this novel in
1948 as a portrayal of life in his home city of Hyderabad (India) as independence
approached. Although geographically far from Pakistan, it relates to the cultural world
from which an important section of the Pakistan élite comes.

702   **The golden tradition: an anthology of Urdu poetry.**
Selected, translated, and with an introduction by Ahmed Ali.   New
York, London: Columbia University Press, 1973. 286p. (Studies in
Oriental Culture, no. 8).

The editor has selected poems, both *ghazals* and longer pieces, from the leading poets
of the 18th and 19th centuries, and has provided an extended and valuable introduction
in which he assesses the poems' literary form and describes the strong religious feelings
behind many of them.

193

703 **Aspects of Ghalib: five essays.**
Ahmed Ali, B. A. Dar, Ainslie T. Embree, Hamid Ahmad Khan,
Mumtaz Hasan.   Karachi: Pakistan American Cultural Centre, 1970.
94p.

As the title indicates, this contains the text of five lectures on the occasion of the
centenary of Ghalib's death. Each author is a distinguished scholar of Urdu literature
or of South Asia more generally. The essays concentrate primarily on the content and
style of Ghalib's poetry. Another volume which was published to mark the centenary
was *Ghalib: two essays*, by Ahmed Ali and Alessandro Bausani (Rome: Istituto
Italiano per il Medio ed Estremo Oriente, 1969 [Serie Orientale Roma, no. 39]).
Ahmed Ali's essay includes the translations of a number of poems, while Bausani
writes in Italian of Ghalib's Persian as well as his Urdu poetry.

704 **Storia delle letterature del Pakistan: Urdu, Pangiâbi, Sindhi, Pasc'tô,
Bengali Pakistana.** (History of the literatures of Pakistan: Urdu,
Panjabi, Sindhi, Pashto, Pakistani Bengali.)
Alessandro Bausani.   Milan: Nuova Accademia Editrice, 1958. 370p.
map. bibliog. (Storia delle letterature di Tutto il Mondo).

A history of the major literatures of Pakistan by a distinguished Italian Islamicist.
More space is devoted to Urdu than to all the other languages put together, and of
course most of the writers covered under this heading belong to other parts of the
subcontinent.

705 **Marxist influence and South Asian literature.**
Edited by Carlo Coppola.   East Lansing, Michigan: Michigan State
University, Asian Studies Center, 1974. 2 vols. (South Asian Series
Occasional Papers, nos 23, 24).

Many South Asian writers were strongly influenced by Marxist ideas, especially in the
years immediately before independence, and they created an important organization
called the All-India Progressive Writers Association. This collection of papers, which
arose out of a 1972 conference, discusses the work of a number of writers in English
and in Indian languages. Ahmed Ali, himself a member of the movement, is concerned
with Urdu writers, and Athar Murtuza with Faiz Ahmed Faiz.

706 **The true subject: selected poems of Faiz Ahmed Faiz.**
Translated by Naomi Lazard.   Princeton, New Jersey: Princeton
University Press, 1988. 133p. (Lockert Library of Poetry in
Translation).

Faiz Ahmed Faiz, who lived from 1911 to 1984, is, together with Iqbal, the most
outstanding figure in 20th-century Urdu literature. Known for his political commitment
to the left both in South Asia and internationally, his poetry touches the human
condition at many different points. His work has been translated into many languages,
and included in many anthologies. The present translation is by an American poet who
herself knows no Urdu and therefore had to work from literal translations. She was,
however, able to work closely with Faiz on the translations as they developed and to
have him explain the nuances and overtones of his poems. Another important set of
translations is by V. G. Kiernan, *Poems by Faiz* (London: George Allen & Unwin,

1971), and in French by Laiq Babree, *Faiz Ahmed Faiz: poèmes* (Paris: Seghers, 1979 [Collection UNESCO d'Oeuvres Représentatives, Série Pakistanaise]).

707 **Another lonely voice: the Urdu short stories of Saadat Hasan Manto.**
Leslie A. Flemming. Berkeley, California: University of California, Center for South and Southeast Asia Studies, 1979. 133p. bibliog. (Monograph Series, no. 18).

The only major study of Manto (q.v.) in English. Flemming begins with a biographical chapter covering Manto's life in Bombay and Delhi before partition and thereafter in Lahore until his death in 1955 at the age of 42. She then discusses the literary context of his work before examining it in detail. She sees both his style and his subjects as making him part of the mainstream of modernist writing in the 20th century.

708 **Versions of truth: Urdu short stories from Pakistan.**
Edited by Khalid Hasan, Faruq Hasan. New Delhi: Vikas, 1983. 273p.

A useful anthology of short stories translated from Urdu to English. All were written in the 20th century but, although it is not always clear, some of them predate partition. Authors covered include Saadat Hasan Manto, Intizar Hussain and a number of others. The translations are by a number of hands, including the editors.

709 **Downfall by degrees and other stories.**
Abdullah Hussein, edited and translated by Muhammad Umar Memon. Toronto: TSAR Publications, 1987.

Five Urdu short stories by a contemporary writer who is concerned with themes of exile and alienation both in Pakistan and abroad. Another selection of his stories, also edited by Memon, was published in 1984: *Night and other stories* (New Delhi: Orient Longman).

710 **Poems from Iqbal.**
Translated by V. G. Kiernan, introduction by M. D. Taseer. Bombay: Kutub, 1947. 133p.

This is a representative selection of Iqbal's shorter Urdu poems, including many of his *ghazals*. Both Kiernan and Taseer knew Iqbal and write with authority on his philosophical and literary achievements. Also included are remarks on the development of Iqbal's poetic thought by Khwaja Abdul Hamid.

711 **The Penguin book of modern Urdu poetry.**
Selected and translated by Mahmood Jamal. Harmondsworth, England: Penguin, 1986. 165p.

This is a broad selection of 20th-century Urdu poets, many of whom are still active. Poets included range from the late Faiz Ahmed Faiz to recent feminist writers, for example Fahmida Riaz. Many of the same poets are represented in another anthology, *Modern Urdu poems from Pakistan*, translated and edited by Anis Nagi (Lahore: Swad Noon Publications, 1974), although the poems chosen are for the most part different.

712 **Journal of South Asian Literature.**
East Lansing, Michigan: Michigan State University, Asian Studies Center, 1963- . biannual.

This well-established journal, originally titled *Mahfil*, covers both English and South Asian languages and regularly carries critical articles on Urdu literature and writers.

713 **Black mirrors.**
Farukh Khalid, translated by Eric Cyprian. London: Jonathan Cape, 1987. 285p.

Translated from an Urdu original entitled *Siah ainey*, this is a narrative of the lives of the inhabitants of a seedy hotel in Lahore. Khalid offers a bleak vision of Pakistan as it was in the 1970s. Only a portion of the original novel has been included in the English version.

714 **Kingdom's end and other stories.**
Saadat Hasan Manto, translated by Khalid Hasan. London: Verso, 1987. 257p.

Manto, who died in 1955, was one of the most outstanding writers of Urdu short stories in the 20th century. He is famous for his powerful stories of the partition period as well as for his portraits of courtesans and other denizens of the Bombay underworld. The volume includes a biographical introduction.

715 **An anthology of classical Urdu love lyrics: text and translations.**
D. J. Matthews, C. Shackle. London: Oxford University Press, 1972. 283p.

Designed primarily as a text for the student of Urdu who has progressed to the point of being able to read poetry, but accessible to others, this is a collection of *ghazals* by 22 poets from the 16th to the 20th centuries. The Urdu text and the translation are printed in parallel, and there are full notes, brief biographies of the poets and appendices on prosody, metre and grammatical features of old Urdu. Another work along the same lines but with an exclusively pedagogical aim is *Classical Urdu poetry*, by Muhammad Abd-al-Rahman Barker, Shah Abdus Salam (Ithaca, New York: Spoken Languages Services, 1977, 3 vols).

716 **Urdu literature.**
D. J. Matthews, C. Shackle, Shahrukh Husain. London: Third World Foundation, 1985. 139p. bibliog.

A succinct and reliable survey of Urdu literature from its 17th- and 18th-century roots to the present day intended for the general reader. There are a number of translations of poems which try as far as possible to give the feel of the original form as well as of the content.

717 **Partition literature: a study of Intizār Ḥusain.**
Muhammad Umar Memon. *Modern Asian Studies*, vol. 14, no. 3 (July 1980), p. 377-410.

The focus of this article is the Urdu short-story writer Intizar Husain. Unlike many of his contemporaries, who were active for example in the Progressive Writers

Movement, Intizar Husain was, Memon argues, conscious of the place of the partition in the broad sweep of Muslim history in the subcontinent. Other Urdu authors who used the partition as a theme are mentioned. Translations of some of the stories discussed have been published in the *Journal of South Asian Literature* (q.v.).

718 Urdu literature: a bibliography of English-language sources.

Frances W. Pritchett.   New Delhi: Manohar, 1979. 162p.

The author describes her work as a 'preliminary compilation' and there is very little by way of annotation, but this is nevertheless a valuable tool for scholar and general reader alike. There are approximately 1,500 entries arranged into general and genre studies, works by and about individual authors, and works on the language itself. Access can be obtained through this bibliography to a remarkably wide range of translations of Urdu poems, novels and short stories.

719 Ghalib: the poet and his age.

Edited by Ralph Russell.   London: George Allen & Unwin, 1972. 131p.

Ghalib was perhaps the greatest of the 19th-century Urdu poets. Born into an aristocratic family in the last days of Muslim power in India, he lived through the dark days of 1857 in Delhi and died when British power was at its height. This volume is composed of five papers originally read at a conference in London in 1969 to mark the centenary of his death. Two chapters, by A. Bausani and the editor respectively, discuss Ghalib's Persian and Urdu verse, while the remaining three are more biographical in nature. More information on Ghalib's life can be obtained from Ralph Russell, Khurshidul Islam, translated and edited, *Ghalib, 1797–1869*, vol. 1 *Life and letters* (London: George Allen & Unwin; Cambridge, Massachusetts: Harvard University Press, 1969 [UNESCO Collection of Representative Works, Indian Series]). This includes the text of many of Ghalib's letters, interspersed with commentary to provide a connected account of his life. Regrettably, the second volume intended to include his poetry has not yet appeared.

720 Three Mughal poets: Mir, Sauda, Mir Hasan.

Ralph Russell, Khurshidul Islam.   London: George Allen & Unwin, 1969. 290p. map. bibliog. (UNESCO Collection of Representative Works, Indian Series).

Intended for a general audience, this book by two distinguished scholars introduces the work of the three most important poets of the 18th century, the first period when Urdu flourished as a literary language. Each had his own distinctive style and purpose, and the authors give each separate treatment, although Mir enjoys pride of place. The poetic forms employed are discussed and there are extensive quotations.

721 A history of Urdu literature.

Muhammad Sadiq.   Delhi: Oxford University Press, 1984. 2nd ed. 652p.

First published in 1964 when it soon established itself as one of the standard works on the subject, the second edition is substantially revised and enlarged. The first half of the book deals with the origins of Urdu and brings the history of its literature up to Ghalib. The second covers the modern period from the Aligarh movement on. As well as chapters on the major poets, Sadiq devotes space to the short story, drama and journalism. Although inevitably, given the range of the work, the treatment of some authors is rather cursory, the judgements always seek to achieve balance. Sadiq is particularly concerned with stylistic questions.

722 A history of Urdu literature.
Ram Babu Saksena.   Allahabad, India: Ram Narain Lal, 1927. 374p.

Despite its age, this remains an important contribution to our knowledge of Urdu literature from its early origins in the medieval period to its flourishing in the 18th century onwards. While the greater part of the work is devoted to poetry, there are substantial sections on prose as well. The work is particularly strong on the biographical side.

723 Classical Urdu literature from the beginning to Iqbal.
Annemarie Schimmel.   Wiesbaden, West Germany: Otto Harrassowitz, 1975. 261p. (*A history of Indian literature*, edited by Jan Gonda, vol. 8, fasc. 3).

Part of a comprehensive survey of Indian literature, this separate work surveys the origins of Urdu in the medieval period up to the beginning of the 18th century, and then deals in separate sections with the 1700-1850 period and with the period bounded by the works of Ghalib and Iqbal. Schimmel has also contributed a shorter review of writing in India in Persian, Turkish and Arabic to the same series: *Islamic literatures of India*, 1973 (vol. 8, fasc. 1).

724 Urdu and Muslim South Asia: studies in honour of Ralph Russell.
Edited by Christopher Shackle.   London: School of Oriental and African Studies, 1989. 205p. bibliog.

The contributions to this *Festschrift* range widely across the field of Urdu literature and its cultural context but with particular emphasis on the 20th century. Apart from poetry, other genres are covered, notably journalism, and there are also papers on the public performance of poetry. A bibliography of works by Ralph Russell is included.

725 Iqbal: his life and thought.
Syed Abdul Vahid.   London: John Murray, 1959. 254p.

First published in India in 1944, this remains an important contribution to an understanding of Iqbal's literary contribution. Three chapters are devoted to Iqbal's philosophy and one to his life, but most of the book deals with his literary output in Persian and Urdu. Vahid also wrote *Studies in Iqbal* (Lahore: Sh. Muhammad Ashraf, 1976, 2nd ed.), in which he compares Iqbal with a number of other poets and writers, including Goethe and Rumi.

A course in Urdu.
See item no. 328.

Pain and grace: a study of two mystical writers of eighteenth-century India.
See item no. 380.

The ardent pilgrim: an introduction to the life and work of Mohammed Iqbal.
See item no. 381.

The structure of marriage preferences: an account from Pakistani fiction.
See item no. 391.

Regional

726 **"Hir": zur strukturalen Deutung des Panjabi-Epos von Waris Shah.**
("Hir": towards the structural meaning of the Punjabi epic by Waris
Shah.)
Doris Buddenberg. Wiesbaden, West Germany: Franz Steiner
Verlag, 1985. 156p. bibliog. (Beiträge zur Südasienforschung Südasien-
Institut Universität Heidelberg, vol. 95).
The author sees *Hir-Ranjha*, the most important Punjabi folk epic dating in the form
she studied from the late 18th century, as a local variant of those love epics which end
with the death of the lovers. Applying the techniques of contemporary literary
criticism, she interprets the epic in terms of two codes, the spatial and the kinship,
which allows the student to achieve greater understanding of the significance of the two
lovers and of the inner meanings of the text. She draws particular attention to the
religious meanings of Waris Shah's work. There is a brief English synopsis.

727 **Bulleh Shah: a selection.**
Translated by Taufiq Rafat, introduction by Khaled Ahmad. Lahore:
Vanguard Books, 1982. 243p.
This book contains translations by a Pakistani poet of a selection of the poems of
Bulleh Shah, the 18th-century Punjabi poet. Like most poets of his time, he came from
a sufi background, and his poems reflect both that and the wider mystical traditions of
India. There is a useful scholarly introduction by Khaled Ahmad, although the
translations themselves are not annotated or discussed. The Punjabi text of each poem
(in Persian script) is printed in parallel.

728 **Popular poetry of the Baloches.**
M. Longworth Dames. London: Royal Asiatic Society, 1907. 2 vols.
(Asiatic Society's Monographs, vols 9 & 10). [also published as
Folklore Society annual volume for 1905].
Dames, an early scholar of Baluchi language and literature, spent many years on this
collection of oral literature. In a brief introduction he sets out his understanding of the
nature of Baluchi poetry and its forms. The remainder of the first volume is given over
to his translations of ballads, love songs, religious poems, legends, cradle songs and
riddles. These do not attempt to reproduce the original metrical form, nor do they
simply seek a literal rendering of the original. The second volume contains the
transliterated texts of the poems translated in the first volume, and an essay on the
language of Baluchi poetry.

729 **A Baluchi miscellanea of erotica and poetry: Codex Oriental Additional 24048 of the British Library.**
Josef Elfenbein.   Naples, Italy: Istituto Universitario Orientale, 1983. 156p. (Supplemento n. 35 agli *Annali* – vol. 43 (1983), fasc. 2).

This is a collection of often bawdy folk tales and poetry written down, according to the editor, probably in the early 19th century. The work contains an introduction, a transliterated text and translation, a word list and a photographic reproduction of the original manuscript.

730 **Poems from the Divan of Khushâl Khân Khattak.**
Translated by D. N. Mackenzie.   London: George Allen & Unwin, 1965. 258p. bibliog. (UNESCO Collection of Representative Works, Pakistan Series).

Khushhal Khan Khattak, 1613-89, is generally regarded as the father of Pashto poetry. This is the most scholarly modern selection of his work. Two hundred and sixteen poems have been translated, ranging from the brief quatrains to longer lyrics and odes. There is a short but helpful introduction. There is another selection of his poems translated into English by Evelyn Howell and Olaf Caroe, *The poems of Khushhal Khan Khatak* (Peshawar: Pashto Academy, 1963).

731 **Selections from Rahman Baba.**
Edited and translated by Jens Enevoldsen.   Herning, Denmark: Poul Kristensen, 1977. 191p. bibliog.

Rahman Baba was a popular Pashto poet of the 17th century who, like similar writers, can be appreciated at many different levels of meaning. In this selection 50 *ghazals* are translated into English side by side with the original text. There is an enthusiastic introduction by the editor which gives the limited information that is known about the poet's life.

732 **Panjabi sufi poets, A.D. 1460–1900.**
Lajwanti Rama Krishna.   Calcutta: Oxford University Press, Indian Branch, 1938. 142p. bibliog.

Originally a thesis, this is one of the few systematic treatments of the subject. Rama Krishna discusses in turn eight major sufi poets, and some minor ones, from the late 15th to the 19th centuries. Pride of place is given to Bulleh Shah. For each poet there is a description of his life, so far as details are known, and a discussion of the sufi themes in his work.

733 **Pakistan: literature and society.**
Fahmida Riaz, foreword by Bhisham Sahni.   New Delhi: Patriot, 1986. 124p.

Fahmida Riaz is a well-known Urdu poet. She moved to India during the Zia régime, and there wrote this study of contemporary Pakistani literature. She arranges her material by province and is particularly concerned with the vitality of the regional languages, although she recognizes the importance of Urdu in the Punjab. She is particularly interested in social and political content.

734 **Sindhi literature.**
Annemarie. Schimmel. Wiesbaden, West Germany: Otto
Harrassowitz, 1974. 41p. (*A history of Indian literature*, edited by Jan
Gonda, part of vol. 8).
This is a brief but comprehensive review of Sindhi literature by the leading foreign
scholar of the subject. Schimmel discusses the importance of sufi themes in Sindhi
poetry, especially that of Shah Abdul Latif, as well as 19th and 20th century
developments.

735 **Shah Abdul Latif: his poetry, life and times. A study of literary, social
and economic conditions in eighteenth century Sind.**
H. T. Sorley. London: Oxford University Press, 1940. 432p. bibliog.
Shah Abdul Latif of Bhit is by general consent the outstanding sufi poet of Sindh. This
book by the leading British scholar of his work is in fact in three distinct parts. The first
is a general study of 18th-century Sindh, the second a critical study of Shah Abdul
Latif's work, and the third a translation of the *Risalo*, or collected poems. Sorley
discusses some of the particular problems in translating this genre of poetry. A
substantial portion of the *Risalo* has also been translated by Elsa Kazi, *Risalo of Shah
Abdul Latif* (Hyderabad: Sindhi Adabi Board, 1965). There are more recent studies of
the poet by Motilal Jotwani, *Shāh Abdul Latīf: his life and work. A study of socio-
cultural and literary situations in eighteenth century Sindh (now in Pakistan)* (Delhi:
University of Delhi, 1975), and by Annemarie Schimmel, *Pain and grace* (q.v.).

736 **Qadir Yar: a critical introduction.**
M. Athar Tahir. Lahore: Pakistan Punjabi Adabi Board, 1988. 141p.
bibliog.
Qadir Yar was a Punjabi poet of the first half of the 19th century. He can be placed in
the *qissa* or narrative tradition (to which belong also the *Hir-Ranjha* poems, q.v.).
Tahir's critical study calls attention to the range of themes, drawn from Islamic and
Hindu sources alike, that Qadir Yar's work encompasses. A translation of Qadir Yar's
masterpiece, *Puran Bhagat*, by Taufiq Rafat has also been published (Lahore:
Vanguard Books, 1983).

737 **The adventures of Hir and Ranjha.**
Waris Shah, translated by Charles Frederick Usborne, edited by
Mumtaz Hasan. London: Peter Owen, 1973. 201p. (UNESCO
Collection of Representative Works, Pakistan Series).
Waris Shah's rendering in the 18th century of the romance of Hir and Ranjha is
generally reckoned as one of the masterpieces of Punjabi literature. Although
Usborne's translation is old, it remains the only available English version. The present
edition was earlier published in Pakistan (Karachi: Lion Art Press, 1966). A scholarly
French edition and translation is also available (*Hīr Vāriṣ Śāh: poème Panjabi du
XVIIIe siècle. Introduction, translittération, traduction et commentaire* [Hīr Vāriṣ Śāh: a
Panjabi poem of the 18th century. Introduction, transliteration, translation and
commentary], vol. 1 *Strophes 1 à 110* [stanzas 1 to 110], Denis Matringe, Pondicherry,
India: Institut Français d'Indologie, 1988 [Publications de l'Institut Français d'Indologie,
no. 72]).

Punjabi in Lahore.
See item no. 339.

Pain and grace: a study of two mystical writers of eighteenth-century India.
See item no. 380.

Storia delle letterature del Pakistan: Urdu, Pangiâbi, Sindhi, Pasc'tô, Bengali Pakistana. (History of the literatures of Pakistan: Urdu, Panjabi, Sindhi, Pashto, Pakistani Bengali.)
See item no. 704.

The bazaar of the storytellers.
See item no. 767.

English

738 The murder of Aziz Khan.
Zulfikar Ghose. London: Macmillan, 1967. 315p.

Set in the Punjab, this is a story of social change and the accompanying tensions. It revolves round a farmer, Aziz Khan, and the efforts of a *nouveau riche* family to dispossess him. The underlying theme is the clash between the values of rural and industrial societies.

739 Kim.
Rudyard Kipling. London: Macmillan, 1949. 413p. (Centenary edition).

First published in 1901 and reprinted many times since, *Kim* is perhaps Kipling's most famous work. The story begins in Lahore, with Kim astride the Zam-zamah gun, although his travels, actually and metaphorically, take him far away from his original existence as an orphan in the city. Kipling's father had been curator of the Lahore Museum and Kipling himself had started his adult life as a journalist in the city. Some of his short stories have a Lahore background, including 'The city of dreadful night'. Kipling's use of Lahore in his writing is discussed in Angus Wilson, *The strange ride of Rudyard Kipling* (London: Secker and Warburg, 1977).

740 Delusions and discoveries: studies on India in the British imagination, 1880–1930.
Benita Parry. London: Allen Lane the Penguin Press, 1972. 369p. bibliog.

A critical study of a number of British authors who wrote about India. The chapters on Kipling, Flora Annie Steel, and Edmund Candler are particularly relevant to the Punjab. Parry argues that Steel and Candler saw India as essentially alien and exotic. Only Kipling and especially Forster used their Indian experience to do justice both to India and to human experience. A work on a related subject is Shamsul Islam, *Chronicles of the Raj: a study of literary reaction to the imperial idea towards the end of the Raj* (London: Macmillan, 1979), which deals *inter alia* with Masters and Kipling.

741   **Wordfall: three Pakistan poets.**
Taufiq Rafat, Malik Kureishi, Kaleem Omar, edited by Kaleem
Omar. Karachi: Oxford University Press, 1975. 78p.

A representative selection of poems by three contemporary Pakistani poets writing in
English. Many of the poems reflect themes directly related to Pakistan life and
experience.

742   **Shame.**
Salman Rushdie.   London: Jonathan Cape, 1983. 287p.

Rushdie is the author not only of *Shame* and *Midnight's children*, a study of India's
experience since independence, but of *The satanic verses*, which caused a storm of
controversy when first published in 1988. Many Muslims regard it as blasphemous. In
Shame he applies his 'magical realist style' to the history of Pakistan. No historical
figures are named but few readers will be in doubt of who might have been in the
author's mind when he refers, for example, to Raza Hyder and 'the virgin Ironpants'.

743   **The crow eaters.**
Bapsi Sidhwa.   London: Jonathan Cape, 1980. 283p.

Herself a Parsi, Bapsi Sidhwa has written an affectionate satire, first published in
Lahore in 1978, on the small but prosperous Parsi community in Pakistan. The central
character, Faredoon or Freddy Junglewalla, makes his way in life in Lahore in the first
half of the 20th century to become the undisputed leader of his community. 'Toady,
philanthropist and shrewd businessman', he is capable of dealing with the British on his
own terms but has less success with his mother-in-law Jerbanoo, a richly comic figure.
Another novel by Sidhwa which focuses on the Parsi community of Lahore but against
the sombre setting of the partition period is *Ice-candy-man* (London: Heinemann,
1980).

744   **The 13th house.**
Adam Zameenzad.   London: Fourth Estate, 1987. 202p.

Zameenzad's first novel tells the story of an ordinary man caught up in a series of
events beyond his control until he finishes up having lost everything. While the
description is often comic, the thrust of the book is to emphasize the helplessness of
the individual.

My beautiful launderette *and* the rainbow sign.
See item no. 319.

The Arts

General

745 Museology and museum problems in Pakistan.
Edited by Saifur Rahman Dar.   Lahore: Lahore Museum, 1981. 331p.
maps.
This volume is in fact the proceedings of a training course for museum staff in
Pakistan, but there is much useful information on Pakistan's museums both included *en
passant* in the general contributions and also in special sections.

746 Repositories of our cultural heritage: a handbook of museums in
Pakistan.
Saifur Rahman Dar.   Lahore: Lahore Museum, 1979. 127p. map.
bibliog.
This volume gives details of contents, opening hours, etc. for Pakistan's 33 largest
museums, brief notes on sixteen more and a list of a number of others. The author
gives a fair summary of the material held by the museums he writes about and is not
afraid to make critical comments.

747 The cultural heritage of Pakistan.
S. M. Ikram, Percival Spear.   Karachi: Oxford University Press, 1955.
204p.
In a series of separate essays held together by an initial chapter by S. M. Ikram on
'The pattern of Pakistan's heritage', a number of distinguished Pakistani scholars
outline the country's cultural heritage in the visual and plastic arts, in Urdu and
Persian and in the regional languages. In many areas, of course, it is the Muslim
traditions of the whole subcontinent which are described. Two concluding chapters
cover religious and intellectual developments. Although dated in some respects, the
book remains a useful survey of the subject.

Visual arts

748 Art in Pakistan: early years.
Jalaluddin Ahmed.   London: Kegan Paul, Trench, Trubner, 1972.
19p.

Apart from the brief introduction which describes the emergence of modern painting in Pakistan in the 1940s and 1950s, this book consists of 72 colour reproductions of works by Pakistani painters. The artists represented include 'traditionalists' such as the well-known Abdul Rahman Chughtai as well as younger painters such as Sadequain who have been influenced by contemporaries elsewhere in the world. Earlier versions of the present work were published in Pakistan.

749 Pahari paintings and Sikh portraits in the Lahore museum.
F. S. Aijazuddin, foreword by W. G. Archer.   London; New York: Sotheby Parke Bernet; Karachi; Delhi: Oxford University Press, 1977.
101p. bibliog.

As W. G. Archer notes in his foreword, the Lahore museum has one of the finest collections of *pahari* paintings, i.e. miniature paintings produced under the influence of Mughal styles in the small states of the Punjab hills and in the Sikh states of the plains. As it happens, the hill states fell to India's share in 1947, although many of the Sikh portraits would have been painted in what is now Pakistan. This excellently produced volume is a catalogue of the museum's holdings. There are colour reproductions of sixteen paintings, and black and white ones of the rest.

750 Sindhi tombs and textiles: the persistence of pattern.
Ethel-Jane W. Bunting, foreword by George F. Dales.   Albuquerque, New Mexico: Maxwell Museum of Anthropology and University of New Mexico Press, 1980. 76p. map. bibliog.

The purpose of this extensively illustrated work is to draw attention to the continuity of motif between the stone tombs which are found throughout Sindh and the hand-blocked textiles produced locally.

751 The gardens of Mughul India: a history and guide.
Sylvia Crowe, Sheila Haywood, Susan Jellicoe, Gordon Patterson.
London: Thames & Hudson, 1972. 200p. maps. bibliog.

The formal gardens laid out by the Mughal rulers of India, with their interweaving of water, trees and flowers, have always attracted attention. The present work is designed for a generally interested audience but is carefully documented and illustrated, with extensive quotes from the memoirs of the Mughal emperors and from European travellers. There are many photographs and copies of miniatures, although most are in black and white. The only surviving garden in Pakistan is the Shalimar garden in Lahore, but several of the most famous are located in Kashmir, and in any case the gardens are an integral part of Indo-Muslim culture. An earlier book on the same subject is Constance Mary Villiers-Stuart, *Gardens of the Great Mughals* (London: A. & C. Black, 1913).

752 **Crafts of the Punjab.** vol. 1. *Murree Hills.*
Has-Saan [*sic*, Hassan] Gardezi. Lahore: Punjab Small Industries
Corporation, 1986. 119p. bibliog.

A glossy and well-produced survey of both design and production techniques. The
book has a number of good colour illustrations.

753 **The calligraphers of Thatta.**
M. A. Ghafur. Karachi: University of Karachi, Institute of Central
and West Asian Studies, 1968 (2nd imp., 1978). 90p. map. bibliog.
(Institute of Central and West Asian Studies Publication no. 5,
Monograph Series no. 1).

Thatta, located near Karachi, was one of the major political and cultural centres of
Sindh throughout the pre-colonial period, and there are abundant archaeological
remains there. The focus of Ghafur's work is the wide range of examples of calligraphy
to be found on tombs and mosques, and photographs of many of them are included.
Most date from the 16th, 17th and 18th centuries. As well as describing the examples,
the book contains biographical details of the craftsmen and some historical information
on Thatta itself.

754 **The art and architecture of the Indian subcontinent.**
J. C. Harle. Harmondsworth, England: Penguin, 1986. 597p. 2 maps.
bibliog. (Pelican History of Art).

This comprehensive work on the subject covers a number of topics relevant to
Pakistan, including finds from Harappa and Mohenjo-daro, Gandhara art and
sculpture, Mughal painting, and Indo-Islamic architecture.

755 **Indian miniatures in the India Office Library.**
London: Sotheby Parke Bernet; Karachi; Delhi: Oxford University
Press, 1981. 559p. bibliog.

The India Office Library holdings of miniatures are among the richest in the world and
include such jewels as the Dara Shikoh album. This complete catalogue gives a
comprehensive history of the collection and deploys the latest scholarly work in its
entries for individual paintings. 568 items are listed but many cover several pieces and
the collection totals some 1,700 paintings. Seventeen of the best paintings are
illustrated in colour and there are smaller black and white reproductions of many
others. The collection includes the highest examples of Mughal court painting as well
as many provincial pieces from the 18th and 19th centuries, including a few from the
Punjab, mainly from the hills (*pahari* paintings).

756 **Textiles of Baluchistan.**
M. G. Konieczny. London: British Museum, 1979. 77p. map. bibliog.

This work describes in detail the techniques, materials and patterns used in textile
production in Baluchistan. Over half the book is made up of colour and black and
white photographs, mostly of items from the collection of the Museum of Mankind in
London. A few of the items illustrated are floor coverings, but the majority are bags of
various types or harness trappings.

757 **Architecture in Pakistan.**
Kamil Khan Mumtaz. Singapore: Mimar, 1985. 206p. maps. bibliog.
A well-produced and presented survey of Pakistan's architectural heritage both imperial and local, together with a review of post-1947 developments. The author's judgements are measured and informative. Mosques, palaces, public buildings and domestic housing are all included.

758 **Lahore: the city within.**
Samina Quraeshi, with an essay by Annemarie Schimmel. Singapore: Concept Media, 1988. 292p.
This is a lavishly illustrated and produced evocation of Lahore in which the photographs and reproduced miniatures have equal place with the text. All phases of the city's history are covered, but greatest attention is given to the Mughal heyday.

759 **The emperors' album: images of Mughal India.**
Stuart Cary Welch, Annemarie Schimmel, Marie L. Swietochowski, Wheeler M. Thackston. New York: Metropolitan Museum of Art, 1987. 318p. bibliog.
Published in connection with an exhibition held in New York in 1987, this volume contains a detailed catalogue, with excellently reproduced illustrations, of the Kekorvian album. The highlights of the album are a collection of miniatures painted for the emperors Jahangir and Shah Jahan. There are also three introductory essays on specific aspects of Mughal painting. Many other exhibition catalogues have been published and often provide valuable information on Mughal painting, for example Stuart Cary Welch, *Imperial Mughal painting* (New York: George Braziller, 1978).

Architecture and art treasures in Pakistan: prehistoric, protohistoric, Buddhist and Hindu periods.
See item no. 90.

Lahore past and present (being an account of Lahore compiled from original sources).
See item no. 177.

Multan: history and architecture.
See item no. 200.

Music and dance

760 **The rāgs of north Indian music: their structure and evolution.**
N. A. Jairazbhoy. Middletown, Connecticut: Wesleyan University Press, 1971. 222p. bibliog.
This is an introduction to the subject for those with no previous acquaintance with it but who wish to acquire a systematic knowledge of the theory of Indian music and the

musical principles underlying the evolution of the ragas. It is at the same time the exposition of Jairazbhoy's own original views. The book is accompanied by a record of musical examples recorded by the well-known Vilayat Khan.

761 **Sufi music of India and Pakistan: sound, context and meaning in Qawwali.**
Regula Burckhardt Qureshi. Cambridge, England: Cambridge University Press, 1986. 265p. bibliog. (Cambridge Studies in Ethnomusicology).

Qawwali is a musical genre that is intimately linked to sufi religious practices and *qawwali* songs are performed at shrines throughout India and Pakistan. This study, based on fieldwork in both countries, deals with *qawwali* from an ethnomusicological perspective which treats the music as music and at the same time as a performance in a religious context.

762 **The new Grove dictionary of music and musicians.**
Edited by Stanley Sadie. London: Macmillan, 1980. 20 vols. maps. bibliog.

There is a comprehensive survey of South Asian music in volume 6, p. 69-166, by Harold S. Powers (et al.) which covers classical styles of music, as well as dance. In volume 14, p. 104-12, Regula Qureshi reviews Pakistani music, which in this context means primarily folk music. In her article she looks at the social role of the performers, instruments, and musical structures. There are brief entries elsewhere in the *Dictionary* for performers, instruments and styles. Extended entries for almost all the instruments used in South Asian music can be found in *The new Grove dictionary of musical instruments*, edited by Stanley Sadie (London: Macmillan, 1984. 3 vols).

763 **Khyāl: creativity within north India's classical musical tradition.**
Bonnie C. Wade. Cambridge, England: Cambridge University Press, 1984. 314p. 2 maps. bibliog. (Cambridge Studies in Ethnomusicology).

Khyal is a style of singing which emerged in north India in the mid-18th century and is now the dominant classical form. Within the genre there are a number of *gharanas* or traditions defined in terms of their physical locations, none of which happen to be in Pakistan, although a number of prominent Muslim exponents moved to Pakistan at or shortly after partition. Wade discusses in detail the most important *gharanas* in terms both of their histories and of their distinguishing stylistic characteristics. The musical illustrations are transcribed in such a way as to allow the trained reader to understand the finest points of vocal technique and style.

764 **Music in India: the classical traditions.**
Bonnie C. Wade. Englewood Cliffs, New Jersey: Prentice Hall, 1979. 252p. map. bibliog. (Prentice Hall History of Music Series).

Designed as an introductory text 'for the uninitiated Westerner', this book reviews the basic categories of Indian music – melody and metre – and discusses the various performance genres. Some degree of general musical knowledge is assumed and the descriptions are often quite detailed, but there are also chapters which seek to place the music in its cultural context. In addition to an annotated bibliography there is a discography and a filmography.

Folklore and Festivals

765 **Mataloona: Pukhto proverbs.**
Translated by Akbar S. Ahmed, with preface by Olaf Caroe. Karachi: Oxford University Press, 1975. 2nd rev. ed. 60p.

Mataloona is the Pukhto (Pashto) for proverbs, and Ahmed argues that in them can be found much of the essence of Pukhtun culture. Each proverb is printed in the original Pukhto, then in a literal translation, and finally in an apt English version, sometimes with parallel proverbs from other cultures. The introduction links the proverbs to the characteristic features of Pukhtun culture. The original edition was published in 1973.

766 **The beggar saint of Sehwan and other sketches of Sind.**
Adrian Duarte. Karachi: Oxford University Press, [?1975]. 98p.

A collection of pieces contributed by the author to the *Illustrated Weekly of India* and other magazines in the 1933-44 period. Many subjects are covered, for example the title piece on the shrine of Kalandar Lal Shahbaz at Sehwan, cock-fighting in rural Sindh, Sindhi wrestling, puppet shows, early English travellers, and the origins of the postal service in the province.

767 **The bazaar of the storytellers.**
W. L. Heston, Mumtaz Nasir. Islamabad: Lok Virsa, [c.1987]. 349p. bibliog.

This volume can be read both as a collection of modern folk tales translated from Pashto and as a study in the evolution of a folk tradition. The stories included in the volume were originally copied down from cassette tapes on sale in Peshawar. The stories themselves are in the traditional sung form but the themes are modern as well as traditional.

768 **Folk tales of Pakistan.**
Laxman Komal. New Delhi: Sterling, 1976. 112p.

A collection of fifteen folk tales, mainly from Sindh, written in a simple and attractive style. There is a brief introduction but no indication of the provenance or background of the individual stories.

769 Tales of the Punjab told by the people.
Flora Annie Steel, notes by R. C. Temple, illustrated by David Gentleman.   London; Sydney; Toronto: Bodley Head, 1973. 310p.

First published in 1884 as *Wide-awake stories* and then in its present form in 1894, this is a classic collection of folk tales collected by the wife of a British official (her life is covered in her autobiography [q.v.] and in a modern biography by Violet Powell [q.v.]). Each story is retold in a simple style suitable for children but there are extensive scholarly notes by Sir Richard Temple, himself an expert on folk tales, which are also included in the modern edition. A collection of folk tales which relies extensively on Steel and Temple for its source material is *There was once a king (folk-tales of Pakistan)*, retold by Sayyid Fayyaz Mahmud (Islamabad: Lok Virsa, [c.1981], 271p.).

No five fingers are alike: cognitive amplifiers in social context.
See item no. 389.

Mass Media

General

770 Press in Pakistan.
S. M. A. Feroze. Lahore: National Publications, 1957. rev. ed. 192p.
This consists largely of an annotated list of titles in English, Urdu, and other languages, both past and current but it also has some more general historical information. There are sections on news agencies and the press laws. The value of the work is diminished by the absence of an index.

771 Journalism in Pakistan: first phase, 1845 to 1857.
Abdus Salam Khurshid. Lahore: Publishers United, 1964. 122p.
A survey of early newspapers published in English and in local languages from the area that became Pakistan. Thirty-three of the titles listed belonged to the West and only two to the East.

772 Punjab Muslim press and the Muslim world, 1888–1911.
Ikram Ali Malik. Lahore: South Asian Institute, University of the Punjab, 1974. 66p.
This monograph reproduces on a thematic basis extracts from the Punjab press in order to illustrate the enthusiasm of the Punjab Muslims for the pan-Islamism that was then emerging and the critique of British imperialism that it implied. Almost all the extracts are from the Urdu press but most of the original files no longer exist and they are given here in the translations made for British officials. Even so, it is possible to get some feel from them of the tone of the press at the time.

773 **Fernsehen in Pakistan: entwicklungspolitische Bedeutung eines Massenmediums.** (Television in Pakistan: the developmental political significance of a mass medium.)
Stefan R. Melnik. Bochum, West Germany: Studienverlag Dr. N. Brockmeyer, 1978. 260p. bibliog. (Bochumer Studien zur Publizistik- und Kommunikationswissenschaft, vol. 19).

The focus of this study is the question of how far television in Pakistan has been used to support development objectives. Although he outlines many difficulties, the author is cautiously optimistic about the extent to which television can be used for such purposes. The work as a whole contains a considerable amount of information on the history of television in Pakistan and on financial, programming and other aspects of its operation.

Public opinion and political development in Pakistan, 1947–1958.
See item no. 475.

Newspapers

774 **Dawn.**
Karachi: Pakistan Herald Publications, 1942- . daily.

The longest established of the English-language newspapers in Pakistan, it was originally founded by Jinnah in 1942, replacing an earlier weekly publication. It now stands for a broadly liberal perspective. It has good coverage of economics. A weekly edition, *Dawn Overseas Weekly*, is also available.

775 **The Frontier Post.**
Peshawar: Zari Press, 1985- . daily.

Established after the end of the Martial Law period in 1985, the *Frontier Post* grew rapidly to become the major English-language newspaper in the North-West Frontier Province. Somewhat idiosyncratic in its editorial line, it is very concerned with the issues of Afghanistan as they impinge on the province.

776 **The Muslim.**
Islamabad: Islamabad Publications, [c.1979-]. daily.

The main newspaper published from Islamabad, the *Muslim* despite its title is a liberal newspaper whose lively and well-informed coverage have made it prime reading for the diplomatic community in the Pakistan capital as well as for civil servants and intellectuals. It also boasts the distinction of having had the first woman editor in the country.

777 **The Nation.**
Lahore: The Nation Publications, [c.1986-]. daily.

Right of centre but more liberal than its Urdu stablemate *Nawa-e-Waqt*, the *Nation* has a good reputation for local Punjab coverage.

778   **The Pakistan Times.**
Lahore: National Press Trust, 1947- . daily.

The *Pakistan Times*, founded in 1947, has gone through many vicissitudes. During the 1950s it was identified as a radical newspaper, but after the 1958 coup it was in effect taken over by the government and in 1964 handed over to the control of the National Press Trust.

Periodicals

779   **Herald.**
Karachi: Pakistan Herald Publications, 1970- . monthly.

A thick, glossy magazine for the Pakistan middle class which covers everything from serious articles on politics and economics to fashion, sport and film. Many of the best English-language journalists in the country write for it. Some of its former staff members have established a rival monthly, *Newsline* (Karachi: Newsline Publications, 1989-).

780   **Journal of the Research Society of Pakistan.**
Lahore: University of the Punjab, 1964- . quarterly.

The Research Society of Pakistan is an autonomous body concerned to promote scholarly activity, especially relating to the Muslim heritage of Pakistan. Its journal carries articles, not always of the highest quality, in English and Urdu on historical, literary and religious topics. *Pakistan Journal of History and Culture* (Islamabad: National Institute of History and Culture, c.1980- . biannual), which is produced by an official institute, covers much the same ground.

781   **Pakistan Pictorial.**
Islamabad: Pakistan Publications, 1949- . monthly.

This general interest magazine first started life in 1949 as *Pakistan – A Quarterly*; from 1952 it became *Pakistan Quarterly*, and then from 1973 onwards, with a break in 1977, *Pakistan Pictorial*. It has always carried a wide range of articles on different aspects of life in the country. It is not entirely clear what the target audience is.

782   **Viewpoint.**
Lahore: Mazhar Ali Khan, 1975- . weekly.

A distinctly unglossy and often rather idiosyncratic magazine that at its best includes some of the best critical journalism in Pakistan. A wide range of topics is covered in each issue, some oriented towards immediate events, others towards longer-term issues.

Newsletter of Baluchistan Studies.
See item no. 336.

Reference Works

783 The Far East and Australasia.
London: Europa Publications, 1969- . annual. bibliog.
Pakistan is represented in this standard yearbook by articles on geography, history and economy, and by a statistical survey and directory giving details of the country's major institutions. In all, the entry is between 30 and 40 pages.

784 Pakistan: an Official Handbook.
Islamabad: Government of Pakistan, Directorate of Films and Publications, Ministry of Information and Broadcasting. annual (sometimes irreg.).
This annual publication offers a review of government programmes and achievements mainly in the field of economic development. The tone is inevitably bland but a considerable amount of information can be derived from it. Its predecessor was *West Pakistan Yearbook*.

785 Pakistan Year Book.
Edited by Rafique Akhtar.   Karachi; Lahore: East & West Publishing Company. 1973- . annual.
Probably the best of the general reference works which seek to cover Pakistan. Its presentation and content has improved in recent years. Each issue contains a large number of short, unsigned articles arranged under the general headings of 'the land and the people', 'the cultural heritage', 'the government and its services', and 'the economy'. The coverage is somewhat uneven, but in general each article includes historical and current information. A limited range of statistics is provided.

The Cambridge encyclopedia of India, Pakistan, Sri Lanka, Nepal, Bhutan and the Maldives.
See item no. 18.

Bibliographies

786 Bibliography of Asian Studies.
Ann Arbor, Michigan: Association of Asian Studies, 1941- . annual.
Published until 1967 as a special issue of the *Journal of Asian Studies* (before 1956 called *Far Eastern Quarterly*), this bibliography lists a wide range of European-language scholarly articles and books on all aspects of Asian studies. Up to 500 titles a year can be found in the Pakistan section, in addition to references in the general sections. Two cumulative versions of the earlier bibliographies, arranged both by author and by subject, have been published (Boston: G. K. Hall). These cover 1941–65 and 1966–70 respectively. South Asia was included in the scope of the bibliography only from 1955.

787 South Asian history, 1750–1950: a guide to periodicals, dissertations and newspapers.
Margaret H. Case.   Princeton, New Jersey: Princeton University Press, 1968. 561p.
This bibliography is organized into sections dealing with periodical literature, dissertations, and newspapers, and within the first two categories is further subdivided by broad topic. Some but not all of the nearly 7,000 entries have brief annotations. Separate author and subject indexes are provided.

788 A select bibliography of periodical literature on India and Pakistan, 1947–70.
Compiled by Pervaiz Iqbal Cheema.   Islamabad: National Commission on Historical and Cultural Research, 1976, 1979, 1984. 3 vols.
A compilation of over 5,000 entries from 575 journals covering an enormous range of topics, although there are no annotations. Subjects covered include cookery, sports, forestry, education, and folk tales, as well as the more common areas such as economics and foreign affairs. The journals that have been scanned include well-known academic periodicals but also a number of weekly and monthly magazines

published in South Asia, the USA and Britain. All sources are in English. The first volume deals exclusively with Pakistan, the second with India, and the third with both.

789 **Pakistan central government and quasi-governmental organisations: a preliminary directory and list of IDS library holdings 1947–1971.**
J. A. Downey. Brighton, England: Institute of Development Studies Library, [c.1976]. (Occasional Guides, no. 5).

Based on the holdings of the Institute of Development Studies at the University of Sussex, this lists many of the often confusing publications of government ministries, their departments and other government organizations. Downey gives valuable details of the organization and functions of each issuing body.

790 **Asian Social Science Bibliography with Annotations and Abstracts.**
Edited by N. K. Goil. Delhi: Hindustan Publishing Corporation (earlier Vikas), 1966- . annual.

This work continues two earlier series, *The Southern Asia Social Science Bibliography* and *South Asia Social Science Abstracts*, published annually from 1952. From 1956 in part, and from 1957 in full, Pakistan was included in the coverage. In the last issue available approximately ten per cent of the entries related to Pakistan.

791 **Library literature in Pakistan.**
S. J. Haider. *International Library Review*, vol. 20, no. 1 (Jan. 1988), p. 65-100.

The author reviews and describes a wide range of literature on libraries and librarianship in Pakistan, including periodicals, conference proceedings, official reports and classification schemes in use in the country. The article could also serve as a history of librarianship in Pakistan.

792 **Pakistan government and administration: a comprehensive bibliography.**
Compiled by Garth N. Jones, Shaukat Ali (vol. 1). Peshawar: Pakistan Academy for Rural Development, 1970-74. 3 vols.

This is a largely unannotated but very wide-ranging bibliography which focuses on the activities of government but also includes material on the history of Pakistan, foreign relations and even literature. As well as books and articles, unpublished dissertations and papers are included. The entries are arranged by subject, and there is an author index. The circumstances of compilation were such that each volume covers the whole field and is arranged according to the same categories. The entries overlap in terms of date of publication.

793 **Bibliographical control in Pakistan.**
R. Mohammadally. *International Library Review*, vol. 18, no. 1 (Jan. 1986), p. 33-56.

This article examines critically the major instruments available for the bibliographical control of what is published in Pakistan, notably the *Pakistan national bibliography* (q.v.) and the Library of Congress's *Accession list* for Pakistan/South Asia. He concludes that both are far from satisfactory.

794 **The Pakistan National Bibliography.**
Islamabad: Government of Pakistan, Ministry of Education,
Department of Libraries, 1962- . annual (sometimes irreg.).

From 1962 onwards, all books in whatever language published in Pakistan and received under the provisions of the 1962 Copyright Ordinance have been listed in an annual volume. Comparisons can usefully be made with the *Accessions list – Pakistan* (since 1981, *Accessions list – South Asia*) produced by the Library of Congress. An attempt was made with UNESCO help to produce a retrospective bibliography for the 1947-61 period, but the project had a difficult history. Only one fascicule appears to have been produced (in 1973).

795 **South Asian civilizations: a bibliographical synthesis.**
Maureen L. P. Patterson, in collaboration with William J. Alspaugh.
Chicago; London: University of Chicago Press, 1981. 853p. 2 maps.

This monumental bibliography contains over 28,000 entries on all aspects of the subject. Although the entries are not annotated, the headings are well chosen to give as clear an insight as possible into the interconnections between the subjects covered.

796 **South Asian bibliography: a handbook and guide.**
Edited by J. D. Pearson. Hassocks, England: Harvester Press;
Atlantic Highlands, New Jersey: Humanities Press, 1979. 381p.

Compiled under the auspices of the South Asia Library Group in Britain, this work contains a number of accurate and detailed descriptive articles, arranged both by country and by subject, on the bibliographical resources available for study on South Asian topics. The chapter on Pakistan by Qazi Mahmudul Haq describes 92 bibliographies on a range of subjects. Aspects of Pakistan are included in most of the subject chapters. This volume is likely to stand for some time as the starting point for any research student or scholar. A related set of papers, but more diverse in scope and oriented more specifically towards libraries in Britain, is *South Asian studies*, edited by Albertine Gaur (London: The British Library, 1986 [British Library Occasional Papers, no. 7]).

797 **Analytical catalogue of publications on Pakistan.**
Akhtar H. Siddiqui. Islamabad: Pakistan Institute of Development
Studies, [?1984]. 380p. (PIDE Library Publication, no. 7).

This bibliography contains brief annotations on 1,361 items on economic development and related topics held in the library of the Pakistan Institute of Development Studies. It is particularly good on government publications.

Settlement and social change in Asia.
See item no. 424.

The economy of Pakistan: a select bibliography.
See item no. 617.

Indexes

There follow three separate indexes: authors (personal and corporate); titles; and subjects. Title entries are italicized and refer either to the main titles, or to other works cited in the annotations. The numbers refer to bibliographical entry rather than page numbers. Individual index entries are arranged in alphabetical sequence.

Index of Authors

221

223

225

Index of Titles

B

Subject Index

Birds 46
Birmingham (Britain) 314
Board of Talimat-i-Islamia
    501
Boatbuilding techniques
    676
Boats
    fishing 676
    river 676
Botany
    Bahawalpur 7
    Baluchistan 7
Bradford (Britain) 314, 318
Brahui 345
Brahui people 410
    see also Baluchistan
Breastfeeding practices 296
Bristol (Britain) 317
Britain
    relations with Pakistan
        569
Brohi, A. K. 352
Budgetary policy 636
Bugti tribe 14
Bulleh Shah 727, 732
Burnes, Alexander 54
Businessmen 601, 651, 656
    and politics 467
    overseas 315, 323-4

C

Cabinet Mission Plan 248
    see also History
Calligraphy 753
Camels 677
Candler, Edmund 740
Caste among Muslims 387,
    394, 401, 413
Cattle stealing and politics
    388
Censuses 291-4, 302
    history 295, 297
Ceremonies and rites
    in Punjab 421
China
    arms supplies from 555
    relations with Pakistan
        555, 557, 561, 573,
        576, 581-2
Chitral (Northern Areas)
    210, 416

cultural anthropology
    416
guidebook 82
history 210
languages 334
Christianity
    history 311-12
    periodicals 309
Christians 310, 317
    Goan 306
    in Karachi 400
Chughtai, Abdul Rahman
    748
Churchill, Winston S. 242
Class structure see Social
    structure
Climatic conditions 27
Coal 24
Cock-fighting 766
Cognitive ontogeny 389
Commonwealth and
    Pakistan 569
Commonwealth
    Conference, 1949 243
Constitutions 487
    1956 455, 501, 518, 523,
        527
    1962 255, 479, 524, 527
    1973 468, 507, 525
    8th Amendment to 1973
        Constitution 525
    appropriate forms 275
    crisis of 1954 527, 535
    during Zia period 448
    framing of 251, 455-6,
        483, 488, 508, 518, 527
Congress, Indian National
    216, 222, 248
Contraception, use of 296
Cookery 19, 79, 788
Corruption 56
Coups see Military role in
    politics
Credit institutions see
    Banking
Cripps, Stafford 242
Culture 8, 11, 17-18
    adab 152
    bibliography 795
    government policy 509
    Indo-Muslim 751
    Northern Areas 416
    of Pakistan 163, 747
    periodicals 142

sharif 147
    value systems 441
Cunningham, George 278

D

Dance 762
Dara Shikoh album 755
Dardic group of languages
    345
Daudzai (North-West
    Frontier Province)
    project 428-9
Dawn 475
Defence see Armed forces;
    Foreign relations;
    Indo–Pakistan
    relations
Delhi 126
Demography see
    Population
Dera Ghazi Khan (Punjab)
    407
Dictionaries
    Punjabi 325
    Sindhi 343
    Urdu 328, 331-2, 337
Dissertations on Pakistan
    792
Drama
    Urdu 721
Drug addiction 427

E

Earthquakes 197
Economic advisers, foreign
    634, 688, 693
Economy 3, 6, 8, 16, 18,
    31, 34, 108, 447, 487,
    594-620, 633, 646-7,
    650, 779, 783-4
    Bhutto period 263, 484
    bibliography 424, 617,
        797
    choice of techniques 616
    development 30, 115,
        258, 608, 612, 614-16,
        618, 633, 649, 654
    exchange rates 652-3
    growth and equity issues
        602, 614

News agencies 770
Newspapers 205, 475,
    770-2
    Dawn 774
    Frontier Post 775
    Muslim 776
    Nation 777
    Pakistan Times 778
    Urdu 328
    see also Mass media
Nomads
    Baluchistan 418
    Qalandar 389
North-West Frontier
    Province 22, 402
    administration 173
    Afghan refugees 300,
        307
    gazetteer 42
    geography 25
    history 5, 173, 182, 188,
        195, 198, 209, 215,
        233, 238, 273, 278,
        288, 551
    Khudai Khidmatgars 288
    newspapers 775
    politics 489-90, 494
    Pukhtunistan issue 68,
        288
    Pukhtuns 5, 21-2, 198,
        209, 405-6, 414, 494,
        765
    pukhtunwali 403, 414,
        434
    rural development 428-9
    social change and family
        size 301
    social structure 13, 21,
        23, 209, 386, 402-3,
        405-6, 411, 413-14
    travel 66, 68, 70
    tribes 5, 173, 404
    women's position 434
    see also Pashto
Northern Areas 35, 422
    archaeology 422
    cultural beliefs 416
    ethnology 422
    geography 25
    geology 33, 65
    guidebooks 80, 82
    history 169, 210, 422
    impact of tourism 425
    languages 334, 345

princely states 261
religions 367, 415
scenery 2
social structure 409
travel 53, 61-2, 64, 71-2,
    75, 77
Novels
    English 738-9, 742-4
    Urdu 391, 701, 713
Nuclear fuels 24
Nuclear issue 547, 554,
    575, 579, 586, 589, 591
Numismatics 122

O

O'Dwyer, Michael 280
Oil price rise 599
Oil reserves 24
Operation Searchlight 260
Ornithology 46
Oxford (Britain) 321

P

Pagaro, Pir of 15
Painting 747
    miniature 749, 754-5,
        759
    modern 748
    Mughal 755, 759
    pahari 749
    Punjab 755
Pakhto *see* Pashto
Pakistan
    ethos 17
Pakistan Fertility Survey
    296
Pakistan Institute of
    Development
    Economics 634
Pakistan National Alliance
    482
Pakistan National
    Bibliography 793-4
Pakistan Observer 475
Pakistan People's Party
    134, 252-3, 453, 470
Pakistan Times 475
Pakistanis abroad 313-24
    Britain 313-15, 317-21,
        323-4

Europe 320
    Middle East 315-16, 322
Parsis 743
Partition of India as
    literary theme 717,
    743
Parwez, G. A. 347, 370
Parwiz, G. A. *see* Parwez
Pashto 765
    see also Folk tales;
        Languages;
        Literature; Poetry
Pataudi, Sher Ali Khan
    281
Patrimonial theories of
    political organization
    107
Patti (social unit) 394
Patwaris (local officials),
    role of 110
Periodicals
    archaeology 94
    Baluchistan 336
    Christianity 309
    culture 142
    current affairs 782
    economy 610, 612-13
    foreign relations 449,
        568
    geography 28
    history 142, 144, 207,
        780
    Iqbal studies 365
    Islam 366
    literature 712
    politics 449, 782
    South Asian Muslims
        142
Persian *see* History;
    Literature; Poetry
Peshawar 181
Photographs 1-2, 20, 79,
    81, 683, 753
Piaget, Jean 389
Pirs *see* Sufism
Planning *see* Economy
Poetry
    Baluchi 728-9
    epic 726
    English 741
    ghazals 700, 702, 710
    Iqbal 371
    Pashto 730-1
    Persian 381, 719, 725

Wheat marketing 660
Wilcox, Wayne A. 263
Wildlife preservation 49
Women 13, 56, 432-44
  19th century 285
  bibliography 443
  impact of education 438
  in Karachi 436
  in villages 408
  Islamization and 433,
    440, 522
  legal position of 432-3,
    435, 504
political participation
  439
status and fertility 303
Women's Action Forum
  440
World Fertility Survey 296
Wrestling 766

Y

Yearbook 785

Z

Zat (social unit) 401
Zia period (1977-88) 71,
  73, 259, 266, 452-4,
  456, 463, 465-6, 470,
  473, 480, 493, 496,
  499, 505, 507, 509,
  513, 516, 522, 531, 627
Ziauddin Barani 135
Zone of peace proposal
  558

Map of Pakistan

This map shows the more important towns and other features.

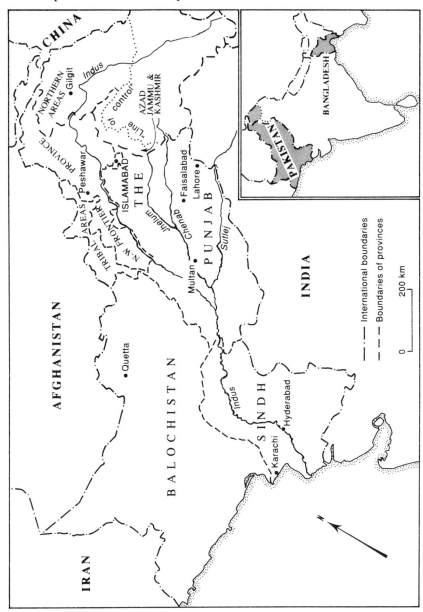